Volume 20

Advances in
Librarianship

Volume 20

Advances in
Librarianship

Edited by
Irene Godden

The Libraries
Colorado State University
Fort Collins, Colorado

Academic Press
San Diego   London   Boston   New York   Sydney   Tokyo   Toronto

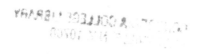

This book is printed on acid-free paper. ∞

Academic Press, Inc.
525 B Street, Suite 1900, San Diego, California 92101-4495, USA
http://www.apnet.com

Academic Press Limited
24-28 Oval Road, London NW1 7DX, UK
http://www.hbuk.co.uk/ap/

International Standard Serial Number: 0065-2830

International Standard Book Number: 0-12-024620-1

PRINTED IN THE UNITED STATES OF AMERICA
96 97 98 99 00 01 BC 9 8 7 6 5 4 3 2 1

Contents

Mexican and U.S. Library Relations
Robert A. Seal

Developing Site Licensing with Particular Reference to the National United Kingdom Initiative
Liz Chapman

Domain of Adult Fiction Librarianship
Liangzhi Yu and Ann O'Brien

Librarian–Faculty Partnerships in Instruction
Evelyn B. Haynes

Preservation and Digitization: Trends and Implications
Eric C. Shoaf

Contributors

Numbers in parentheses indicate the pages on which the authors' contributions begin.

Daniel E. Atkins (47), School of Information and Library Studies, University of Michigan, Ann Arbor, Michigan 48109

Stella Bentley (27), Davidson Library, University of California, Santa Barbara, Santa Barbara, California 93106

Joseph A. Boisse (27), Davidson Library, University of California, Santa Barbara, Santa Barbara, California 93106

Liz Chapman (123), Institute of Economics and Statistics Library, University of Oxford, Oxford OX1 3UL, United Kingdom

Karen M. Drabenstott (47), School of Information and Library Studies, University of Michigan, Ann Arbor, Michigan 48109

Evelyn B. Haynes (191), Social Sciences and Humanities Reference Librarian, Colorado State University Libraries, Fort Collins, Colorado 80523

Arnold Hirshon (1), Lehigh University, Bethlehem, Pennsylvania 18015

Ann O'Brien (151), Department of Information and Library Studies, Loughborough University, Loughborough, Leicestershire LE11 3TU, England

Robert A. Seal (69), Texas Christian University, Fort Worth, Texas 76129

Eric C. Shoaf (223), Brown University Library, Providence, Rhode Island 02912

Liangzhi Yu (151), Department of Information Management, Nankai University, Tianjin, People's Republic of China

Preface

As editor of *Advances in Librarianship* for the past 5 years, I have been struck by the plethora of topics that could be considered "advances" in the field and the dearth of authors who can find the time to write the type of thorough, scholarly analyses typical of this publication. Moreover, authors must struggle with rapid developments that will simply not hold still for leisurely analysis; often, a snapshot description and some informed speculation are all that is possible. I am therefore pleased that in this twentieth volume of *Advances in Librarianship* I have been able to find, with the expert help of my editorial board, a group of authors, who, while discussing the uncertainties inherent in describing a field in flux, nevertheless both provide analysis and indicate direction.

The lead contribution for this volume, "Running with the Red Queen: Breaking New Habits to Survive in the Virtual World," by Hirshon, expands on the thought of "too much change too soon." Libraries are no longer a sequestered refuge, buffeted as they are by changes in the scholarly publishing process, constantly increasing customer expectations, shrinking budgets, and the demands to keep pace with rapidly changing technologies among other things. It does indeed seem, as Hirshon quotes from *Alice in Wonderland*, that "it takes all the running you can do to keep in the same place" and "if you want to get somewhere else, you must run at least twice as fast as that." Hirshon develops his topic by discussing customer service expectations and strategies for meeting them in the foreseeable future. He concludes that the days of stability and predictability are gone forever and, to paraphrase the caterpillar's advice to Alice, "We will get used to it in time."

Rethinking and reshaping their organizational structures is one way many libraries have attempted to respond to rising demands. Many reorganization plans have attempted to flatten the organizational structure, the goal being more empowered line employees (and fewer managers) who would be self-directed and more efficient and give better service. Joseph Boisse and Stella Bentley, in "Reorganizing Libraries—Is Flatter Better?" review the management theory behind horizontal organizations, the factors that drove libraries to change, the factors that typically affect success or failure, and the issues that need to be seriously considered before this approach is adopted.

As libraries are forced to change, library and information science programs also are being asked to change. They must educate a "new breed of librarian," one who is a leader and a technical expert and who has been exposed to more traditional values and skills. Karen Drabenstott and Daniel Atkins, in their contribution "The Kellog CRISTAL-ED Project: Creating a Model Program to Support Libraries in the Digital Age," describe one school's "bold action plan" to deal with "the revolution upon us," a plan that includes not only a new curriculum and new approaches to teaching and learning, but also a number of linked research projects that will help shape what they foresee as an interdisciplinary educational program "to produce graduates who will create and manage a broad set of knowledge-work environments including but not limited to libraries."

Internationalization of business, scholarly communication, and communication generally are other areas in which librarians have become more involved as global interdependence is creating new links and obligations. Robert Seale, traces the relationship between Mexican and U.S. libraries in a comprehensive treatment of this subject. He begins with an overview of Mexican librarianship and then covers library cooperation in Mexico, a history of U.S.–Mexican library interaction, organized acquisition of Latin American materials, the status of library education in both countries, and current cooperative projects. He ends with suggestions for future activities, such as resource sharing, and discusses the potential impact of the North American Free Trade Agreement.

Liz Chapman explores the potential of licensing—a legal agreement between publishers of serials and libraries—as a possible solution to the well-known "serials crisis." Existing licensing projects are reviewed briefly, and a pilot project now under way in the United Kingdom is described. Of special value is a section on the potential impacts of licensing on publishers, serials agents, and, of course, libraries and their users.

While high-profile issues such as organizational accountability, restructuring, technological developments, high costs of serials, rising user expectations, and internationalization, tend to dominate the current professional literature, it is sometimes forgotten that traditional library services are ongoing and in demand. Certainly, activities such as the acquisition and loaning of fiction, including reader advisory services, are alive and well in public and, to a lesser extent, in academic and special libraries. Two UK authors, Liangzhi Yu and Ann O'Brien, provide a thoughtful description and analysis of what they call "the domain of adult fiction librarianship," that is, the provision of adult fiction in libraries, including collection development promotion and reference services. In addition to describing their own research approach, they include a review of prior and suggested research.

Academic librarians have believed for a long time that closer cooperation with faculty in the various disciplines is the best way to teach students more effectively and consistently. Yet, the influence of the library faculty is rarely strong enough to effect an integrated program except perhaps in smaller 4-year institutions. Evelyn Haynes, in "Librarian Faculty Partnerships in Instruction," describes the typical relationship of the academic library with its parent institution; faculty perceptions, understanding, and attitudes; and the challenges library faculty have to overcome to be successful in maximizing the unique contributions the library and its faculty are capable of making to the educational enterprise.

One of the more elegant solutions that technology has put within our grasp (if not as yet within our reach) is the digitizing of large amounts of text for purposes of preservation and potentially much improved access and delivery. As with other breakthrough technical developments, the road from technical feasibility to actual implementation, is, not surprisingly, rather complex. However, because the potential is so inviting in the United States, a number of major pilot projects have been launched to begin to digitize certain collections and to establish procedures that can be used for further application. Eric Shoaf, in "Preservation and Digitization: Trends and Implications" discusses the concepts of preservation and access that led to these projects. He summarizes the advantages and possible disadvantages of digitization as a preservation option and lists the key factors that need to be in place for this option to become the major preservation or access tool.

Given that this volume, the twentieth for the serial and my fifth as editor, represents somewhat of a milestone, I thank the present and past members of the editorial board, Nancy H. Allen, Harold Borko, Michael K. Buckland, Karen Horny, Frederick C. Lynden, Charles Martell, W. David Penniman, and Bendik Rugaas, for being proactive in contributing their ideas and expertise. Because of the small number of board members, each individual gave quite a bit of his or her time. I also thank my administrative assistant, Betty M. Espinoza, for her work as project director for these volumes. Her enthusiasm and attention to detail, as well as her ability to keep authors, editorial board, and publishers informed and happy, have made the task of completing each volume both possible and pleasurable.

Irene Godden

Running with the Red Queen
Breaking New Habits to Survive in the Virtual World*

Arnold Hirshon†
Lehigh University
Bethlehem, Pennsylvania 18015-3107

I. Introduction

After running through the forest for quite some time, Alice asked the Red Queen, "Are we nearly there?" The Queen replied, "Nearly there! Why, we passed it ten minutes ago!" When they finally stop running, Alice remarked in great surprise, "Why, I do believe we've been under this tree the whole time! In *our* country, you'd generally get to somewhere else—if you ran very fast for a long time."

"A slow sort of country!" replied the Queen. "Now, *here* you see, it takes all the running *you* can do to keep in the same place. If you want to get somewhere else, you must run at least twice as fast as that!"

The problem should sound familiar. For some time, libraries have not fit the stereotypical image of the quiet, sequestered physical refuge from the world. Librarians are buffeted constantly by increasing customer expectations and by the inability to keep pace with new technology. These two factors have become inextricable. As fast as we run, we cannot keep pace. For all of the effort, sometimes the only visible outcome seems to be frustration and stress.

Some in the profession assert that technology itself is causing this problem and that the best way to relieve the stress is to reassert the importance of the "human imperative" over the "technological" one. For example, DeVinney (1994) asserts that academic librarians need to develop a vision that *excludes:*

* This paper was originally prepared for presentation at the Australian Library and Information Association Reference and Information Services Section Conference in Adelaide, Australia, in September 1995. The author thanks Karen Karykis for the invitation and for her assistance in making this trip possible.

† *Note:* The author formerly was University Librarian, Wright State University, Dayton, Ohio. This fact is significant within the context of this chapter.

putting support staff at reference desks to answer routine questions; referring complex questions to librarians; eliminating reference desks; substituting discipline-specific expert computer systems for library staff; replacing telephone reference with electronic mail; and providing fee-based document delivery. Instead, she believes librarians should "forge a vision that emphasizes the human imperative to connect with others . . ." (DeVinney, 1994, p. 91).

By this argument, the increased use of technology takes librarianship away from an inherent mission to provide personalized service. This is a false dichotomy. We can no longer perpetuate romantic myths about the quality of services we provided in the past. To do so ignores the long lines of customers who waited to see a librarian, the endless hours librarians spent answering repetitive and routine questions, and the wrong answers dispensed by librarians. Customer service and technology are not diametrically opposed. *Effective* use of technology can enable professional staff to do professional work.

Although both customer service demands and the increasing use of technology undoubtedly cause stress, the combination of the two factors intensifies the overall tension significantly. Figure 1 illustrates this point.

Point "A" represents a library with a low level of customer service and a low use of technology. Library services are highly ineffective, but the working environment for staff is the least stressful. The only staff who would find this state desirable would be those who see customers as an interruption to an otherwise enjoyable day and technology as something best ignored. The highest priority for this staff is a secure job with good pay. They are likely to realize neither.

Point "B" illustrates high customer service expectations, but little use of technology. This is a low stress environment for technophobic customers

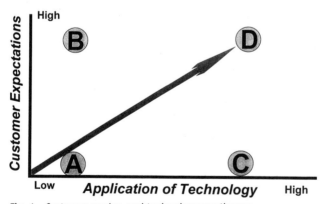

Fig. 1 Customer service and technology continuum.

and staff, but it is virtually impossible today to provide a high level of academic library customer service without information technology.

Point "C" is at the opposite extreme of point "B," with a high use of technology but a low level of customer service. It is technology for its own sake. Although this may create a low stress environment for staff who enjoy playing with electronic toys, this scenario fails to recognize that the true purpose of information technology is to improve customer service.

Point "D" is a "high-tech and high-touch" library. For better or for worse, in today's library, the high level of customer demand can be met only through the effective employment of information technology. Unfortunately, this also creates the greatest amount of organizational stress.

II. Reinventing Reference: What It Is Not

The confluence of increased expectations for customer service and the accelerated pace of integrating information technologies spurred much of the recent discussion in academic libraries about "rethinking," "reinventing," or "reengineering" the reference function. While many of the ideas raised by this debate were sound, they were mostly ideas that have been around for decades. For example, in 1938, Reece described then-current developments in academic university libraries such as campus messenger service deliveries to faculty offices, bibliographic courses for under-graduate students, elimination of catalogs in card form, and an early system of mechanization to charge out books. That same year, Garnett (1938) described an undergraduate course on how to use the library and the creation of an information desk to make assistance more accessible and informal.

The "rethinking reference" movement has had many proponents. Among the recent explorations of this topic were works by Ford (1986, 1988) and Campbell (1992). A seminal event in the rethinking reference movement was the Library Solutions Institutes at the University of California, Berkeley, and at Duke University in 1993, at which Campbell was the keynote speaker ("Rethinking Reference," 1993). Perhaps the most frequently cited specific case study in reinventing reference was the work by Massey-Burzio and her colleagues (1992) at Brandeis University. The primary contributions of the "Brandeis Model" were the replacement of a professionally staffed reference desk with a paraprofessionally staffed information desk and the creation of a reference consultation office.

Although the rethinking reference movement did promote some reconsideration of tactical approaches for providing reference services, it cannot be said to have resulted in radical changes to the strategic concepts for service delivery. To set a context for further discussion, the following summarizes the minimum standards for customer services and technology for reference services in an academic library today. These features reflect current mainstream thinking, not necessarily the service model for the twenty-first century; however, academic libraries not yet at this level are in danger of being left in the backwaters of the profession.

A. Customer Services

1. The traditional reference desk has been replaced by the following (Ewing and Hauptman, 1995)[1] (LaGuardia, 1995) (Lewis, 1995) (Mardikian and Kesselman, 1995)[2] (M. Morison, 1995)[3] (Steele, 1993)[4]:
    a. Paraprofessionals providing basic information services at an information desk.
    b. Reference librarians "roving" to seek customers in need of assistance (Bregman and Mento, 1992).
    c. A consultation office near the reference area staffed by librarians (Massey-Burzio, 1992).
2. The library has regular and formal mechanisms to receive customer feedback (suggestion boxes, focus groups, surveys, etc.).
3. Outreach librarians meet regularly with every academic department to provide faculty with expert training, collection management support, etc.
4. All library staff wear name tags to make themselves easily identifiable to the customers.
5. The library provides clear, concise, and attractive printed and online user guides.
6. Signage, which is readily apparent to locate appropriate service areas, incorporates the principles of good visual design. The text is concise, avoids jargon, and meets the needs of persons with disabilities.

B. Technological Environment

1. All public workstations are high-performance microcomputers (e.g., employ a Pentium CPU or higher), have at least 16 MB of memory (and preferably more), and support sound and video delivery.

[1] Ewing and Hauptman argue that reference desk time often is filled with nothing to do, the reference interview is overrated in importance, and reference desk personnel ignore patrons while working too in-depth with individuals.

[2] Mardikian and Kesselman address, in part, the use of reference rovers at point of need, cooperative reference over the network, instruction over the network for distance learning, development of user interfaces, development of expert systems, and partnerships with faculty for teaching and research.

[3] The article proposes value-added, tailored reference services, shrinking reference collections, less of a geocentric organizations, and paraprofessional staff negotiating routine requests.

[4] The author explores flatter organizational structures, knowledge navigators, paraprofessionals providing reference service, reengineering, and specialized generalists.

2. The workstation provides one-stop shopping. All electronic information services (e.g., online catalog, CD-ROM network, locally mounted databases, World Wide Web resources) are accessible at the same workstation, which provides access to a library-maintained Web home page (or other common interface) and the campuswide information system (CWIS). Simple context-sensitive online user assistance is available to respond to frequently asked questions.
3. The library makes available a wide range of networked online indexes and abstracting services, and full-text and image databases.
4. Workstations are housed at ergonomically designed work spaces and are situated so reference librarians can easily monitor workstation use and provide customer assistance.
5. Service requests (e.g., to ask reference questions, place interlibrary loan requests, etc.) can be performed electronically (Bristow, 1992; Still and Campbell, 1993) and by telephone.
6. All electronic services are available with full graphic user interfaces from high-speed connections at remote locations (e.g., offices, dormitories, PPP or SLIP connections for high-speed dial access).

Although every academic library may not currently meet all of these standards, this list does represent mainstream thinking for desirable practices today. However, we must begin to look for more significant changes. If librarianship is to continue as a vital partner in the educational enterprise, there must be further changes in how we cope with the two major *environmental* factors—customer service delivery and keeping pace with rapid changes in information technology—relative to four key *organizational* factors—the underlying service infrastructure, changes in strategic directions, considerations as to where we work, and evaluating the way in which we work. These relationships can be thought of as a grid, which is illustrated in Table I. The remainder of this chapter addresses each of these factors.

In the discussion that follows, the customer service issues are primarily discussed in terms of changes to the current environment to build the new information organization. By contrast, the technological changes are discussed primarily in terms of future changes that will enable us to change and grow. As we forge a new environment for library services, it is the intersection of these two themes that will form our course of action.

III. Meeting Increasing Customer Expectations

Customer service was not a concept invented by total quality management experts. For example, Cesar Ritz, the Swiss hotel proprietor, is attributed

Table I   Key Change Areas for Librarianship

Area of change	Customer service solutions	Technology solutions
Infrastructure	Prepare and articulate a customer service plan.	Expand bandwidth & apply artificial intelligence.
Strategic directions	Strategically disregard the customer to develop innovative services.	Accommodate commercialization of the Internet.
Where we work	Redesign workplaces and work spaces.	Adapt to virtual workplaces.
The way we work	Collaborate with information partners.	Apply new learning technologies.

with saying in 1908, "Le client n'a jamais tort" ("The customer is never wrong") (Ritz, 1992).[5] The modern equivalent of the quote has become "the customer is always right."

High-quality reference service traditionally was seen within the context of two functions of reference: answering specific questions at the point of need and providing "bibliographic" instruction to assist customers to help themselves. It has been the point-of-need function that has received the greatest attention in the "rethinking reference" movement thus far. The basic problem with most point-of-need service is its inherent inefficiency. Whether a librarian sits at a traditional reference desk or "roves," much of the effort is still devoted to answering repetitive questions that often do not require professional-level intervention. Staff productivity suffers because the answers must be given on a one-to-one basis. This customer dependency relationship continues in large measure because it has become a comfortable habit.

If we have made little effort to affect meaningful changes in point-of-need services, we have done even less with the instructional function. Instructional programs at many academic libraries are inefficient and ineffectual. Too much of what passes for instruction is little more than a "tour and tell" of the building or of bibliographic resources. Classroom instruction needs to move beyond talking heads to include more "live-and-learn" and hands-on experiences, interactivity, and self-paced and media-based instruction. We must create educational experiences that students want to participate in rather than merely endure. Only in this way can we reduce the labor intensity and increase the return for the investment in technology.

It is ironic that we perpetuate these pedagogically flawed instructional methods given that these programs not only are ineffective, but also often

[5] According to the *Oxford Dictionary*, the quote was originally recorded by R. Nevill and C. E. Jerningham. (1908). *Picadilly to Pall Mall.* p. 94.

cause unneeded stress on staff. For example, at Wright State University, reference librarians were giving personalized 50-minute presentations for each section of the required first-year undergraduate English course. In this 50-minute segment there was little time to do more than provide a fast "show-and-tell" presentation, followed by students working on customized reference question exercises. In addition to the great stress on reference librarians to accommodate well over 3000 students a year, it is doubtful that many students found the experience to be educational or enjoyable. This instructional method was later replaced by a self-guided audiotape tour. Each student checked out a portable tape recorder and headset from the circulation desk at his or her convenience and walked through the library unobtrusively. It was not high technology nor was it innovative, but it was inexpensive, easy to implement, and much more effective than the system it replaced.

A. Changing the Infrastructure: Developing a Customer Service Plan

If an organization expects to delivery high-quality services, it is important to establish a shared benchmark for the library staff and the customers to judge what constitutes quality service. To do this, the library must clearly articulate and publicize its service standards. For example, at Wright State University (1995) this statement is a published brochure, "Our Commitment to Customer Service." [The full statement also appears as an appendix in Wehmeyer, Auchter, and Hirshon (1996).] The brochure is in two parts. The first part contains broad pledges that apply to all service areas, such as "we will provide courteous, prompt, and accurate service to every customer." The second part consists of specific quality measures for each customer service, such as "we will acknowledge you immediately at any service desk and serve you within 3 minutes or call additional staff" or "we will respond personally to your signed suggestions within 5 working days." It is this section of the document that gives the specific context and meaning (Wehmeyer, Auchter, and Hirshon, 1996).

There are certain principles that should underlie a customer service statement. The statement should be written from the perspective of the customer, not the staff. The focus should be on frequently used customer-apparent services, not on background operations that may be important for effective functioning, but of which customers are unaware. The statements should be clear and concise, and avoid the use of jargon. Statements should be unambiguous and phrased positively. Equivocating words or phrases, such as "generally," "usually," or "whenever possible," should be eliminated. Specific service goals should be measurable. For example, instead of saying that the library will provide "prompt" service, the Wright State statement says "we will meet your research needs when materials are at the bindery by locating acceptable substitutes immediately or providing copies within 48 hours." Such goals commit the organization to stretch to do more and to do so consistently. However, when developing stretch goals, the library should be careful not to create expectations on which it may not be able to deliver.

Successful development and implementation of such a plan requires the involvement of all staff because ultimately the work to make the customer service plan a success will fall on everyone. Staff should be asked to identify potential implementation problems and solutions, recognizing that simply saying "more staff, equipment, or money" is not a solution.

Effective implementation requires an understanding by staff that every transaction is important and that one bad customer experience can cancel out a hundred previous positive ones. Above all, staff should not "pass the buck" and should not "pass the blame." Before referring a customer to another department, staff should be encouraged either to call ahead or to accompany the customer to ensure that someone will be available to provide assistance. At Wright State, effective referral was so important that there is only one statement phrased in the negative, which was done to increase its impact: "We will not give you the runaround. We will provide the assistance you need, or we will put you in contact with someone who can."

Implementation should be a responsibility delegated to each department. To ensure the success of the program, there should also be mechanisms in place to review the performance of the department against the goals. Monitoring throughout the year is important, but the time required to track progress should not impede staff from providing the actual customer service. The measures may vary from department to department. For some departments, formal and regular statistical records to monitor their performance may be appropriate, while other departments may choose to employ informal or casual observation.

This articulation of customer service expectations ultimately helps staff because it clarifies for all staff what level of service the organization intends to deliver. Eliminating the ambiguity can also relieve the pressure to perform too many services for too many people. Library administration must accept the obligation to provide the support necessary to meet the commitments, but all staff must recognize that accountability is everyone's responsibility.

B. Changing Strategic Directions: Strategically and Selectively Disregarding the Customer and Staff to Improve Service

Traditionally, the emphasis of the customer service movement has been on being sensitive to the needs of the customer. Effective techniques to do this include suggestion boxes, focus group interviews, and user surveys. Although effective listening is critical, it is a passive activity that ironically can limit progress. Customers usually know what is available, but not what is possible. Customer services should be based not only on what customers express as their current needs, but also should predict those needs and generate demand for new services. *On occasion*, it is desirable to *disregard* customers *strategically* to give them what they do not know they want. This is not contradictory to listening to the customer, but is a complementary activity. While customer satisfaction is important, Hamel and Prahalad note that "it is equally important to ask which customers are we not even serving" because "[c]ustomers are notoriously lacking in foresight." For example, in libraries, many current services such as online catalogs and indexes were not the result of customer requests but arose from the foresight of visionary thinkers in the profession. As Hamel and Prahalad (1994) have said, "Companies that create the future do more than satisfy customers, they constantly amaze them." Disregarding the customer must only be done for *strategic* reasons and never out of expediency. Overlooking the immediate needs of the customer as part of a clear strategy to create a new service is very different from disregarding the customer to make life easier for staff.

Sometimes, it may be desirable to disregard the *staff* for the same reason as disregarding the customer: lack of vision. Strategically disregarding customers or staff requires not only a well-developed vision, but also great faith in that vision. There will likely be staff resistance to an idea if its value is not immediately apparent or if it will result in additional work. Staff may claim that "we know what the customer wants." Staff also may overgeneralize customer behavior based on only those customers they serve. For example, all customers of reference services are customers of the library, but many library customers are not customers of reference services at all. To discover the needs of the nonserved population, unobtrusive observation of the entire population can be a good way to learn from the customer.

Knowing when it is the right time to disregard the customer or the staff can be difficult. One good indicator is to recognize when the vision becomes clouded by unimaginative thought. One marketing executive acknowledges that "Our biggest competitor . . . is the way in which people currently do things" (Martin, 1995). A manifestation of unimaginative thinking is when we attempt to protect the customer from changes in systems or services. This is most often done under the guise that "we know what the customer wants" or "the customer cannot cope with so many, or such constant, changes." In other words, we project on the customer changes that we ourselves do not like. We must begin to recognize that to do this may temporarily make life easier for customers or ourselves, but this may do significant damage in the long-run if the organization fails to demonstrate the courage needed to make significant changes. In a technological age, rapid change is becoming the norm, and the ability to adjust to that change is becoming an essential survival skill.

C. Changing Where We Work: Redesigning Physical Space to Enable Organizational Change

Making changes to public spaces is an essential element of any reengineering effort. Vischer (1995) notes that space planning is important because ". . . [s]trategic work-space planning can facilitate and, in some cases, drive reengineering of work processes, and can encourage teamwork . . . and instigate other organizational changes" (p. 33). Although the importance of virtual reference services from remote locations will be important (and is discussed later), there is little doubt that for the next decade services in physical libraries will continue to affect how customers use virtual resources. Too often, the configuration of the public service space in the library is an afterthought. Rather than reenvisioning an effective space that is aesthetically pleasing, library reference areas tend to gain functions over time. Slowly the space becomes cumbersome, overgrown, ill-conceived, and user-unfriendly. For example, Cargill (1992) observes that most reference areas create an illusion "of a barrier between the practitioner and the patron, between the information disseminator and the recipient" (p. 83). Even in new buildings, the reference area can become an architect's dream but a working librarian's nightmare. For the reengineering of reference services to be effective, a thorough review and reconceptualization of the physical space is essential.

Every library building presents its own unique challenges. What works in one building or with one type of clientele may not be effective in another. Whenever a library is undertaking a serious or comprehensive review or reengineering of its services, it is essential to review whether changes are necessary to the physical environment. As noted earlier, many libraries recently reengineered their reference services to replace the reference desk with an information desk, to open a consultation office, or to introduce new systems that incorporate a wide variety of emerging networked electronic library services. Anytime a library contemplates such large-scale changes, there should be a concomitant review of space utilization to ensure that the physical environment fully enables the changes envisioned to the services. Old reference areas, designed to deliver a different type of service (if ever truly designed at all), and new service models are inherently incompatible. To rectify the many existing physical problems with the reference area and to better incorporate the planned services, it is best to envision the area as an empty space. There should be no limits as to where to locate services and operations. This will doubtless require an iterative process in which many physical configurations will be considered and discarded.

When designing the new reference services for a networked information environment, there are some basic principles a library should consider in reconceptualizing the service area.

1. Customers should be able to see readily from anywhere in the service area where to go for help. Staff should have a clear line of sight of customers in need of assistance.

2. Workstations should be clustered near the service area. The clusters should have ergonomically designed stations that do not obstruct lines of sight. Whenever possible, customers should face the service personnel, rather than have the backs of the customers facing the service area. There should be sufficient space to expand the number of workstations.

3. Reference stacks should be arranged so service personnel can look down as many of the aisles as quickly and easily as possible (especially when roving). If there is a permanent desk, staff should be able to look straight down the aisles from the desk.

4. If there are other service points in the area, the walking path and sight lines should be unobstructed so that customers can be directed quickly and easily.

5. Signage should be neat, large, and applied judiciously. Too many signs, whether neat or sloppy, become visual noise that obstruct communication rather than enhance it. The library should ban handwritten signs, laser-printed signs in all black letters with no borders, and little pieces of paper taped to the border of computer screens.

6. The space around workstations should be neat and free of extraneous brochures and signs.

7. If there is a reference consultation office, it should be located very near the reference area. The space should be sufficiently equipped to provide effective service and be soundproofed to allow for conversation without disturbing others.

Too often library service areas are ill-conceived or not conceived at all. Effective space planning is critical to effective service delivery. Logical space configuration does not necessarily need to cost a great deal of money. The expenditure of even modest funds on planning and renovation can yield benefits far in excess of their cost in terms of increased staff efficiency and improved customer perceptions.

D. Changing the Way We Work: Engaging in Collaborative Efforts to Improve Customer Service

Libraries probably have had a history of collaborative efforts greater than most corporate or academic organizations. Yet even with a tradition of cooperation, libraries still were reticent to collaborate because to do so inevitably raised concerns about having to cede institutional independence, or that the cooperation might result in the strengthening of an institutional competitor. However, in the global economy of today, such collaboration is vital to organizational survival. Effective customer service increasingly requires that libraries engage in meaningful collaborative efforts so that we can provide more collectively than we can provide alone. Every collaborative effort may not be desirable. To ensure that the effort will be mutually beneficial, it is essential for an institution to understand the agendas, opportunities, challenges, and drawbacks of its various strategic partners. Any strategic alliance involves compromises. Nonetheless, effectively managed cooperation can improve circumstances for each institution.

A dynamic example of library collaboration is OhioLINK (Hirshon, 1995). Initially this statewide network consisted largely of state-assisted academic institutions and two private research institutions, but other private academic institutions came onboard later. OhioLINK provides each member institution with a local and union online catalog, shared online research databases, and full-text retrieval services. Through the central online catalog it is possible for customers to initiate direct requests for borrowing books from other libraries. There is a daily ground delivery service, and most requests are available to the borrower within 3 days or less of the request.

OhioLINK provides member libraries with substantial opportunities to engage in strategic alliances that have had a dramatic effect on customer services, particularly in the development of digital library services. The State of Ohio provides central categorical funds to OhioLINK so member libraries, at no cost to their institutions, may obtain many online resources that complement those that the local institution provides locally. These funds are in addition to the ongoing funds received by each local institution. A basic tenet of OhioLINK is that a strong local commitment to the continued purchasing of materials is essential; without such materials to share, OhioLINK would be an empty shell. By leveraging institutional and OhioLINK funds, member institutions benefit from a rich mix of abstracting and indexing services, full-text periodical articles and books, and online reference resources. Freed from having to expend local funds for these purchases, member libraries can rededicate institutional funds for purchasing additional collections and digital resources.

Collaboration need not be limited to interinstitutional alliances. In addition to external partnerships for effective customer service, libraries also must develop internal alliances with other campus-based information partners (Shapiro and Long, 1994). For example, there is increasing cooperation by libraries and campus-computing organizations to design and deliver Internet services, to provide faculty and student training, and to develop the campuswide information system. In some cases this collaboration is resulting in formal changes to the reporting or organizational structure. There currently appears to be a growing trend for academic institutions to formalize this arrangement and to name a "chief information officer" for the institution who is responsible for libraries, computing, media services, and telecommunications. Some might assert that this is simply a repeat of a pattern seen in the early and mid-1980s (Hirshon, 1988), but growing evidence shows that the current integration is more widespread and deeper than before. An informal survey done by the author in February 1996 revealed that there are nationally at least 64 academic institutions with chief information officers who have line responsibility for libraries and computing. Evidence also shows that more institutions have this option under active consideration. The list of institutions cuts across all academic types, from colleges through research institutions.

Even in institutions that are not combining these operations, there is an increased expectation for collaboration. There is a clear indication of a shift in institutional thinking as to how to use technology to provide customer services and how customer services must drive the application of technology. Technology, resources, and services are coalescing and causing this new breed of organization to foster interorganizational collaboration. This result also may be one of the first signs of a major shift in philosophy for higher education, moving from the model of the solitary faculty member to one of strong team collaboration and interaction to become a learning organization.

IV. Customer Services and Technological Change: Past and Future

The need to improve customer service will constantly increase over the next decade, but the likelihood is great that the increased demand will not be matched by a considerable increase in library budgets for additional staff. Effective implementation of technology will be essential for libraries to provide customers with more, and more innovative, services in the future. This may seem a modern management phenomenon, but not only were libraries early adopters of technology to improve customer service, but they also were early predictors as to how technology would change how people gained access to and used information. To understand how information technology may affect customer services in the future, it is instructive to reflect for a moment on some of the more visionary ideas of the past half-century.

"[C]omparisons between the university libraries of today and those of a hundred years ago are virtually meaningless—the two belong in different categories" (Arlt and Lund, 1937). These words, written in 1937, resonate today. For example, Wilson (1936)[6] predicted widespread use in libraries of photocopiers, computerized library systems for circulating library materials, and expansive use of mass storage. While the reality may not have come in the same form that Wilson predicted, his broad vision was remarkable for its time.

A seminal prediction in information management was Vannevar Bush's Memex, which 50 years ago presaged the modern online catalog and World Wide Web. Bush described Memex as a device for individual use that would be a "sort of mechanized private file and library . . . [that] stores all his books, records, and communications, and which is mechanized so that it may be consulted with exceeding speed and flexibility. . . ." Memex could be "operated from a distance" and had "slanting translucent screens, on which material can be projected for convenient reading." The input device was a keyboard (Bush, 1945). Twenty five years later, Bush (1970) explained further that "The heart of the idea is that of associative indexing whereby a particular item is caused to select another at once and automatically. The user of the machine, as he feeds items into it, ties them together by coding to form trails. . . . Here is where the ability of the digital computer to learn from its own experience . . . comes into play. . . . It can do more than this; it can build trails for its master" (p. 190). The enabling technology was decades away, but Bush's vision encompassed online computer storage and catalogs, retrieval of full-text documents, computer workstations, automated filtering mechanisms, predictive searching, remote access, artificial intelligence, and hypertext.

In a more popular vein, in 1963 and 1964 the Sheaffer Pen Company[7] ran a series of advertisements about what life would be like in the twenty-first century. The constant theme of the series was that the fountain pen would continue to be essential in the next century. Many of the library-related inventions predicted came to pass (again in different forms), including a voice-activated portable electronic language translator, a wrist-watch-size television, and a portable purse-size videophone with speed dialing. Perhaps the most prescient example was electronic mail using a portable networked device that looks amazingly like an Apple Newton, but upon which one wrote with (of course) a Sheaffer fountain pen (1964/1965). Sheaffer may not have been too far off in predicting the viability of the fountain pen; even in our

[6] For a further discussion of Wilson's article, see Hirshon (1988).

[7] Sheaffer Pen Company. (1963–1964). Advertisements appeared as follows: The wrist-watch television appeared in two places (*National Geographic*, June 1963, and *Time*, November 13, 1964). The videophone appeared in multiple publications, including *Time* (June 7, 1963). The checkbook appeared in multiple publications, including *Time* (March 20, 1964). The credit card ring appeared in multiple publications, including *Time* (March 15, 1964). The Newton-type electronic mail slate appeared in multiple publications, including *Time* (December 4, 1964).

digital world, WordPerfect software continues to use as its logo the nib of a fountain pen to represent the epitome of fine writing.

Also in 1964, the Council on Library Resources commissioned Bolt, Beranek, and Newman (BBN) to prepare *Toward the Library of the 21st Century*. This is the company that "designed the first modem, chose the @ symbol to address electronic mail and built . . . the original computer network from which the Internet evolved" (Zuckerman, 1995a). The 1964 BBN library report envisioned a computer-based system with remote access from home and office. Full documents were stored, retrieved, and delivered to the computer workstation. Audio playback was available, as was high resolution of art reproductions. The system would ". . . deduce answers to questions asked, and not only find answers that are already stored in its information memory. Accepting questions and giving answer in natural, written English, the library will draw upon deductive principles and associative [indexing] techniques for organizing information. Also, it will have checked each new piece of information received, to see whether that piece substantiates, contradicts, or merely repeats information stored previously" (Bolt, Beranek, and Newman, 1964, p. 10). BBN also described work on a prototype system called Symbiont, which consisted of electric typewriter connected to a light pen and cathode-ray tube display to enable entry and editing of online text (Bolt et al., 1964, pp. 31–34).

In all of these cases, the new technology was envisioned as enabling people to do their work faster and better. *As we look to the future, customer service clearly will remain as the primary objective and driver for change, but information technology remains the major enabler of that change.*

Technology can enable customer service, but it can be a two-edged sword. The changes wrought by technology can be disorienting and stressful for staff and customers. However, it is important to recognize that often it is not the technology with which it is difficult to cope, but change itself. Daniel Bell remarked that Mark Twain's Connecticut Yankee at King Arthur's Court "was able to introduce quickly all kinds of wonderful inventions from the nineteenth century, but he foundered when he sought to change the religion and monarchy—a lesson in the comparative recalcitrance of technology and belief systems in social change" (Bell, 1967, p. xxiii).

As libraries develop new customer-driven services, it will be essential to know not only the trends in information technology, but how those changes might affect customer services. A few examples of current breakthroughs in computing and telecommunications may be instructive:

1. Architext Software is developing a search engine capable of searching by concept by scanning millions of documents and retrieving relevant items even when the desired keyword does not appear anywhere in the article. The

searcher can request an abstract for each reference provided or ask the search engine to retrieve similar articles (Reese, 1995).

2. A company called "The Other 90%" is developing a "mind-driven technology," a computer input device to replace the keyboard and the mouse. The device fits on the fingertip and detects changes in your heart rate, in body temperature, and in the nervous system. The searcher can therefore enable body reactions to control actions and replicate a learning experience (Fefer, 1995).

3. A scanning laser opthalmoscope will allow persons who are visually impaired to read words on a computer screen ("A Seeing-Eye Helper," 1995). Although developed as a means for researchers to probe the inside of the eye, we can imagine the potential to adapt it to become an optically driven navigational device for computers.

4. At the Massachusetts Institute of Technology, the "Things That Think" project is dedicated to designing "computer intelligence into everyday products" such as "shoes able to calculate the time it will take to walk to a given location." The project is focusing on "new sensing technology, new networking technology, and a kind of artificial intelligence that makes once-inanimate objects responsive to human needs and emotions" (Markoff, 1995).

The practical application of these changes to libraries may be many years away. Nonetheless, these ideas should cause us to consider the tremendous shifts in how we think about technology and how that technology will change libraries.

V. Adjusting to the Technological Changes of the Future

We may not be able to predict the precise nature of future customer demands, but it is clear that a strong technological infrastructure will be essential to create an effective information environment for that new world. Therefore, we must understand the nature of changes that will likely occur and begin to predict how those changes will affect our future customer services. There are at least four technological trends relative to the key factors noted earlier that will change the nature and quality of library customer services in the future: changes in telecommunications bandwidth and the application of artificial intelligence, the commercialization of the Internet, the growth of the virtual workplace, and the expanding use of instructional technology.

A. Changing the Infrastructure: Expanding Bandwidth and Applying Artificial Intelligence

Probably no development in technology will transform information delivery more than increases in bandwidth to enable the transmission of large quantities of information across network lines. This will be possible because of advances in hardware [such as fiber and plastic optics, asynchronous transfer mode (ATM), cable modems, and ISDN] and software (such as Java). Although many of these technologies (particularly in hardware) have been available for some time, the recent commercial and popular demand for Internet-based services on the World Wide Web (WWW) is driving the need for higher and higher bandwidth. By one estimate, in the two years and a half years from January 1993 to July 1995, there was a worldwide increase from less than 21,000 Web sites to more than 120,000 (http://www.nw.com/zone/WWW/report.html).

As little as 10 years ago, nearly the entire information universe was text and data driven. Today, there is a need for high-resolution animation, video, high-grade sound reproduction, and real-time teleconferencing. Increased bandwidth is therefore required not only at the backbone and office, but also remotely at home. In the United States, cable television and telephone companies are vying for the rights to provide these multimedia voice, video, and data services. Each claims that its new technologies will use existing standard telephone copper wires or coax cable to enable these high bandwidth services. In countries such as Australia, the movement is to bypass coaxial cabling (as is used for cable television in the United States) and to go directly to fiber-optic cabling directly to every home.

These and other technologies will not only speed the transfer of information, but will change the nature of the information being transferred. The critical development is not the technology itself, but the application of that technology to enrich the information available to the customer. These technological advances will make possible a much wider range of research and instructional services. For example, the large-scale distribution of high definition images and sound (including real-time video and true interactivity) over the Internet will change not only what information is used in instruction and research, but where and how that information is deployed and exploited. As with the growth of personal computers over the past decade, competition and demand will drive constant and dramatic increases in bandwidth power with concomitant decreases in cost. With these changes in the infrastructure it will be possible to deliver a far wider range of networked information services than previously possible. Communication changes will provide high speed connectivity not only in the office and the home, but through cellular technology to any computer at any place, including on the road.

This bandwidth is essential because a key element to the future of higher education will be distance learning. The secondary effect on libraries service delivery will be profound. There is already an obvious trend of the library being less place bound, but this trend line will spike dramatically. Libraries may continue to play a role as a navigational assistant in the use of these information resources, but only if the library has systems in place to assist these remote customers. Librarians must become expert not only at navigating this new telecommunications environment, but also in assisting faculty and students to integrate the technology into their coursework and research. Libraries must also develop digital archives that ensure the preservation of digital information so customers will continue to have an ever-expanding array of information.

To organize and provide access to information in a vastly different electronic world will require tools that go well beyond the capabilities of current systems. To meet this challenge, libraries will need to develop and apply artificial intelligence and smart systems. For four decades there have been predictions about the imminent blossoming of artificial intelligence (AI) and practical applications for it. Within this context, AI includes a number of different technologies, including *fuzzy logic* (which allows the computer to establish rules to make a close approximation of matches to information queries), *expert systems* (which replicate the deductive reasoning process), and *data warehousing* or *information harvesting* (which uses the computer to collect information from databases on one or more systems to derive new forms of information). AI also includes *neural networks*, which attempt to replicate the way in which the human brain works by using inductive logic (Abu-Mostafa, 1995).

Currently, AI methodologies such as fuzzy logic, information harvesting, expert systems, and neural networks are being combined to create more refined systems in which the whole of the combination is stronger than the sum of its AI parts. Related developments in information processing, such as natural language processing, enable users to frame questions in standard English phrases. According to one survey, currently more than 70% of America's top 500 companies are using AI applications in some way or another (Port, 1995). Eventually these techniques will become less expensive and become more affordable for integration into library systems. For example, AI holds tremendous promise to improve current awareness information services by combining precoordinated profiles with cumulative search histories to make search results more user responsive. Based on the search request placed by the customer, it will also become more practical to have the system select the appropriate databases to search and to search those databases simultaneously. The customer will then receive a merged search result based on the databases searched. While some librarians fear that this customer empowerment may result in a lower quality search result or that librarians will be put out of a job, it is also possible that there will be real benefits to these new systems. With new forms of information being developed at a far more rapid rate than the typical person can absorb, librarians can ensure their future as navigators if they continue to be pioneers of the new technology.

B. Changing Strategic Directions: Commercialization of the Internet

There has been a massive growth of interest about the Internet over the past few years. Where much of the initial interest was based on the use of electronic mail, today the major driver has been the growth of information services available on the World Wide Web. The Web has made it practical for the first time to transmit not only interactive data and images, but also voice and video at a relatively low transmission cost.

The Web is already becoming crowded with home pages of individuals, nonprofit organizations, and commercial information providers. How long many of the Web servers now online will *stay* online is a matter of some debate. Even in the commercial sector, the value of the Internet is under question. One skeptic noted that "Right now it is like an enormous library with no card catalog. People look around and leave" (Churbuck, 1995). Nonetheless, whole industries are developing to exploit anything associated with the Web. Netscape Communications in August 1995 had the best opening day for a new stock in Wall Street history (Zuckerman, 1995b). With the entry of Sun Microsystem's product "Java," the Web is being re-imagined as a much more interactive medium, and one in which the network itself and the software may eventually become one.

As with any such developments, there is obviously the danger of too much hype and too much fiscal overspeculation. Although it is much too soon to predict the eventual corporate winners and losers, collectively the industry has high expectations that the Web and the Internet will drive technology during the next 10 years in the same way that personal computers and networking did during the past 10 years. With so many major corporations investing heavily in the Internet, the Internet is no longer the academic preserve it was. What was a free and common good may soon be an expensive and limited commodity as commercial entities refine mechanisms for charging for information and for making the system more secure. The looming question is whether the Gresham's Law of the Internet will take hold, with "bad money" driving out "good resources" because only the heavily capitalized industries (and for libraries, commercial publishers) can afford to pay.

Regardless of whether one believes that the Internet is creating a new global community or a crass commercial menace, Internet commercialization will change the strategic directions for library customer services. Librarians typically have given away expertise for free. The Internet is creating a new venue for fee-based access and retrieval information services that could provide the necessary capital to continue funding high-cost technology. Ultimately, commercialization of the Internet may be what makes libraries more expensive, more lucrative, and, ironically, more customer-service oriented because it will be the marketplace that will determine which services are essential.

C. Changing Where We Work: The Virtual Workplace

The library information universe traditionally was physically bound by the amount of information that we could house in a building. Librarians regulated the pace of change by regulating how, where, and when that information was available. In contrast, virtual information is constantly and rapidly changing, and is bound by neither place nor time. Today, this virtual information is being accessed by virtual workers from virtual offices.

Telecommuting, or work in the "virtual organization," is rapidly expanding. For example, the Olsten Corporation found that "29 percent of companies permit employee telecommuting, and 86 percent of these firms reported an accompanying productivity increase. Telecommuting is more prevalent in high-tech companies (44%), followed by service companies (37%) . . . Professional-level employees were most likely to be offered the option of telecommuting (cited by 63% of the respondents . . .)" ("Telecommuting Raises Productivity," 1995).

In the commercial sector, the move toward the virtual office is driven largely by an effort to reduce the cost of office space, to improve worker productivity, and to respond to the desire of workers for greater job flexibility. There is a growing list of books and newsletters for workers on how to get started in telecommuting and a Web site (http://www.gilgordon.com).

For every movement there is inevitably a countermovement. There are those who fear that telecommuting has a significant downside. For example, Snider (1995) is concerned about an "environmental disaster of the first magnitude" as huge numbers of telecommuters discover the charms of working at home out in the rural countryside. Others worry about the loss of socialization or sense of stability by not having a workplace to which to report. Davenport notes that in a survey of IBM virtual workers, 77% reported that professional communication at work was somewhat or much worse, and 88% found their ability to socialize with co-workers was worse. Davenport concludes that "The fact is, we don't communicate well in virtual environments" (Davenport, 1995, p. 36). There are also important social concerns. As Davenport notes, "Having an office doesn't just give us a place to sit; it's also a place to get socialized into the culture of the company" (Davenport, 1995, p. 38). Handy (1995) advises that "a sense of place is as important to most of us as a sense of purpose" (p. 42) and "to enjoy the efficiencies and other benefits of the virtual organization, we will have to rediscover how to run organizations based more on trust than on control" (p. 44).

Libraries as places have always been social organizations. The effects of virtuality on our culture will be profound both for staff and for customers.

There already have been experiments in librarians telecommuting to perform original cataloging (Black and Hyslop, 1995). Perhaps not all aspects of librarianship are so hospitable to telecommuting, but the expanding availability of virtual information certainly makes many aspects of virtual reference service more practical. Some reference work can be performed outside the traditional library building. Rather than being employees of the library, reference librarians may well become free-lance workers who provide their services from home rather than from the library building.

For telecommuting customers of libraries, user assistance must be available at all hours to any location in the world. Although simultaneous data and voice communication is common in the business workplace today, it is less common in the home. As remote access becomes the norm, simultaneous communication will become a necessity for effective remote assistance systems. For example, Billings and others described a system that enables the reference librarian to take control of the user's workstation at a remote site and to intervene as needed on the user's workstation (Billings, Carver, Racine, and Tongate, 1994).

As with all changes brought by technology, virtual offices and telecommuting will neither be all good nor all bad. It will be different than what we have done before, but its power must be harnessed. There will be the inevitable experiments, successes, and failures. However, academic libraries cannot afford to ignore the confluence of two major trends: virtual work and distance learning. The outcome is obvious. A rapidly increasing percentage of the country's population will spend at least part—if not all—of their time working outside of the traditional building-bound office environment. As library customers, these people will need information at distant locations. Once people are liberated to work outside of the bounds of the physical organization, they will demand that their advanced learning be moved beyond the boundaries of the traditional campus-based classroom (and, therefore, campus-based library). Adjusting to these profound social changes, which are being caused by technology, will undoubtedly present one of the greatest challenges for library services in the decades to come.

D. Changing the Way We Work: Expanding the Use of Instructional Technology

Despite the many recent reports touting the potential power of technology to improve the learning process, evidence still remains that the adoption of information technology in the classroom has been very slow. Today only a small percentage of college courses nationally use technology to enhance or supplement instruction. However, a recent survey conducted by the American Council on Education of university administrators found that 68% thought it "very likely" that "more courses will use electronic materials," 47% saw it as "very likely" that "more courses will be offered through distance learning," and 90% thought it very likely or possible that class assignments will be submitted electronically within the next 5 years (DeLoughry, 1995). Therefore, while the use of information technology in on-campus instruction and distance learning has thus far been slow, there is reason to believe it will become of great importance in the twenty-first century.

This growth of information technology to foster the learning process will generate new roles for, and expectations of, librarians. If librarianship is to survive in this new world, librarians must find ways to add value to the educational process. It will no longer be sufficient to answer point-of-need questions. Librarians must seek opportunities to become members of the team that designs instructional programs for use in and outside of the classroom. To continue in the passive role of disseminating what others created will no longer be adequate.

These new demands will also require new skills and abilities. Training for reference work must rely less on understanding information sources than on understanding the learning process. Librarians also need expertise both in the application of technology and in visual and educational design principles. The advent of the World Wide Web and home pages has encouraged many people to become their own designers. Unfortunately, having design tools available and having the skills to use them well are not the same thing. Access to a word processor does not make one write like Tolstoy, nor does access to HTML or screen design software make one a system designer. The Web today is cluttered with poorly designed home pages that are all sound and visual fury, but devoid of a logical screen layout or content. The Web has granted the ability to transfer our early lack of skills in creating attractive and informative brochures into the disability to distribute our poor handiwork on an international scale. The basic principles for good screen design are quite similar to the principles that have governed the design of the printed page for the past few hundred years. Unfortunately, many librarians may be skilled in information access, but have not a clue as to the impact of good visual design. Screens that have lots of graphics, buttons, sound links, and video clips can seem dazzling, but the dazzle is worthless if the customer still cannot find the information he or she is seeking.

Whether the expertise is necessary to bring Web resources to the classroom, to assist in the development of course-related home pages, or to develop interactive learning experiences, librarians must become equal partners in the learning process if the library is going to continue as an important player in the emerging high technology university. The retraining of professional staff to deliver these new services will be an essential element in this process.

VI. Coping with the Future

Academic libraries will always have limited funds to invest in staff and in new technology to meet customer service demands. This problem has been made worse not only because organizational downsizing has left most libraries with fewer staff to provide more services, but also because the useful life cycle of automated equipment has gone from being 5 to 7 years down to 1 to 2 years. Few (if any) universities have a plan or adequate *recurring* funding for the replacement and upgrading of computing equipment. The 1993 National Survey of Desktop Computing in Higher Education showed that 44% of those surveyed did not have plans for replacing outdated machines" (Mac-Knight, 1995). The Massachusetts Institute of Technology is one institution that does have a plan. They recommend that "administrators need to stop thinking about computers as though they are buildings. They [computers] are not a capital expense and should not be paid for out of capital budgets. Computers must be amortized and regularly replaced to keep pace with the changes in technology. Second, administrators must acknowledge that technology is not free. The days when technology vendors could afford to equip a campus lab have long since passed" (MacKnight, 1995).

In the absence of a regular plan to replace equipment, often the goal is not to get ahead of the technology curve, but simply to stay even with it. This task is made more difficult when an organization must attempt to predict customer needs in a transitional period in which the technology is rarely stable. Information technology can go from innovative to obsolete without ever having been mainstream either because the technology was too far ahead of its time or because it was not understood or wanted by customers.

Many of the changes in library services over the past decade have not been particularly dramatic. Too often the changes represented new solutions to old problems rather than re-conceptualizing the principles we wished to espouse or the standards we wished to establish. In reengineering terms, we rethought what we did, but not whether we should do it at all. Solutions should follow problems, not the other way around. As we look to the future, not only do we need to break some of our old habits, we also need to break some of our newer ones. To do so, we should start developing new principles for our customer services based on the four key organizational factors discussed in this chapter.

The new infrastructure should emphasize sensitivity to the needs of the customer. Systems and services should rapidly respond to customer information needs, regardless of that customer's physical or virtual location. The technological infrastructure must have high bandwidth and employ technology that can better predict and meet customer needs. The library should maintain only services that benefit the customer and eliminate processes that impede customer service, even when those processes make life easier for the staff. The profession should develop, and individual libraries should implement, standards that regularly measure the quality of customer services.

Changes in strategic directions should occur to create an environment that encourages the development of new programs, resources, and services, even when the change was not requested by, or the value is not immediately apparent to, the customer.

A reexamination of where we work for the near future will require modification of the physical environment in which we provide customer service. Over the longer term, libraries must provide innovative new services that exploit the native environment of the virtual workplace. Customers should find the service environment, whether physical or virtual, welcoming and supportive.

The way in which we work must also change. Professional staff should do only professional-level work. Libraries should seek out and seize opportunities to collaborate with other information partners to develop high-value services. The labor-intensiveness of the work should be kept to a minimum through the effective exploitation of instructional technology.

As we look to define the new information services organization, it is instructive to review Robert Morison's principles for computer operations organizations. His prescriptions apply equally well to libraries. Morison notes that the future of information systems will be based less on system maintenance than on the quality of the services we provide. Information organizations must stop spreading themselves too thin and concentrate on responding to the customer needs of the entire organization rather than on individual users. Given that customers now do much of their own computing themselves, Morison believes information organizations must provide a different type of customer service and must recognize that customers have uneven learning levels. Most importantly, if the information systems staff are to be effective change agents, the staff must be good at changing themselves (R. Morison, 1995).

Libraries have a reputation for being traditional and stable. This future will require a fundamental rethinking of the organizational mind set away from stability and predictability. As Handy (1995, p. 46) wrote, "a necessary condition of constancy is an ability to change." The emerging organization must constantly meet customer expectations through creativity, innovation, and risk-taking.

When Alice was in Wonderland, she engaged herself in a constant process of change and discovery by eating and drinking different foods. As a consequence, she kept growing and shrinking, depending on the food she ate. At one point, Alice remarks to the Caterpillar that "being so many different sizes in one day is very confusing." Nevertheless, Alice must have enjoyed the process because she continued to experiment by eating new foods. Librarians today can empathize with Alice's plight and wonder how best to cope. When one is in the middle of the change process, it is hard not only to see how it will come out, but sometimes to see the significance of what is happening at the moment. The actual changes are often of transient importance. It is going through the process of change that is the most difficult challenge. How is a librarian today to cope with higher customer expectations and the stress of constantly changing new technologies? Perhaps the advice to Alice from the Caterpillar, to whom the process of changing from chrysalis to butterfly is natural evolution, says it best: "you'll get used to it in time."

> "You may call it 'nonsense' if you like," said the Red Queen, "but *I've* heard nonsense, compared with which that would be as sensible as a dictionary!"

References

Abu-Mostafa, Y. S. (1995). Machines that learn from hints. *Scientific American* **272**, 64–69.

Arlt, G. O., and Lund, J. F. (1937). The university library: Some thoughts about its past and some questions about its future. *Library Journal* **62**, 766.

Bell, D. (1967). Introduction. In *The Year 2000: A Framework for Speculation on the Next Thirty-Three Years.* (H. Kahn and A. J. Wiener, eds.) MacMillan, New York.

Billings, H., Carver, I. E., Racine, D., and Tongate, J. (1994). Remote reference assistance for electronic information resources over networked workstations. *Library Hi Tech* **45**, 77–86.

Black, L., and Hyslop, C. (1995). Telecommuting for original cataloging at the Michigan State University Libraries. *College & Research Libraries* **56**, 319–323.

Bolt, Beranek, and Newman (BBN). (1964). *Toward the Library of the 21st Century: A Report on Progress Made in a Program of Research Sponsored by the Council on Library Resources.* Bolt, Beranek, and Newman, Cambridge, MA.

Bregman, A., and Mento, B. (1992). Reference roving at Boston College. *C&RL News* **53**, 634–635, 637.

Bristow, A. (1992). Academic reference service over electronic mail. *C&RL News* **53**, 631–632, 737.

Bush, V. (1945). As we may think. *The Atlantic Monthly* **76**, 106–107.

Bush, V. (1970). *Pieces of the Action.* William Morrow, New York.

Campbell, J. D. (1992). Shaking the conceptual foundations of reference: A perspective. *Reference Services Review* **20**, 29–35.

Cargill, J. (1992). The electronic reference desk: Reference service in an electronic world. *Library Administration & Management* **6**, 82–85.

Churbuck, D. C. (1995). Where's the money? *Forbes* **155**, 100–108.

Davenport, T. (1995). Think tank: The virtual and the physical. *CIO* **9**, 36–37.

DeLoughry, T. J. (1995). Colleges' use of computers nears "take-off stage," report says. *The Chronicle of Higher Education* (July 28, 1995), A22

DeVinney, G. (1994). Rushing toward the Emerald City? *The Journal of Academic Librarianship* **20**, 91–92.

Ewing, M. K., and Hauptman, R. (1995). Is traditional reference service obsolete? *The Journal of Academic Librarianship* **21**, 3–6.

Fefer, M. D. (1995). Fortune visits 25 cool companies: The other 90%. *Fortune* **132**, 162.

Ford, B. J. (1986). Reference beyond (and without) the reference desk. *College & Research Libraries* **47**, 491–494.

Ford, B. J. (1988). Reference service: Past, present, and future. *College & Research Libraries* **49**, 578–582.

Garnett, E. (1938). Information desk at the University of Illinois Library. *Library Journal* **63**, 408.

Hamel, G., and Prahalad, C. K. (1994). See the future first. *Fortune* **130**, 64–70.

Handy, C. (1995). Trust and the virtual organization. *Harvard Business Review* **73**, 40–50.

Hirshon, A. (1988). Vision, focus, and technology in academic research libraries: 1971 to 2001. In *Advances in Library Automation and Networking* (Vol. 2, pp. 215–257). JAI Press, Greenwich, CT.

Hirshon, A. (1995). Library strategic alliances and the digital library in the 1990s: The OhioLINK experience. *The Journal of Academic Librarianship* **21**, 383–386.

LaGuardia, C. (1995). *Desk Set* revisited: Reference librarians, reality, & research systems' design. *The Journal of Academic Librarianship* **21**, 7–9.

Lewis, D. W. (1995). Traditional reference is dead, now let's move on to important questions. *The Journal of Academic Librarianship* **21**, 10–12.

MacKnight, C. B. (1995). Managing technological change in academe. *CAUSE/Effect* **18**, 29–31, 35–39.

Mardikian, J., and Kesselman, M. (1995) Beyond the desk: Enhanced reference staffing for the electronic library. *Reference Services Review.* **23**, 21–28.

Markoff, J. (1995). And now, computerized sensibility. *The New York Times* (May 15, 1995), D6.

Martin, J. (1995). Ignore your customer. *Fortune* **131**, 122–126.

Massey-Burzio, V., *et al.* (1992). Reference encounters of a different kind: A symposium— Brandeis University Library has eliminated its reference desk. *The Journal of Academic Librarianship* **18**, 276–286.

Morison, M. (1995). Reference now and when. *Journal of Library Administration* **20**, 131–140.

Morison, R. (1995). *The New I/S Agenda.* CSC Research and Advisory Services, Cambridge, MA.

Port, O. (1995). Computers that think are almost here. *Business Week (Industrial/Technology Edition)* **3433**, 68–70.

Reece, E. J. (1938). College and university library news, 1937–1938. *Library Journal* **63**, 957–958.

Reese, J. (1995). Fortune visits 25 cool companies: Architext Software. *Fortune* **132**, 145–147.

Rethinking Reference in Academic Libraries: Proceedings of Library Solutions Institute No. 2. (1993). University of California, Berkeley, March 12–14, 1993; Duke University, Durham, NC, June 4–6, 1993. Published by Library Solutions Press, Berkeley, CA.

Ritz, C. (1992). In *Oxford Dictionary of Quotations.* (A. Partington, ed.) Oxford University Press, London.

A seeing-eye helper for the Internet. (1995). *Business Week* (March 27, 1995), 182.

Shapiro, B. J., and Long, K. (1994). Just say yes: Reengineering library user services for the 21st century: Collaborative efforts between the library and the computing center. *The Journal of Academic Librarianship* **20**, 285–290.

Snider, J. (1995). The Information Superhighway as an environmental menace. *The Futurist* **29**, 16–21.

Steele, C. (1993). Millennial libraries: Management changes in an electronic environment. *The Electronic Library* **11**, 393–402.

Still, J., and Campbell, F. (1993). Librarian in a box: The use of electronic mail for reference. *Reference Services Review* **21**, 15–18.

Telecommuting raises productivity. (1995). *HR Focus* **72**, 6.

Vischer, J. C. (1995). Strategic work-space planning. *Sloan Management Review* **37**, 33–42.

Wehmeyer, S., Auchter, D., and Hirshon, A. (1996). Saying what we will do, and doing what we say: Implementing a customer service plan. *The Journal of Academic Librarianship* **22**(3), 173–180.

Wilson, L. R. (1936). The next fifty years. *Library Journal* **61**, 255–260.

Wright State University. (1995). *Our Commitment to Customer Service.* Brochure. (http://libnet.wright.edu/policies/customer-services.html.)

Zuckerman, L. (1995a). Innovator is leaving the shadows for the limelight. *The New York Times* (July 17, 1995), D5.

Zuckerman, L. (1995b). With Internet, cachet, not profit, a new stock amazes Wall Street. *The New York Times* (August 10, 1995), A1.

Reorganizing Libraries
Is Flatter Better?

Joseph A. Boisse and Stella Bentley
Davidson Library
University of California
Santa Barbara, California 93106-9010

I. Introduction

A. The Horizontal Organizational–Management Theory

A horizontal or flattened organizational structure is quite simple to describe—the hierarchy or pyramid (the layers of supervision and management) is reduced or even eliminated in order to reduce the distance between those on the front lines and senior management. In its purest form, the horizontal organization would consist of just two groups: senior management responsible for strategic decisions and policies and empowered employees working together in teams. The teams would be empowered to control the flow and nature of their work and to spend their time on activities that add value for the organization's customers.

The ideas behind the horizontal organization have their roots in current management and organizational theory and practice. Over the years, the literature of management and organizational design has addressed, assessed, and promoted a variety of design models for organizations. Most recently, there have been both scholarly and popular works that have particularly looked at knowledge- or information-based organizations and advocated in turn that such organizations should move to matrix management, strive for total quality management (TQM), transform into the learning organization, and reengineer both the corporation and the management. Many factors in the economic and political climate of the 1990s are forcing organizations in many fields to look at their structure, functions, and processes in order to determine how best to achieve their purposes and compete well in their arena. The primary reasons that are cited for reorganizing by flattening the structure can be categorized into four general areas:

1. Budgetary factors. Many libraries, as well as their parent institutions, have been required to downsize and reduce the number of employees at the same time that they are expected to reduce costs, maintain or increase services, and generally achieve more with less.

2. Delayering. In order to overcome traditional demarcations and remove what may now be seen as unnecessary layers of management, many organizations have tried to decentralize operations, reduce job categories, and work cross-functionally in order to increase decision-making speed and increase the organization's responsiveness to its users and to the changes taking place in the economy and environment.

3. Changing organizational culture. Changing the organizational culture is both a response to the changes within the culture at large and an attempt to empower the workforce and encourage individuals to share in decision making. The employees are encouraged to have a customer focus and are granted autonomy, delegated power, and given the accountability to respond to customer needs. The members of the organization develop a shared vision of the future and esprit de corps. Pervasive expectations are developed by the workforce rather than directives from above. Together, the employees develop high commitment, work in self-managed work teams, and utilize team synergy. Team success is promoted over individual achievement, and accountability is based on clear job requirements and demonstrated results. A culture of continuous learning often pervades the organization.

4. Productivity improvement. In order to compete and survive, many organizations have had to find ways to improve productivity and reduce costs. They have made greater use of information and other technologies, have worked toward improving quality, and have often implemented total quality improvement processes to attain their goals. They want to be able to respond quickly to changing customer needs and to improve customer satisfaction while increasing their competitiveness.

As this list amply demonstrates, much of the thinking behind creating a horizontal structure relies especially on the theories put forth in discussions of total quality management, the learning organization, and reengineering. TQM emphasizes teamwork, culture change, individual responsibility/authority, creativity, accountability at all levels, and enhanced productivity in the quest for strategies to improve quality. According to Senge (1990), the learning organization is one that is continually expanding its capacity to create its future. The shared vision building and team learning that are cornerstones of his learning organization are essential elements of most of the flattened structures that have been created. Downsizing, moving to a horizontal structure, and reengineering are often used interchangeably in some discussions of the trends, but many believe that they are really different processes with

some common features. Hammer and Champy (1993), the gurus of reengineering, say that reengineering is not the same as flattening or delayering
the organization, although reengineering may produce a flatter organization.
They maintain that the problems facing companies result from their process
structures rather than from their organizational structures. They also maintain
that while many corporations claim to have embarked on reengineering programs, a majority of them are doing something completely different—usually
merely downsizing rather than radically changing their processes or current
operations. In comparing TQM and reengineering, they believe that while
both methods place an emphasis on the customer and on process, the two
diverge radically because TQM is about improving something that is basically
okay, whereas reengineering is about radical, dramatic change. They say that
TQM and reengineering are complementary in that TQM can keep the
processes on the right track until radical change—reengineering—is needed.

   With the combination of internal and external pressures facing organizations today, reengineering currently has a definite allure according to Vitiello
(1993, p. 46) because "in an era where corporations have been downsized,
delayered, and de-bottlenecked with disappointing results, the freedom to
chuck it all and start fresh is tempting. Reengineering gives strategists permission to do just that." So, has thinking changed about the appropriateness or
efficacy of the flattened structure as organizations have had experience with
it? Although there are many articles and testimonials about the pros of a
flattened structure and a few on the cons, it is interesting that we have gone
from titles such as "Horizontal organization" (1989), "Making the horizontal
organization work" (1990), "Making organizational change happen: The keys
to successful delayering" (1993), and "Managing a horizontal revolution"
(Brooks, 1995) to titles such as "The myth of the horizontal organization"
(1994), "Flat and happy?" (Hequet, 1995), and "Is the horizontal organization
for you?" (1995) in a fairly short time.

B. Libraries: Pressures for Change

Most libraries are being affected right now by a variety of external and internal
forces. The forces driving organizational changes in libraries are very similar
to the pressures in the private sector—changes in the external and internal
environments that render the old structures ineffective or obsolete.

   At the top of the list of these factor are the serious fiscal constraints that
have been imposed on most libraries in the past 10 to 20 years. Most libraries
have experienced a period of stable or declining budgets and fewer resources
of all kinds, which have essentially mirrored the changing economic situation
in the United States at large. Coupled with this lack of budgetary increases
or at the most very modest increases has been the rapid escalation in the

price of books and journals during the same time—the inflation rate for these materials has been as much as triple or quadruple the general rate annually for several years. As a result, most libraries are canceling subscriptions, moving funds from the operating budget to the materials budget, and still losing ground in the struggle to maintain the collecting levels of even a few years ago.

Rapid and constant technological change is another major factor. Since computer technology was first introduced in libraries about 25 years ago, it has continued to intrude into every area of library activity. There is virtually no single area of library activity that has not been affected by technology. Furthermore, technological applications have been characterized by rapid and constant change both in the applications being used and in the impact on employees and customers. This adoption of technology has resulted in major dislocations within libraries and has been at least partly responsible for some of the other changing factors in the environment. Because libraries have invested significant sums in technology and the use of the technology has promised a more efficient way of doing things, there is frequently an expressed expectation that productivity will actually increase too, despite reductions in staffing. Also, there has been a significant increase in user expectations of what can be done and how rapidly and easily it should be done resulting from the knowledge that libraries have embraced technology so wholeheartedly.

The entire services spectrum is under pressure to increase productivity and to become more effective and efficient, and this is especially true of the public sector. Accountability is the watchword everywhere. There are pressures from the general public and from the parent institution, be it local, state, or federal government or the university, for the library to be more effective and efficient with its use of resources. The bottom line, of course, is to do more with less. There is also a concurrent expectation by both library patrons and the parent institution that quality will improve and that the library and its personnel will be able to meet ever-rising expectations for the amount of services provided as well as for their quality.

Finally, on the external level, there has been considerable change, ambiguity, and uncertainty; some of this is a result of unprecedented technological change, some due to the increasing desire for more services at less cost, and some a result of the general economic situation that has prevailed for some time now. Regardless of the combination of factors leading to this situation, the impact on libraries has been considerable.

Changes in the internal environment are also having an impact on libraries. Many libraries have had to reduce the size of the staff through layoff or by not filling vacant positions in order to revert dollars to the parent institution, fund operations, or fund collections. The adoption of new technologies and the move to integrated systems have changed people's jobs, changed the way they interact with each other at work, changed how they interact with the library's users, and led to a continuous need for training and adaptation. These needs to adapt to change more rapidly, with fewer resources and in many cases fewer staff, have often exacerbated already stressful situations and demonstrated that inefficient procedures and processes need to be addressed. In addition, these situations have also shown that the existing organizational structure does not facilitate timely decisions and adaptation to constant change. At the same time, people's expectations of work and their own roles within their organizations have also been changing.

The factors just outlined have caused a significant level of organizational stress. Library employees are feeling pressured from all sides. They are being bombarded by changes and are being expected to adapt to this change quickly and with a minimum of fuss. The wholesale adoption of technology in libraries has also resulted in radical changes in what library employees do. Individuals have seen their job descriptions change almost annually. The decision-making structure of libraries has come under attack as well because it has been frequently unable to adapt to the need for rapid decision making. It is not surprising that almost every survey conducted in recent years has concluded that staff morale in most libraries is low.

II. The Flattened Library

The status quo, represented by organizational structures that have been in place for decades, has, in the minds of many, been powerless to deal with all of these pressures. This is not surprising since the status quo, by its very nature, is resistant to change. However, at a time when rapid change is occurring around libraries, they simply cannot afford to be resistant to changing themselves. The status quo is organized around processes rather than around people. It is predicated on the assumption that only "management" knows what is best for the organization and that employees should do what they are instructed to do without raising any questions or offering any suggestions. The traditional structure does not foster an ongoing, continuous review of activities and processes. To date, the notion of "continuous improvement" has not been a part of the basic operational culture of our institutions.

But our society has changed over the past decade and, in the opinion of many management gurus, it will be impossible to move a large organization forward without taking into account this basic change in cultural attitudes. The major characteristic of the change to which they are referring is a commitment to value the individual more than the organization per se. This is frequently referred to by using the term "empowerment" when discussing the status of nonmanagerial employees in today's organizations. The notion is that by giving all employees a more meaningful role in decision making within the organization, the overall productivity and quality of the organization will be improved. These same gurus conclude that in order to attain this objective, any organization has to look at radical change.

The conclusion has been reached in many libraries that the existing organization, which may have been put in place many years ago, is unable to respond adequately to current and foreseeable external and internal pressures. A growing conviction has developed that the future demands a more user-oriented and flexible organizational structure that will allow the library's various components to be more self-directed and more adaptable in responding to internal and external pressures. Many libraries have therefore been undergoing organizational changes in order to cope with these pressures and to create an organization thought to be more responsive.

Libraries that have undertaken large restructuring and reorganizing efforts have clearly laid out their reasons for going in this direction. The following comments are from working documents prepared at a selection of institutions that have gone through this process:

> [The new organization] will allow greater input from all staff to solve problems creatively and cooperatively while allowing for flexibility to address new needs created by the electronic environment. (Rader, 1987, p. 1)

> . . . a series of focus group sessions conducted by the University Libraries indicated that library staff and users alike were experiencing a loss of control over their work due to such factors as fiscal constraints, increased productivity demands, and constant technological change. . . . Many staff felt that too much energy was depleted by inefficient procedures and that there was a lack of key personnel with authority to make timely decisions. Above all, there was a growing conviction that the future demanded a more user-oriented and flexible organizational structure that would allow its various components to be more self-directed, and thus more "nimble" in responding to change. (University of Minnesota Libraries, 1994, p. 1)

> The objectives of the reorganization were to improve service, better define processes, reduce duplication of processes, and give the library staff more responsibility for processes. (Fitch, Thomason, and Wells, 1993, p. 295)

> The rapid transformation and automation of services and operations, in combination with fundamental changes in the information, scholarly and economic environments, must encourage a fresh and critical look at long-standing and increasingly dysfunctional structures. In order to remain a vital part of the university, the research library must create a working environment where both the employee and the user recognize and accept new power to exercise creativity and implement change. (Neal and Steele, 1993, pp. 81–82)

An analysis of these and other statements from personnel in libraries that have restructured and flattened shows the following:

1. There is a strong desire to become more responsive to user needs. These libraries make very clear that they intend to focus more on the informa-

tion and service needs of their users. They believe that this focus will result in an improvement to those services. To achieve this end, they want to create a more flexible organization, one that has a greater ability to adapt quickly to the changing environment and that allows more personnel to be involved with front-line activities.

2. The intent is to change the internal culture of their organization in a profound and permanent fashion and to create an organizational culture adaptive to change. The new culture will have improved and more effective communication mechanisms, will foster collaboration among the staff at all levels, and will stimulate creativity and risk taking, which, in turn, will result in an increase in innovation and initiative. The focus of the organization will be redirected to address strategic work rather than business as usual. Finally, the effort will empower employees throughout the organization, creating a more collegial and collaborative working environment, and result in improved morale for all personnel.

3. At the operational level, this restructuring is intended to distribute administrative authority and responsibility more widely throughout the organization in order to develop more efficient operations. By creating flexibility in the structure, it is hoped that the library will be able to manage resources better, define processes better, and eliminate boundaries and the turf wars that have historically existed in libraries. It is hoped that productivity will be increased by integrating key activities and operations, focusing on managing work processes rather than on people, and reducing process duplication and pushing decision making to the lowest possible level within the organization.

The process of restructuring or reengineering libraries is not a simple one. It begins with the development of a strategic vision for the organization, a vision that sets out clearly and unambiguously where the organization wants to be in several years. In the new organization, one of the major tasks of the leadership will be to continually promote this vision both within and without the library. From the vision flows a set of guiding principles upon which the reorganization objectives are based.

An early step in the process has to be the assessment of user expectations, since the reengineered library is dedicated to the highest level of user satisfaction. The library is to become customer focused rather than process focused. Information is sought from a wide variety of sources and that information serves as the basis for identifying users' needs and problems and focusing on quality.

Since creating an environment characterized by creativity, innovation, and risk taking is a major goal, reducing the number of layers in the organization's hierarchy and organizing into teams are very characteristic of most flattened organizations. The teams are centered on specific aspects of the overall functions of the library and are devoted to a continuous assessment of the quality of service and of the mechanisms used for attaining their objectives. Within the teams a system of shared management is implemented. This shared management goes beyond the concept of consultation and frequently settles on a truly collegial management style. In more than one instance, the team leader has been selected by a vote of the entire team. The desired result here is to create a real sense of empowerment among the employees, to facilitate cooperation and collaboration, and to engage them in the ownership of their part of the organization and thereby of the entire organization.

The successful implementation of this kind of radical restructuring necessitates a comprehensive approach to training and education. Staff are interested in participating in the shared governance that a flattened organization implies but will be reluctant to become involved unless they believe that they can contribute productively and meaningfully. A comprehensive and ongoing training and development program provides the basis of individual knowledge and preparation that helps assure success.

From more than a dozen organization charts of flattened libraries that have been examined, three patterns clearly emerge. Models A, B, and C can be characterized, respectively as the grid model (Fig. 1), the horizontal model (Fig. 2), and the circular model (Fig. 3). Model A, the grid model, is a structure that has been used by libraries that have more than one physical location. It carefully takes into account the multiple locations, and the grid is created to accommodate location team facilitators in addition to services team facilitators. Model B, the horizontal model, simply stretches the organization out and does not deal with the location factor, either because there is only one location where library services are provided or because the location factor is not deemed critical to the organizational structure. Model C, the circular model, is a direct adaptation of the quality circle concept to the library's organizational structure.

The most important characteristic to note about all three models is that the traditional pyramidal structure has been clearly eliminated. Although a few delayered libraries still show the administration at the top of the chart, most do not. As Models A and B demonstrate, many place the traditional administrative structure at the bottom of the chart, indicating quite clearly that these libraries have made a commitment to view the library administration as the major "support unit" for the rest of the library. This depiction of the organization's structure is aimed at underscoring the role of the university librarian as the major enabler rather than as the lawgiver. Model C also abandons the traditional pyramidal structure but depicts the chief librarian simply as a team leader for one of the quality circles.

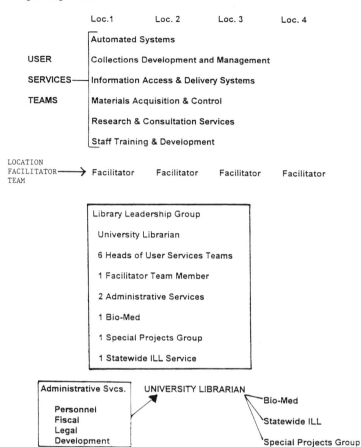

Fig. 1 Model A: Library organization.

In all of the models, the major role of the chief administrative officer is to promote constantly the vision of the organization. That promotion must be directed on the one hand to all of the constituent parts of the organization and, on the other hand, to the external community. In the case of academic institutions, much of the effort of the chief administrative officer will be directed to promoting the vision of the library to the campus community. If the institution is going to understand what is transpiring within the library, faculty, staff, and students must understand exactly what vision is driving the library. One of the biggest hurdles that must be overcome in a library's movement toward a flattened organizational structure is the hesitancy of most administrators to cede what they have traditionally viewed as their "power."

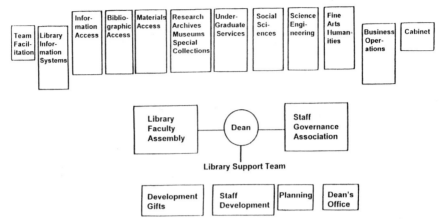

Fig. 2 Model B: Library organization.

In the new structure, the power of the leader lies in his or her ability to inspire the workforce and to motivate them toward the attainment of the established goals and toward the realization of the shared vision.

All of these models rely heavily on the "team" concept in striving to attain their goals. Needless to say, the leaders of the various teams are important players in the overall operation of the library. Teams may differ in internal organization, communication structure, and leadership. Team leaders, who may be appointed or elected, do all the various things that department heads probably did in the old structure, but they do it by exercising leadership skills instead of the traditional management skills. Various documents and

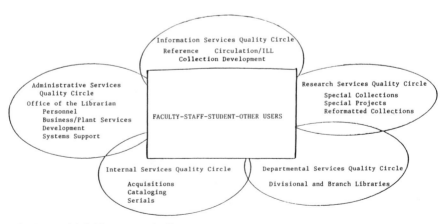

Fig. 3 Model C: Library organization.

statements from libraries that have been dealing with the functional aspects of these new organizations devote considerable space to discussions of the role of the team leader. Some of the key phrases that appear in these documents are: the team leader oversees tasks performed by the team; and he or she ensures consistency of service standards; he or she resolves conflicts among team members; and he or she assists in setting individual and team goals.

The libraries represented by these organization charts have all eliminated various layers of administrative structure. The purpose in doing so has been to reduce the number of layers or steps in the decision-making process, so that in theory only individuals who actually "add value" to the decision are included in the process. The teams that have been established are closer to the customers and to the day-to-day operations of the library. The team members are better equipped to provide users (customers) the kind of quality service to which the organization is committed. In the delayered library, the teams are empowered to take the initiative to solve problems and to improve services based on their intimate and first-hand knowledge of user needs.

As has been shown, the movement to a flatter organization in libraries, patterned on what has been occurring to a considerable extent in the corporate structure, is relatively new. It came about as the result of observations by all involved that radical steps were needed to deal with the radical changes in the internal and external environments. The goal of the effort has been to refocus the organization and to thereby make it possible for it to cope with a variety of problems brought on by the many changes in the internal and external environments.

III. The Flatter Organization: Success Factors, Problems, and Other Issues

A. Success Factors

Those who have studied organizational change have identified a number of factors that are most apt to lead to a successful reorganization. A library that is contemplating movement from the traditional hierarchical structure to a flattened structure should use these factors as guidelines to help ensure the success of the effort:

1. The organization is ready, willing, and able to change—there is a sense of urgency about the need for radical change at all levels, and the case for change is compelling, urgent, and constantly refreshed.

2. The organization's leadership is truly committed to change and is willing to take the steps necessary to make the change happen. Top manage-

ment lays the foundations for success—it mobilizes, organizes, and energizes personnel.

3. The organization develops a clearly defined vision and critical success factors for the accomplishment of the vision based on customers' needs. The vision and the critical success factors are communicated widely and are understood throughout the organization.

4. The organization funnels its energy toward goals that will improve its performance, and the focus of change is on overall process performance.

5. Top management is ready and willing to deal with any personnel and management issues that are necessary to facilitate the radical change. Obsolete assumptions and processes are abandoned. Appropriate means and methods are used to motivate performance and to deal with poor performers. Those who cannot change are removed, and new leadership is brought in when necessary.

6. The organization must build on small steps and make continuous progress toward the new structure.

7. Employees must have clear expectations about their new roles as individuals and as team members in the new structure. They must understand that the new structure defines and values skills and competencies rather than titles and salary scales.

8. Members of teams must know how to work together and why they are working together; training is provided for new responsibilities and team roles.

B. Despite the Best Laid Plans—Problems Often Encountered

Even though all of the success factors may be present, organizations can still flounder or even fail during the implementation stages as they attempt to make the radical structural changes from a hierarchical to a flattened structure or even after the implementation has been completed and the organization is functioning under the new structure. Although some of the following issues might not seem too much to overcome when the people involved in the change truly want to have a new structure, each of these can be the final straw that prevents a successful transition or implementation. If two or more are present, the flattened organization is likely, at the very least, to be flawed and less than an optimal performer or doomed to failure in the worst case scenario.

A significant problem that can be an impediment to success is failed expectations. Often, people can get caught in the trap of putting too much faith in the process rather than in the results. People may be so ready for change and so sure that the change is being done at the right time that they do not undertake the change process with the degree of intensity and focus that it requires. Critical success factors must be established, and ways to maintain accountability and measure success must be agreed on in order to ensure that the process is moving the organization in the correct direction. Likewise, inflated expectations for the impact of the changed structure may lead to disillusionment and a loss of faith in the process if the change is too little, too late, or undertaken at too high a cost.

Then there is the double-sided problem of changing too much or too little in a given time frame. There needs to be a balance both in terms of the amount of time to devote to the change process and in the number of activities that are being changed at any one time. Trying to change everything at once can lead to total chaos—it may be better to change parts one at a time so that there is a sort of controlled chaos, with only some parts in chaos at any one time. If the implementation is done too fast, people may not have time to adapt to radical change and the inevitable resistance of some may be exacerbated. If, however, the change process takes too long to implement, there is the danger of a lack of timely results, and the resulting lack of progress and frustration may doom the process as people lose interest and confidence, and believe that there is not a strong commitment on the part of top management.

Another important issue is allowing employees an appropriate amount of time to adapt to their new empowerment or change in power for those who are no longer middle managers, and the roles of teamwork and individual accountability. People who have been locked into a hierarchical structure for their entire working careers cannot be expected to bloom suddenly once the hierarchy has been eliminated. Department members, who may have had varying degrees of influence and impact on decisions but without the responsibility, are now expected to function in a more collegial environment with shared responsibility for both decision making and for the results. In addition, the transformation of the role from middle manager to team coordinator or just team member may be especially difficult for individuals who are no longer department heads or assistant directors.

The existing skills and expectations of employees must be gauged and taken into account during the process, and appropriate training must be provided at all steps of the transformation, even after the new structure is in place. Too often, even though they desire a flattened organization, the employees may lack the needed skills and frame of mind for the new roles they will assume. The skills to function successfully as a team leader are very different than those of the middle manager. Whereas the head of the reference department was a department head with 10 direct reports who was expected to provide direction, prescription, control, and coach the department members, the coordinator of the information services team has 10 teammates and is expected to provide guidance, coordination, and empowerment while serving as a playing coach. Most employees do not know how to function in a team environment. Moving to a team structure may be especially trying and chaotic for professionals who are used to working independently and do not automatically know how to work effectively with other people and, as a result, may not take readily to the idea. There must be enough time and funding to provide appropriate and adequate training. Another difficulty in moving to a team-based structure is that the teams might not gel because of the emphasis on individualism within our society. Even in our team sports, there is a great deal of concentration on individual exploits and glorification of the role of the star or most valuable player.

Overcoming employee fear and resistance can be one of the greatest hurdles for the successful implementation of a flattened organization. Many employees may experience role ambiguity at the prospect of moving to a team environment; they do not know what it means to be a team member. Change is almost always difficult for people, and many employees may have a great deal of anxiety over whether they will have a job and, if so, whether they will be able to perform the new job successfully. Such fears can be heightened by concerns about their future and their status in the new structure—in a flattened organization, what will the career path be? How are salaries set if the old career paths no long exist? If my middle management position has been eliminated, what has happened to my status in the organization? However, there are employees who are very comfortable in their present roles in the organization and who may not want the responsibility that accompanies empowerment and increased authority. Some may especially resent being asked to take on responsibility without a concomitant increase in salary.

Equally difficult can be employee cynicism—is this just the latest management fad? Since corporations tried it last year, and the books describing it are now on the best seller lists, is it inevitable that the library will do it this year or next year, or after Library XYZ has done it? If they have already been managed by objectives and gone through a management review and analysis program in the 1970s, done a public services study in the 1980s, subsequently tried quality circles in the 1980s and the learning organization in the 1990s, and then been downsized or rightsized in the early 1990s, it is easy to see that cynicism about reengineering, flattening the organization, or whatever else seems to be the latest model can run very deep. Many may believe that the new organization offers them nothing but more turmoil and failed promises when they are already pressured just trying to cope with the many factors noted earlier.

Another potential problem area is the failure to focus on overall process performance during the transition. Clear performance goals must be established immediately as teams are created. The teams and all of their members must be accountable for what they do and the outcomes of their performance.

The organization must review and modify policies to motivate all personnel and provide additional training for employees with poor performance records. In addition, management must deal with employee resistance; steps have to be taken to implement career changes or disciplinary action if needed.

Group decision making itself can be an impediment to the successful functioning of the flattened organization. Suppose that the delayering process itself has gone well, and the organization has been able to take the necessary steps while avoiding or compensating for the many pitfalls that could have derailed the process. Team identities have been created, individuals trust their teammates and feel very positive and prepared for their own roles on the team; teamwork is thriving; and the team has expanded its capabilities and is formulating its goals. Are the goals being translated into action? Are the desired outcomes being accomplished? Are good decisions being made? Can the team, as a team, make the most of its differences, take risks, discover new insights, and leap to new conclusions? Or, does the group decision-making process produce mediocrity and the status quo as the team members manage their relationships and work to ensure consensus and harmony? Do the team leaders and administrators accept mediocre decisions in order to facilitate and support the decisions made by teams?

Finally, one of the greatest impediments to a successful change or organizational structure is the failure to reach closure in the change process. The process takes on a life of its own, and the organization may lose sight of the reason for its existence. Personnel become so engrossed in techniques that the methodology or process of change itself often becomes the purpose of existence, and the organization fails to achieve its very raison d'être. Delegation may give way to abdication rather than the team responsibility and accountability that was envisioned. As a result, the organization may be weakened rather than strengthened. The flatter organization may be less focused and effective than was its hierarchical predecessor.

C. Other Issues

Several other issues need to be addressed that may be especially relevant to libraries that have flattened their structures. An issue of particular concern in libraries is career development. Historically, chief library administrators have been selected from among the ranks of individuals who have moved up in the organization and have had experience at various managerial levels. In a flattened structure, apart from the chief administrative officer of the organization, at most one or two individuals will gain that kind of experience. What remains to be seen is whether the new mode of operation will develop the skills among these individuals to move into the top position. And, of course, it remains to be seen if recruiters of chief library administrators will be willing to make appointments of individuals who have not climbed the traditional management ranks. Certainly the model exists for such promotions to take place: faculty members frequently move into senior management positions in colleges and universities with virtually no administrative experience. However, that has not been the traditional approach in the appointment of chief library administrators.

In almost all of the documents about restructuring in libraries, one of the desired results has been the elimination of turf wars. It is easily seen that with the elimination of the traditional rigid, hierarchical distinction between technical and public services, the turf war between these two divisions can be eliminated. However, will that translate to no turf wars in the new organization? At least one library has raised this question and found that additional steps have to be taken if turf warfare is indeed to be minimized. In any organization, loyalties tend to build around some kind of structure. In the flattened organization, loyalty to one's team is ranked high on the list of desiderata. Will this loyalty to the team simply shift the turf warfare to a different arena or level?

Any organization that undertakes to move in this direction must be willing to review its system of rewards because current systems for rewarding employees are based on the traditional hierarchical structure. This challenge presents a special problem for most libraries. The problem arises from the fact that libraries are a part of a larger organization and the reward system for the library is part of the overall human resources program of the parent organization. In most of the corporate examples cited in the literature, the entire company has gone through the process of restructuring. As a result the reward system for the entire corporation has been reviewed and altered, frequently in very significant ways. All of the libraries whose organizational structure was reviewed for this project are indeed part of larger institutions. In no case has the entire institution gone through the kind of restructuring that the library has embraced. The authors were able to identify only one library that has tackled the challenge of redefining the system used to reward its employees. In that case, it took a major concession on the part of the university administration for this to occur.

In the books about reengineering (Champy, 1995; Hammer and Champy, 1993), much is made of a system of evaluation that is collegial. The team evaluates each of its members. They work as a collective group in doing so. There have been varying degrees of success of such a system. It is not likely that it will be implemented any more easily in the public or academic sector than it has in the corporate sector.

Some of these potential problems will be addressed through education and training. One characteristic of the reengineered organization is the need for extensive training of all employees. The success of a model where everyone is empowered and everyone is involved in decision making and problem solving rests to a great extent on the ability of employees to engage in these activities. That ability in turn necessitates an informed and well-trained work force. Because of the rapid changes taking place in our culture, and because of the constant changes that technology brings to the workplace, any library that reengineers itself will have to devote significantly more resources to training and development than has been done in the past. The training effort has to be extended to all employees for the model to succeed.

Accountability must go hand in hand with empowerment. While decisions have, in the past, been made near the top of the pyramid, decision making is pushed further down in the organization when the pyramid goes. Most employees are quick to state that they enjoy this change because it makes their work more interesting and they can control their own destiny more. However, some are slightly less enthusiastic when it is pointed out that along with the empowerment goes the need to accept responsibility for making decisions, establishing goals, and translating goals into action.

One of the biggest challenges to those in the traditional structure will be the changed role of the chief administrative officer. Actually, the role will be both reduced and increased. It will be reduced when considered in the traditional sense of holding the power in the organization. It will be increased, however, since it is that individual who is responsible for continually nurturing the new organization, promoting the vision, and coordinating the effort of the team leaders. In many ways, the new structure will make the role of the chief librarian more interesting and more challenging.

IV. Conclusions

Despite intense internal and external pressures, it may be very difficult to effect change in an established culture, especially when the agents of change themselves are partly responsible for the problem. While the end result may look alluring, the process to get there can collapse. Even when the process to change may work, the new structure may not turn out to be feasible. History and experience show us time and again that there is no one right structure—organizations have been effective using a variety of structures. In addition, few organizations consist of only one structure; hybrid structures exist in almost every organization consisting of more than a few employees. Different processes have different characteristics and often thrive in different structures. Some libraries have flattened part of the structure (just public services, for example), but have retained a more traditional hierarchical organization for the other functions. What may be right for a particular type of organization or for an organization at one stage of its development may not work at all for other organizations or for different stages in the life cycle of an organization. It is often easier to blame or praise the structure than to look at other factors that may have led to success or failure. In hindsight, we can often easily see what worked or did not work, but it is rarely possible for us to look at the present or future and decide what structure is or will be the best.

Is flatter better? It is too early to tell with any degree of certainty whether this strategy has been successful. Many libraries that are moving to a flatter structure and even those few that have delayered are still in the process of training, overcoming obstacles, and coping with the myriad steps that need to be taken to change the organization and its culture. There is a considerable risk of chaos both during and after the transition if the traditional organization (hierarchy) is not replaced with a structure of some sort that provides the necessary coordination and feedback to ensure that the library is truly efficient, effective, and meeting the needs of its users. It remains to be seen if the flatter organization is that structure or if other organizational design models will emerge that are most appropriate for the library.

References

Bellante, N. D. (1994). Implementing a horizontal management structure. *Human Resources Professional* **7**, 28–32.
Boykin, J. F., and Babel, D. B. (1993). Reorganizing the Clemson University Libraries. *Journal of Academic Librarianship* **19**, 94–96.
Brooks, S. S. (1995). Managing a horizontal revolution. *HRMagazine* **40**, 52–58.
Caudron, S. (1994). Teamwork takes work. *Personnel Journal* **73**, 41–46+.
Champy, J. (1995). *Reengineering Management: The Mandate for New Leadership*. HarperBusiness, New York.
Duck, J. D. (1993). Managing change: The art of balancing. *Harvard Business Review* **71**, 109–118.
Euster, J. (1990). The new hierarchy: Where's the boss? *Library Journal* **115**, 41–44.
Fitch, D. K., Thomason, J., and Wells, E. C. (1993). Turning the library upside down: Reorganization using total quality management principles. *Journal of Academic Librarianship* **19**, 294–299.
Floyd, S. W., and Wooldridge, B. (1994). Dinosaurs or dynamos? Recognizing middle management's strategic role. *Academy of Management Executive* **8**, 47–57.
Garvin, D. A. (1993). Building a learning organization. *Harvard Business Review* **71**, 78–91.
Giesecke, J. R. (1994). Reorganizations: An interview with staff from the University of Arizona Libraries. *Library Administration & Management* **8**, 196–199.
Hammer, M., and Champy, J. (1993). *Reengineering the Corporation: A Manifesto for Business Revolution*. HarperBusiness, New York.
Hequet, M. (1995). Flat and happy? *Training* **32**, 29–34.
Johnson, P. (1990). Matrix management: An organizational alternative for libraries. *Journal of Academic Librarianship* **16**, 222–229.
Kotter, J. P. (1995). Leading change: Why transformation efforts fail. *Harvard Business Review* **73**, 59–67.
Lam, K. D., Watson, F. D., and Schmidt, S. R. (1991). *Total Quality: A Textbook of Strategic Quality Leadership and Planning*. Air Academy Press, Colorado Springs.

Lee, S. (1993). Organizational change in the Harvard College Library: A continued struggle for redefinition and renewal. *Journal of Academic Librarianship* **19**, 225–230.

McCarthy, C. K. (1995). "How do you flatten an AUL? Making the transition from a hierarchical organization." Paper presented at the Seventh National ACRL Conference, Pittsburgh, PA, March 29–April 1, 1995.

Neal, J. G., and Steele, P. A. (1993). Empowerment, organization, and structure: The experience of the Indiana University Libraries. *Journal of Library Administration* **19**, 81–96.

Rader, H. (1987). From the director. *Cleveland State University Libraries Newsnotes for Library Staff* **321**, 1–2.

Riggs, D. E. (1992). Strategic quality management in libraries. *Advances in Librarianship* **16**, 93–105.

Senge, P. M. (1990). *The Fifth Discipline: The Art and Practice of the Learning Organization.* Doubleday, New York.

Stoffle, C. (1993). "Organizational transformation: New structures for new realities." Paper presented at the ALA 112th annual conference, New Orleans, LA, June 24–July 1, 1993.

Stoffle, C. (1995). "How we are different." Paper presented at the ALA 114th annual conference, Chicago, June 23–28, 1995.

Sullivan, M. (1992). The changing role of the middle manager in research libraries. *Library Trends* **41**, 269–281.

Sweeney, R. T. (1994). Leadership in the post-hierarchical library. *Library Trends* **43**, 62–94.

University of Minnesota Libraries. (1994). *Task Force on Restructuring the Libraries Final Report.* University of Minnesota Libraries, Twin Cities.

Vitiello, J. (1993). Reengineering: It's totally radical. *Journal of Business Strategy* **14**, 44–47.

The Kellogg CRISTAL-ED Project

Creating a Model Program to Support Libraries in the Digital Age

Karen M. Drabenstott and Daniel E. Atkins
School of Information and Library Studies
University of Michigan
Ann Arbor, Michigan 48109

"It was the best of times. It was the worst of times . . . ."

If these words must sound familiar to you, then you recall Charles Dickens' opening statements in his *A Tale of Two Cities*—a novel about *revolution*. We have used these statements to open this chapter because they characterize the momentous events and advances occurring today that serve as the impetus for redefining the University of Michigan's School of Information and Library Studies. We are in the midst of a revolution so profound that it will affect the lives of people around the world—how they go about their daily business and interact with others in their workplaces, homes, schools, and communities. The revolution is forcing us to restructure a profession that is in serious jeopardy of becoming obsolete, irrelevant, or marginal to the needs of an educated society.

Chaos accompanies revolution. It brings on uncertainty about the future, upsets the status quo, blurs distinctions between and even eradicates traditional roles, creates turmoil, and sets into motion a plethora of new, unexpected problems. Today's revolution will effect change with unprecedented speed. Never in the history of the world will we have had so much change in so short a period of time (Leyden, 1995).

I. The Revolution upon Us

We are in the midst of a revolution that has several fronts—technology, networking, and information. Today's revolution in technology represents the best of times in that we are able to easily buy off-the-shelf computer technology that sits on a desktop and provides more power, functionality, memory, and storage space than OCLC's first computers that filled up entire rooms and required around-the-clock monitoring by a team of technical staff. It is also the worst of times because advances in technology are occurring with such lightning speed that the cutting-edge hardware we buy today is obsolete by the time we place it on our desktops tomorrow. If we continue to wait, we will wait for a good long time because whenever we are prepared to buy, we hear reports of the imminent release of a stunning new machine that delivers all the punch and power that we want. Its release brings on more reports of even more versatile machines with capabilities that surpass those that we are about to purchase.

The revolution in technology is also challenging and exhilarating. We have the opportunity to shape, fashion, and blend new and emerging technologies in different ways that allow us to streamline tasks, effect processes, and accomplish the unthinkable. For example, scientists, warm and comfortable in the familiar surroundings of their own institutions, monitor computer-driven instruments that collect atmospheric data in the most remote, forbidding regions of Greenland and, at the same time, use computer technology to conduct face-to-face meetings that include the discussion of incoming data from such instruments (Committee on a National Collaboratory, 1993). While the best of times is apparent in the blending of technologies that makes this scenario possible, it comes with a tremendous cost in the time and energy required to keep up with changes in technology and the introduction of new ones.

The Internet looms largely on the networking front. We are constantly bombarded by news stories that cite millions of collections and Internet servers, tens of billions of Internet users, billions of packets sent per year, and exponential increases in every aspect of the Internet. When a major blizzard hits the northeast United States, newspapers flash bulletins about storm-weary Easterners who alleviate their cabin-fever blues with long hours of Internet chat, browsing, and exploration (O'Harrow and Corcoran, 1995). The worst of times reared its ugly head for the many Internet travelers who had difficulty connecting to the Internet and major network providers due to the heavy volume of traffic that was created by the chaos of the storm.

In large measure, this is the best of times because of the vast reservoir of information that is available at our fingertips through networking technology. No longer do we have to trudge to the library to search an aging, stale card catalog, finger and scan endless rows of neatly packed cards looking for hints on a worn and smudged card that describes a book having the potential for answering one's question, fetch it from the maze of lonely bookshelves, haul it to a photocopier, and feed an endless supply of nickels, dimes, and quarters into the machine to make copies of relevant chapters and passages.

In contrast, networked information is easy to access, update, and maintain. Vast amounts of data are available on networked machines that are searchable at megabit and gigabit speeds. We can order computers to scan entire texts looking for the exact words to answer our question. When we find the right passage, a few clicks will enable us to download the passage, paragraph, or entire paper into the machine at our fingertips. This is the best of times!

While networks feature access to thousands of collections and servers, the pathways for finding useful information are seldom paved, well-lit, broad, sweeping avenues. They are not even dirt paths that are occasionally impassable due to mud, snow, falling rocks, trees, or debris. They are trails that have barely formed by repeated chance footsteps and are hardly distinguishable from the surrounding wilderness. We can lose our way or proceed for long periods of time down a dead end only to retrace our steps and start anew. Traffic jams are akin to arriving at an enemy camp where we could become waylaid for an unknown period of time. This just may be the worst of times. Yet, today's adventurers on the Internet are undaunted by tasks of surveying uncharted territories, discovering the most fruitful pathways, and introducing order through the construction of paved roads, traffic controls, maps, directories, and so on.

On the information front, we are facing an unprecedented glut of information. Where publishers and professional associations once stood guard, carefully scrutinizing and evaluating the quality of the printed word, the marriage of information technology and networking is making it possible for anyone with a computer, modem, and Internet access to become an author and publisher on any topic under the sun. There is also the enormous problem of finding the right information to answer questions, make decisions, or increase one's knowledge and understanding about the world. The difficulty of finding information is compounded by today's hybrid information environment of print-on-paper and digital artifacts. In addition, the form, content, and expression of digital artifacts are constantly evolving into new representations that defy our best efforts to harness them using tools that were developed to organize a much more stable genre. This is definitely the worst of times.

II. Life on the Battlefront

Long accustomed to organizing printed materials available at their home institutions, librarians must face the reality of a vast, distributed web of data, information, and knowledge that large portions of society will seek because it is dynamic, available every hour of the day and night, and compelling in its form and expression. No longer relegated to finding the information they want in passive, immutable expressions of black ink on white paper, users of networked information have texts, images, numeric data, full-motion video, multimedia, sound, data feeds, and live links at their fingertips around the clock.

Networked information is not pipe dream of technology gurus or wayward computer hackers in search of a rest stop along the information superhighway. It is here now and it is growing at breakneck speed.

Towering above the battlefield of the revolution are today's libraries. They have been stable, enduring institutions that have guarded the physical knowledge base of an educated populace, community, or society for hundreds of years. Librarians are geared to handle the world of print material. How will they respond to the challenge of networked information? This is not a question of digital material replacing printed material. The volume of networked information is growing exponentially, and an ever-increasing number of information seekers are abandoning the printed world and favor searching new sources of digital information for any number of reasons, especially their accessibility on a 24-hour basis. The revolution is forcing us to redefine a profession that is in serious jeopardy of becoming obsolete, irrelevant, or marginal to the needs of an educated society. How will librarians respond to the urgent need to re-examine the mission of the library and their roles as librarians?

Librarians and library educators are at a critical juncture. They must make bold decisions, identify and clearly articulate their opportunities, and set out aggressively to seize them.

III. Taking Bold Action at Michigan

Support from the W. K. Kellogg Foundation has enabled the School of Information and Library Studies (SILS) at the University of Michigan (UM) to embark on radical change of its instructional program. The *impetus* for taking this bold action is our *vision* of the ongoing revolution in technology, networking, and information and the changes it is likely to effect across the broad spectrum of human life. We cannot now fully define this future but we are certain that profound change is underway. We are presently at the horseless carriage stage of creating new knowledge-work environments that meet the needs of people, organizations, and communities. Libraries, as traditional centers of knowledge work, have the right—even the responsibility—to take the leading role in defining and shaping the future and seizing opportunities to invent new approaches to serving people's information needs.

Similarly, there are ample opportunities for library schools to reinvent themselves in broader, more multidisciplinary ways. There is intellectual and professional turf to be seized. There are new opportunities for future-oriented professional education that are not currently being addressed by information and library studies, computer science, and management information systems programs as they now exist.

1. Schools of information and library studies are not sufficiently addressing future-oriented educational needs. Data, information, and knowledge are becoming even more critical to modern life, and technology is providing a vast array of opportunities to augment the print-on-paper, place-based library to meet these demands. The basic values of librarianship—service to people, education to meet information needs, an ethic of broad access, quality of information, and guardianship of knowledge for the future—have never been more important. For a variety of reasons, few information and library studies schools seem to have the resources or the capabilities to lead into this future. In fact, such schools continue to be closed or are severely curtailed even as we step into the age of knowledge (Woodsworth et al., 1994).

2. Computer science and engineering programs, although they produce the professionals to create the incredible enabling technologies, have not taken a sufficiently holistic view of systems and have ignored the human and nontechnical dimensions of the information systems of the future.

3. Management information systems education has focused on a relatively narrow context of maximizing productivity and profitability of commercial enterprises. It has emphasized mission-critical access to data and information—not information access for all citizens.

The University of Michigan's SILS is responding by building a national, multidisciplinary collaborative consortium to define new professional specializations to serve society's needs for information access in the rapidly emerging age of digital data, information, and knowledge. We aspire to educate new information professionals with broad competency and a holistic view of information systems. We want our graduates to understand users of information and to be committed to using and shaping current and emerging digital systems technologies to solve problems of information access, organization, and preservation in hybrid environments that feature both print and digital forms of human communication. We expect our graduates to be leaders in transforming the products, services, and processes of organizations in fundamental ways with the aid of information technology.

IV. Activities Leading up to the Award

Appointed Dean of the School of Information and Library Studies in summer 1992, Dan Atkins received a mandate from the administration of the University of Michigan to effect a radical change in SILS. The new SILS mandate was threefold: (1) define and deploy an educational program that produces knowledge resource management professionals for the twenty-first century, (2) pursue an interdisciplinary program of research and development that increases general understanding and knowledge of systems for information access and collaboration, and (3) be a "skunk works" for the application of information technology to the "knowledge mission" of the university. SILS faculty responded to this mandate in several ways:

1. They established a base-line digital information environment and Information Technology Support Organization, together with a faculty-written report on how it should relate to the SILS instruction and research institution.
2. They conducted a preliminary study to determine the feasibility of defining core knowledge and skills.
3. They enhanced the faculty with joint, adjunct, and affiliate appointments from other schools, colleges, and university service units, and enriched the intellectual life of SILS with workshops and study groups that investigated the future of libraries and definitions of digital libraries.
4. They charged a design and development team with the building of an information system to access electronic journals, structured documents, and digital, scholarly communications.
5. They challenged the SILS faculty to work in concert with one another and collaboratively with faculty from related and allied disciplines in the pursuit of grants from government agencies.

These and other activities laid the groundwork for the SILS faculty to respond to the W. K. Kellogg Foundation's interest in investing in a coordinated program of "human resources for information systems management" (HRISM). In fall 1993, SILS faculty proposed an ambitious initiative to the W. K. Kellogg Foundation that would produce the human resources required to lead in the creation, organization, management, and dissemination of information in the twenty-first century and to reduce barriers of all kinds that restrict people's access to information. The Kellogg Foundation responded by awarding SILS a $4.3 million grant and making SILS the flagship of its HRISM program.

V. Kellogg CRISTAL-ED Goals and Phases

The goal of the Kellogg CRISTAL-ED (Coalition on Reinventing Information Science, Technology, and Library Education) Project at the University of Michigan's School of Information and Library Studies are to:

1. Build a coalition to reinvent an information and library science learning environment that produces information and library leaders for the digital information world.
2. Conduct joint pilot projects to support research, hands-on learning, creation of "living specifications," and continuing education.
3. Apply collaboratory ideas to distance-independent learning, perhaps by creating a federated (virtual) school.

The Kellogg CRISTAL-ED Project is divided into several phases to achieve project goals. Figure 1 depicts these phases over a 6-year time period.

SILS faculty and administrative staff devoted much of 1993 to building a shared vision and undertaking tasks that led up to the submission of a proposal to the Kellogg Foundation. Since the award of the grant in spring 1994, SILS faculty have focused much of their attention on defining the new core curriculum and learning environment. Intense periods of committee work are periodically punctuated by full-school retreats that enable SILS faculty to discuss and resolve issues that affect that school as a whole.

The new learning environment includes new approaches to learning. For example, faculty do much less lecturing and testing of students. Instead, faculty now engage in project-based learning in which they present basic principles and assign projects that reinforce these principles and require students to work collaboratively to build new tools, resources, or methods. Other new approaches to teaching include distance-independent learning, co-ops, internships, fieldwork and other experienced learning modes, and pilot projects.

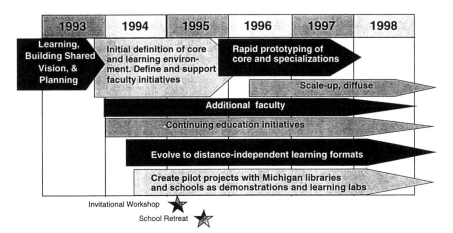

Fig. 1   Kellogg CRISTAL-ED project phasing.

Two new faculty members bring considerable expertise and experience in the areas of human–computer interaction and archives and records management, while faculty from several University of Michigan schools, colleges, and departments—School of Business Administration, College of Engineering, Psychology Department—also have joined the SILS faculty through joint appointments. Searches for new faculty will continue throughout the grant. Existing faculty are working together in the planning and design of a new educational program; they have been conducting an ongoing "virtual conference" through listserv discussions with interested individuals around the world and garnered information and ideas at an invitational workshop held in Ann Arbor in April 1994. Through activities such as these, the Michigan experience is forwarding a new model for other universities and facilities to consider, while involving leaders and ideas from others, worldwide. Up-to-date information on Kellogg CRISTAL-ED Project activities is accessible through the project's World Wide Web (WWW) presentation (see Fig. 2). Throughout this chapter, we include URLs (Uniform Resource Locators) that readers can consult using their WWW browsers for additional and the latest information.

VI. A New Curriculum

A. Early Efforts

In winter 1993, Dean Dan Atkins gave the following charge to a task force composed of SILS faculty and students: "Is there a core of concepts, theory, skills, knowledge, experience which provides the basis for a broader array of future-oriented professional practice in information systems and services, including but not limited to current forms of libraries?" Deliberations led the Core Curriculum Task Force to conclude that such a core indeed exists. The task force as a whole identified five core components and divided into five subtask force groups to study and recommend content for a new core curriculum: (1) Organization of Information, (2) Information Systems Analysis and Design/Delivery Tools, (3) Evaluation, (4) Users and Access, and (5) Management and Professional Competence.

Our study of core curriculum was one of several tasks that led up to our submission of a grant proposal to the Kellogg Foundation. We concluded that we needed to introduce radical change to our instructional program.

In the 1994–1995 academic years, SILS faculty made major progress in planning for the new core curriculum. Besides deliberating over core curriculum content in a half-dozen task forces, faculty introduced major changes to four existing core curriculum courses—Searching, Automated Databases,

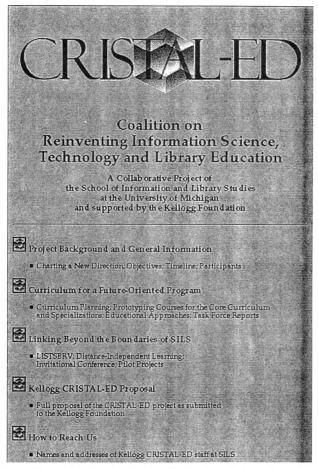

URL: http://sils.umich.edu/Publications/CRISTALED/KelloggHomePage.html

Fig. 2 Kellogg CRISTAL-ED project.

Organization of Information, Technologies for Information Management, and Sources of General Information—through the rapid-prototyping method. Faculty have taught two of these four core courses more than once and made significant changes to the structure and content of these courses every time they have taught them.

Despite the presence of an elaborate organizational structure, core curriculum task forces and faculty who were making changes to core courses found it difficult to coordinate their activities. In addition, faculty felt the need to spend a lengthy period of time discussing concerns of an immediate nature. For these reasons, faculty planned and participated in a day-long, off-site retreat to assess their progress to date, coordinate their activities, and try to resolve the "nitty-gritty" of curriculum change. Chief among the outcomes of the retreat was the creation of a faculty core curriculum team.

B. Rapid Prototyping a New Core Curriculum

The SILS faculty team that volunteered to create a new, integrated core curriculum offered this new core in fall 1995, in the form of a single, six-credit course. The team of three faculty members took equal responsibility for the content of this new core curriculum. The course dealt with three themes: the life cycle of information from creating through editing and publication, collection, organization, representation, retrieval, reading, and use, with particular emphasis on organization, retrieval, use and decision making on the part of professionals, and the importance of context in understanding why certain formats, sources, and organizational structures arose. Course objectives were to:

1. Develop an understanding of the principles that underlie information storage and retrieval systems and appreciation of the interrelationships between effective information searching and the organization and description of information, interfaces, and command structures.
2. Develop the ability to think critically about why and how we provide intellectual access to information.
3. Gain familiarity with some established tools and models for organizing information; develop familiarity with, and ability to search in, a basic core of general, print, and electronic-based sources of information.
4. Develop skills in the evaluation, selection, and use of sources, including formulating effective search strategies.
5. Consider the changing nature of information resources and the process by which such sources are/will be published, organized, represented, retrieved, used, and archived.

The final project requires students to synthesize acquired knowledge and skills in the course of designing and giving structure to an encyclopedia native to a distributed networked environment. Design teams composed of four to six students must address issues such as taking advantage of content available through the Net, keeping the encyclopedia current, organizing content, enabling people to search and browse content, marketing the encyclopedia, handling user feedback, and ensuring quality, authority, and comprehensiveness. Students are expected to produce a World Wide Web-accessible report that outlines specifications and design details for the encyclopedia. Some design teams will probably produce a prototype of a functional encyclopedia by the end of the course.

C. Parallel Efforts

Several faculty task forces are at work on efforts that are parallel and complementary to the rapid prototyping of a new core curriculum. The Curriculum Visions Group, an operating committee for the new curriculum, has charged task forces with the development of a new curriculum that will initially feature six specializations: (1) future systems architecture, (2) human–computer interaction, (3) librarianship, (4) archives and records management, (5) digital documents/digital publishing, and (6) organizational information systems. Figure 3 represents our vision of the new curriculum.

Students entering the school will come from a variety of academic backgrounds and possess varying levels of technical expertise, analytical skills, and knowledge of local information infrastructures. We propose to offer introductory workshops for students who do not enter the new program with the requisite skills and knowledge expected of incoming students. During their first semester of enrollment, all incoming students will be required to take one or more core courses that will account for the majority of credit hours during their first semester of enrollment. The size of the incoming class and personal constraints imposed on students because of funding, current

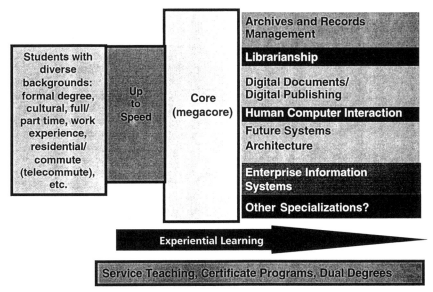

Fig. 3 Vision of our new curriculum.

employment, and personal obligations may require us to offer the core curriculum in different forms to accommodate student needs. Course work beyond the core curriculum will be divided into six specializations:

1. Future Systems Architecture—Graduates will create and apply computational technologies that support, augment, and replace decision makers in complex social institutions.

2. Human–Computer Interaction—Graduates will design and develop technologies that fit into their organizations and work practices, the work to be done, and the capabilities of users.

3. Librarianship—Graduates will work in hybrid (print-on-paper and digital) environments and integrate new and emerging information technologies in the course of handling data, information, and knowledge throughout all phases of the life cycle of information.

4. Enterprise Information Systems—Graduates will assume management positions in providing information systems for profit and not-for-profit organizations of all sizes and administer such systems in the service of people.

5. Archives and Records Management—Private corporations, government entities, colleges and universities, religious orders, special libraries, manuscript repositories, and archives will employ our graduates who will manage archival materials according to a set of principles that respect the personal, organizational, historical, business, and/or technological environments in which they were created.

6. Digital Documents/Digital Publishing—Graduates will find employment opportunities in museums, libraries, publishing, and the entertainment industry where they will organize, manage, create, or market new digital forms of human communication and expression.

Task forces charged with curriculum planning connected with each of the six specializations will not only make recommendations concerning content within their specialization, but they will also make recommendations concerning the core's content and form(s). A task force charged with the development of the new core curriculum will take up these recommendations, paying special attention to topics that none of the specializations have identified but topics that students should know, e.g., evaluation methods, statistics, economics of information, in their deliberations, planning, and efforts to design the school's new core curriculum. This task force will also learn from faculty who have up to four semesters of experience in core curriculum prototyping, including the most recent prototyping effort involving the six-credit core course.

At the present time, both specialization and new core curriculum task forces are in fact-finding and planning stages of the curriculum development process. Their deliberations will focus on:

1. Courses that students are required and encouraged to take, including the major topics that each course covers and the amount of time per topic.

2. Labs, projects, culminating experiences, internships, and/or work co-ops that students would be required and encouraged to do, including collaboration with students who are enrolled in other specializations.

3. Faculty in the school who are prepared or who require preparation to teach courses (and the amount of time they need), faculty in the UM who teach in recommended areas, and recommendations for additional faculty and needed expertise.

We do not expect that specialization curricula will be entirely self-contained, but they will feature course offerings across several specializations. We also may entertain proposals from students who want to design their own educational programs in the fulfillment of educational objectives that they have set for themselves and in the pursuit of career goals that are on the cutting edge of new information technology.

While we have tried to be inclusive regarding our definition of specializations in the new curriculum, we may add new ones in the near future, or consolidate, restructure, or redefine the six specializations that we have identified to date. Somewhat later in our planning, we will also need to address evaluation, continual revision, and refreshing of established specializations to ensure that our program remains viable and sensitive to the lightning-swift changes in information technology.

VII. New Approaches to Teaching and Learning

A. Project-Based Learning

In traditional classrooms, learning means reading textbooks, listening to lectures, taking tests, and completing homework assignments using paper and pencil. SILS is committed to project-based learning. This new approach to education features educators and learners who participate in collaborative, constructive, and authentic activities. They have access to timely, dynamic information resources and to members of scientific and professional communities who are shaping our present and future with new discoveries, insight, and knowledge.

Today's technologies provide collaboration tools such as real-time video conferences, live-screen sharing, virtual worlds, group chat, Usenet news, and electronic mail. From a technological perspective, this arsenal of collaborative media is historically unprecedented. From an educational perspective, we are still striving to define the place for these new media with regard to the needs of learners. The collaborative media just listed were primarily technology driven; the goal was to see what the new technology would support. Project-based education enlists these new technologies to facilitate learning.

Nearly all courses that have undergone significant change through rapid prototyping have incorporated project-based learning. An example of project-based learning is Professor Joseph Janes' Internet Public Library (IPL) course (ILS 726). Earlier iterations of ILS 726 focused on visions of the future of the library profession and intellectual property issues in the electronic domain. In the winter semester of 1995, Professor Janes took a different approach—he challenged students to explore the issues involved in the merger of networking and libraries by actually planning, building, and running a public library for the Internet community.

An experimental project, the IPL is a World Wide Web presentation that blends the traditions and culture of libraries with the dynamic and sometimes chaotic world of the Internet, to help people find information and learn (URL:http://ipl.sils.umich.edu). IPL has the following resources and services:

1. Reference center with a substantial ready reference collection as well as mechanisms for submitting live reference questions to IPL staff via a MOO (a multiuser object-oriented environment that is an interactive system accessible through telnet by many users at the same time).
2. Youth division that features original stories, a listserv for discussions of children's books, a science project, and materials for help with science and mathematics.
3. Services to librarians division that provides librarians and other information professionals with resources on using the Internet for their work, also allowing them to share professional information.
4. Exhibit hall that currently features materials from the collection of the Museum of African American History in Detroit, Michigan.
5. Classroom where individuals or organizations can teach others independent of time and distance.
6. Other resources and services, e.g., reading room, building directory, annotated guide to web searching tools, listserv, and conferences.

The initial design, development, and operation of IPL were collaborative efforts of students enrolled in ILS 726 in the winter semester of 1995. IPL development challenged students to rethink the roles and significance of libraries in today's increasingly distributed and digital world and to reconfigure the public library in a merging of traditional library services and networked, information technologies. In subsequent semesters, students have built upon this ambitious beginning of the Internet Public Library by expanding and enhancing services and introducing new ones using Internet-based technologies.

B. Distance-Independent Learning

A goal of the Kellogg CRISTAL-ED Project is to design a flexible, modular academic program that delivers key units of core knowledge and skills, is replicable by other schools of information and library science/studies, and can be implemented in a variety of methods (via traditional courses, distance-independent education, continuing education, and so on). SILS faculty began experimenting with distance-independent technologies in two courses.

Technologies used in these two courses included the following.

1. HyperNews

To facilitate discussion between students outside of the classroom, classes used networked discussion tools to create a forum for questions and discussion. The popular solutions are UseNet news or Confer; however, neither satisfied our needs as well as HyperNews. HyperNews provided easy access to the discussion by users familiar with the web and browsers. Anonymous access from anyplace on the Internet and local administration solved these problems, and persistent hypertext messages enriched the discussion.

2. CU-See Me

One goal of the courses was to set up intercampus communication between students. We sought a way of communicating beyond keyboard-based methods like electronic mail, discussion groups, and file exchange. Cornell University had developed the CU-See Me software that created video-conferencing links between computers on the Internet—working between both Macs and PCs. CU-See Me uses inexpensive video cameras and digitizing boards to send live video to users anywhere on the Internet. It offers a real-time solution to communication and provides students an opportunity to meet their remote peers face to face.

3. Timbuktu

In addition to discussion and file exchange software, we found that Timbuktu software greatly contributed to collaboration. It gave students and faculty the ability to view and control the same computer screen. Thus, collaborators could give intercampus presentations, brainstorm with partners at a remote site, and contribute to the progress of joint assignments in a timely fashion.

4. Vistium

Vistium is a product from AT&T that permits stable video conferencing across ISDN phone lines. (ISDN stands for Integrated Services Digital Network—a method for higher-speed communication). Classrooms were linked by Vistium video connections, allowing student participation and interaction during lectures and discussions.

5. CD-ROM Lectures

Another approach that is in development stages (and was not used in the first two courses) is the creation of several course modules in CD-ROM lecture format. This would provide a modular approach to instruction where desktop and full-room conferencing, World Wide Web documents, collaboration tools, and electronic mail are used as appropriate for the tasks.

Distance-independent technologies were used to teach "Sources of General Information" simultaneously at the University of Illinois at Urbana–Champaign. This course focused on the nature, evaluation, and use of basic bibliographies, dictionaries, directories, handbooks, indexes, and yearbooks, as well as reference works for statistical and biographical data, in a variety of print, digital, and other formats. Some course objectives were rather traditional. Examples were:

1. To develop familiarity with the basic core of general sources of information.
2. To develop skills in the evaluation, selection, and use of sources, including effective search strategy.
3. To develop and understanding of how reference sources are accessed and users are educated to their use.

Other course objectives focused on distance technologies and their integration into the learning environment. These objectives were:

1. To explore shared teaching by faculty located at a distance.
2. To explore partnering students on two campuses.
3. To test use of video/audio/text-based delivery mechanisms and consider how each may be applicable to a range of learning experiences (e.g., classroom lecture, group work, one-on-one meetings with faculty, group discussion).
4. To migrate the course to anytime, anyplace status through development of various digitally based modules.
5. To evaluate the effectiveness of technology-based instruction.

"Impact of New Information Resources: Multimedia and Networks" involved students simultaneously in Berkeley and Ann Arbor, and used the same distance-independent technologies. Students examined past predictions (e.g., Goodbye Gutenberg), currently available services (Prodigy, America Online, San Francisco Chronicle's The Gate, listservers and newsgroups, Time Magazine, multimedia CD-ROMs, etc.), and future delivery mechanisms (Media Lab's Newspaper of Future, movie delivery to the home, etc.) to determine how people now get their news, culture, and other information at a time when new technology is making the shift from broadcasting to narrowcasting more feasible.

Students, faculty, and guest lecturers used distance technologies to query each other during class and to hold group discussions and collaborate on projects. Students divided into working groups to focus their studies during the course of the semester. Each group consisted of students from both campuses. Group members in each city held weekly meetings and periodically communicated with one another using distance-learning tools like CU-See Me. From time to time, groups were given class time for discussions.

VIII. Pilot Projects

A major part of the new learning environment is the creation of several plot projects with Michigan libraries, museums, and schools. These projects are being carefully selected because they will serve as "living laboratories" for students, faculty, and practitioners. That is, they will be "living specifications" of new information environments to meet the needs of Michigan citizens. These pilot projects will be carefully evaluated and will hopefully serve as models for adoption in many other places.

Although full-scale pilot-project deployment will characterize later years of the Kellogg CRISTAL-ED Project, two projects are underway at the current time. The Flint Community Networking Initiative (FCNI) is the first "living laboratory" supported by the Kellogg CRISTAL-ED Project (URL:http://www.flint.lib.mi.us/fpl/GFCNI/gfcni.html). Funding provided the impetus for the development of a collaboratively funded, multiyear project which officially started with the dedication of the Community Networking and Training Center at the Flint Public Library in Flint, Michigan, on March 10, 1995. The objectives of FCNI are to:

1. Create an information infrastructure which will foster a viable community civic network built on emerging information technologies.
2. Provide extensive training to a core group of librarians who will act as trainers of librarians, community leaders, and a cadre of volunteer trainers.

3. Develop a sustainable approach to information delivery that is supported by the strengths of the public library (free to all, a public forum, provision of a wide variety of resources in an organized way).
4. Create a living laboratory which will inform and educate information professionals in the twenty-first century.
5. Revolutionize the way public libraries and the professionals who practice in them provide information to their communities and think about their practice.

FCNI's funding model reflects the collaborative model of community information networks in that it includes support from several organizations— Apple Library of Tomorrow (ALOT), Community Stabilization and Revitalization Project (CSR), Library of Michigan, Flint Public Library (FPL), and the Mideastern Michigan Library Cooperative. As a prelude to the Flint Community Networking Initiative, in fall 1994, CSR funded an extensive Internet training project for 30 librarians from both FPL and area public and academic libraries. Between September and December of 1994, training was held at the University of Michigan–Flint campus computing laboratory. The opening of the FPL's Community Networking and Training Center in March 1995 has provided the infrastructure to continue preparing the Flint-area librarians to assume a leadership role in the development of the emerging community network. The vision for this resource center that contains state-of-the-art microcomputers, software, and networking equipment is that it will become a friendly meeting place which provides public access to the Internet, facilities for training a wide range of users, and a studio for the creation of community information resources.

At the present time, librarians in the training group are learning how to create WWW-based documents. Trainees will serve as auxiliary Internet/ WWW trainers in future months. The lab will also be used periodically for basic Internet workshops which are part of the Library of Michigan's Internet Training Initiative. In addition, librarians who wish to develop Internet services tour the lab and seek advice. The lab will also provide opportunities for SILS students to assist volunteers and library staff in the design, development, and operation of the Flint Community Information Network. The initiative will also involve students in the acquisition of programming and content for the network through negotiation, visits, demonstrations, and discussions with local community leaders, merchants, public service agencies, and other representatives of the community.

A second Kellogg CRISTAL-ED pilot project is the Cultural Heritage Initiative for Cultural Outreach (CHICO) (URL:http://www.sils.umich.edu/ Publications/chico/CHICO.html). CHICO's goal is to prepare professionals who can provide access to cultural heritage materials that will be available to a broad array of audiences by using information and collaboration technologies.

An underlying premise of the CHICO initiative is that pilot projects can help explore how to make the vision of scenarios of the future possible and to educate knowledge professionals who will be key players in these future-oriented settings. To broaden and enhance access to cultural materials, CHICO will develop pilot projects and a curriculum program which serve as models for using advanced information and collaboration technology. CHICO project staff will work with members of the art, education, and information professional community to design, deploy, and test the models. Partnerships will be forged with the information, arts and entertainment industries to leverage resources and publicize the initiatives. In CHICO, students will work with professionals in museums, archives, and other cultural heritage repositories to help design services which can bring museum resources to diverse venues, such as K–12 classrooms, community centers, and college classes.

Several projects are already in place at SILS which serve as starting points for the CHICO. Examples are:

1. SILS Art Image Database Project, which is developing, deploying, and evaluating a digital database of images in art and architecture, utilizing classification.
2. Getty Trust's Museum Educational Site License Project which is testing models of classroom use of digital images provided by museums.
3. Mellon-sponsored Making of America Project which is a collaborative project involving SILS, UM libraries, and Cornell University in the building of a significant collection on the development of the United States.

CHICO will also build on existing curricular strengths at SILS to create the knowledge base needed to prepare professionals in creating, sharing, and providing "anytime and anyplace" access to cultural heritage materials.

IX. Impact of Large-Scale, Interdisciplinary Research Projects

Joining the Kellogg CRISTAL-ED Project in enriching the learning environment for SILS faculty and students are several large-scale, interdisciplinary research projects in the area of digital libraries. Teams of UM faculty with formal affiliations in SILS, computer science, economics, education, and the university libraries were awarded a $4 million grant through the Digital

Library Initiative funded by the National Science Foundation (NSF), the Advanced Research Projects Agency (ARPA), and the National Aeronautics and Space Administration (NASA). These teams are creating an architecture and working prototype called the University of Michigan Digital Library (UMDL) which will broker access to millions of digital collections, services, and resources in ways that are easy, relevant, and timely for people to use (URL:http://http2.sils.umich.edu/UMDL/HomePage.html). The prototype focuses on digital collections in the areas of earth and space sciences and is initially for use among high school students, public library users, and academic library users.

A related project is JSTOR—a digital library to support research and scholarly inquiry in the arts and sciences (URL:http://index.umdl.umich.edu/jstor/). JSTOR is supported by a grant from the Andrew W. Mellon Foundation and will initially consist of about 10 journal titles in the areas of economics and history. Some JSTOR titles such as *The American Economic Review* and *The American Historic Review* stretch back to the late nineteenth century. Besides providing leverage for the UMDL Project, JSTOR will provide digital-library researchers with opportunities to compare and contrast the searching strategies of digital library users who are searching timely and up-to-date digital-library collections such as UMDL with the JSTOR digital-library collection that is retrospective and historical in its scope and coverage.

Another project that is related to the UMDL Project and features an interdisciplinary research team is the recently begun Middle Years Digital Library (MYDL) Project, an NSF-funded initiative. MYDL will be an extension of UMDL and will provide ready access to a broad range of information resources, from traditional books, magazines, and newspapers, to data sets, scientific instruments, computer-based research tools, and collaboration with peers and mentors. The MYDL Project team is determined to use this opportunity to find ways to engage middle-school students in science at a critical time in their development, i.e., when students develop cognitive ability and experiences to participate substantially in the process of doing science but all too often lose interest in science and in school altogether.

SILS students, especially doctoral students, are full and active participants in these large-scale research projects through appointments as research assistants on design and development teams for the user interface, collection search and retrieval, and on evaluation teams for overall system impact and evaluation. Masters-level students are invited to undertake directed research projects that involve study of digital-library users or uses.

SILS faculty have brought the experience of these large-scale, interdisciplinary research projects into their classrooms. Several new courses have been inspired by these projects and/or enlist the digital library as a test bed for student study and research.

X. Conclusion

In our curriculum planning efforts, SILS faculty are not merely renaming courses or adding a few courses to reflect advances in computer technology. We are engaging in a complete and deep evaluation and restructuring of our entire educational program. While we remain firmly committed to instilling the traditions and values of librarianship in our graduates, we feel that it is time to do this as part of an even broader agenda—as part of a new, larger, and more diverse multidisciplinary school.

We are convinced that a need exists for an augmented set of professional programs to produce graduates who will create and manage a broad set of knowledge-work environments including but not limited to libraries. We will provide our students with a broad, holistic education in technology, behavioral and social sciences, a grounding in specific application domains, and instill a visceral commitment to meeting real human needs. Graduates of our program will assume leadership positions in libraries and other information-intensive organizations and apply themselves to solving problems of information access, organization, and preservation in hybrid environments that feature both print and digital forms of human communication. We also want our graduates to become experts in human–computer interaction, in computer-supported work, in information technology and organizational design, in electronic records management, in the design and production of new information goods, in information policy issues and resolution of intellectual property issues, and in the creation and application of computational technologies that support, augment, and replace decision makers in complex social institutions.

SILS faculty are now in the process of building such a new school. We are currently exploring a new, more encompassing name for the new school. We are planning for a student body that is growing in size and intellectual breadth. We are creating a multidisciplinary faculty that is enhancing our humanities focus with expertise in technology, behavioral sciences, and social sciences. We have also adopted the "Borromean rings" as a symbol for the unique, multidisciplinary synergy we are hoping to achieve in enhancing our faculty and in developing a new educational program. The symbol is three, symmetric interlocking rings, no two of which are interlinked and in which removing one destroys the synergy (see Fig. 4).

The School of Information and Library Studies of the University of Michigan has evolved and changed over the 70 years of its existence. In response to today's revolution in technology, networking, and information that is radically changing how knowledge is created, disseminated, used, and preserved, we are taking bold action by building a national multidisciplinary collaborative consortium to define new professional specializations to serve

Computer,
Information,
Library Sciences

Behavioral,
Organizational
Sciences

People in Society

Fig. 4 Borromean rings.

society's needs for information access in the rapidly emerging age of digital data, information, and knowledge. We must continue to change into a new, more encompassing educational program if our program is to stay the same—a vital, viable, and relevant learning environment that is committed to meeting the information needs of people in society.

References

Committee on a National Collaboratory (1993). *National Collaboratories: Applying Information Technology for Scientific Research.* National Academy of Sciences, National Research Council, Washington, DC.

Leyden, P. (1995). On the edge of the digital revolution. *Star Tribune*, June 4, part I, p. 1.

O'Harrow, R., and Corcoran, E. (1995). Snowed in but still in touch with the office. *The Washington Post* (January 9), A03.

Woodsworth, A., et al. (1994). *The Future of Education for Librarianship: Looking Forward from the Past.* Council on Library Resources, Washington, DC.

Mexican and U.S. Library Relations

Robert A. Seal

Texas Christian University
Fort Worth, Texas 76129

I. Introduction

A. Overview and Purpose

For many years, librarians in the United States have interacted with their colleagues abroad. One of the earliest instances of "foreign library relations" was the very first American Library Association conference in Philadelphia in 1876, which attracted a number of international visitors. Since that meeting, American libraries have worked with their counterparts around the globe for a variety of reasons. Contact with Latin America libraries began in earnest after World War I and has continued ever since. Because of the close geographic proximity to and historical and cultural links with Mexico, there has been a natural alliance between the librarians of these two countries. This has been especially true in the border region.

This chapter examines recent library interactions involving the United States and Mexico, providing a review of the literature and commentary on current and potential future cooperative endeavors. However, due to space considerations and a dearth of literature describing early work, the focus is limited to the past 30 years, with only selected references to earlier activity. The potential impact of the North American Free Trade Agreement (NAFTA), recent developments in telecommunications and computer technology, and a rising number of "grass roots" binational conferences and projects all make this a good time to review our relationship, librarywise, with our neighbors to the south.

To place the subject of U.S.–Mexico library relations in context, this chapter begins with a brief overview of Mexican librarianship in Section II. Topics include types of libraries, professional activities, library education and research, the impact of technology, obstacles to library development, and sources of information on Mexican librarianship. Whenever possible, the reader is referred to key works in the literature that provide more detailed information. There are also selected references to the broader topic of U.S.–

ADVANCES IN LIBRARIANSHIP, VOL. 20
Copyright © 1996 by Academic Press, Inc.

Latin American library relations to provide a framework for a discussion of work with Mexico, as well as to emphasize and give credit to key organizations such as the Organization of American States, the Seminar on the Acquisition of Latin American Library Materials (SALALM), the Library of Congress, and others whose activity in libraries in Latin America ultimately affect our relations with Mexico.

Section III addresses library cooperation within Mexico itself, also to put the relations between our two nations in context. This portion of the chapter covers, among other things, the climate for cooperation, obstacles to collaboration, economic considerations, and specific recent examples of resource sharing in Mexico.

The core of this chapter is Section IV, "U.S.–Mexico Library Interaction," which begins with an overview of U.S. involvement in Latin America before moving to the more specific issue of work with Mexico. Topics presented include historical background, key players, exchanges, conference activities, association interaction, library schools, state-to-state programs, and miscellaneous cooperative projects.

The chapter ends with a look to the future in Section V, reviewing the advantages of continued and increased cooperation, obstacles to collaborative work, and the impact of NAFTA. A particular focus is on two key questions: "What can the United States offer to Mexican libraries?" and "What can Mexico provide to American libraries?" Potential future activities to promote and strengthen ties between the United States and Mexico also are presented.

B. Scope

The phrase "library relations" can have a variety of meanings in the context of international activity: one-on-one interactions between librarians, the purchase of foreign imprints, attendance at conferences, the exchange of personnel, interlibrary loan, library school programs, etc. This chapter includes all of these and more; however, the exploits of individual librarians who visit Mexico (and vice versa) to work, lecture, and consult are not discussed at any great length. It should not be construed that the work of individuals is not important, rather that such activity is infrequently documented and there are too many instances to address in any meaningful way.

Instead, the emphasis here is on relations in terms of cooperative projects and programs, learning and resource-sharing activities in which both Mexico and United States benefit from working together. While the goal of international relations is often a concrete thing, e.g., the exchange of publications, information, or personnel, the end result is often intangible, e.g., a better understanding of another culture, language, and a way of doing things.

C. Research Undertaken

A brief word is in order regarding the research process for this piece. A thorough review of the U.S. literature revealed almost no books and a relatively small number of articles addressing U.S.–Mexico library relations, and very few pieces addressing Mexican librarianship per se. Articles on U.S.–Latin American interactions were more common and often useful. Searching the Mexican literature was even more problematic. There is not much "Mexican library literature" to begin with and it is not widely available in the United States. In the case of both American and Mexican literature, many sources on this topic are very much out of date.

So while there has been a long history of cooperation and other interaction, there is little in print, especially recently, to describe it. In addition to bibliographic research on site in the United States and Mexico City, other means of gathering information were employed, such as personal interviews, conversations at conferences in Mexico, and information from colleagues via e-mail and listservs. The end result is a review of primarily recent examples of U.S.–Mexico library relations from the literature of both countries, supplemented by information and opinions from colleagues on both sides of the border.

II. Mexican Librarianship: A Brief Overview

A. History

The first libraries in what is now present-day Mexico consisted of "large collections of hieroglyphs that narrated the artistic, scientific, religious, and war experiences of its inhabitants, as well as their traveling and the prosperity and magnificence of pre-Columbian Mexico" (Fernández de Zamora, 1976, p. 4). These massive archival collections were kept in temples under the supervision of Aztec priests. With the arrival of the Spanish in 1521, these "libraries" were destroyed along with the civilization that had created them (Peñalosa, 1953).

The clergy who came to the New World to convert the indigenous population were instrumental in bringing culture and learning to Mexico. They brought the first printing press in 1544 (Peñalosa, 1953) and established the first library on the North American continent in 1534 (Fernández de Zamora, 1976). From that time up until the early twentieth century, overall library development in Mexico was erratic, often nonexistent, and adversely affected by war and revolution.

There are few books on the history of libraries in Mexico, although several articles provide an overview of the topic. Heliodoro Valle (1923) wrote a brief piece on librarianship in Mexico in which he described, among other things, major libraries in Mexico City. More recent and very insightful panoramas were done by Peñalosa (1953) and Fernández de Zamora (1976), the latter an in-depth study with a lengthy bibliography of sources from the Mexican library literature. Fernández de Zamora (1987) also compiled a detailed chronology of twentieth-century library developments in her country.

B. Present Status of Mexico's Libraries

1. Public Libraries

Prior to 1983, public libraries were not well developed in Mexico. In 1921, a Department of Libraries was established by the Secretary of Education, José Vasconselos, who also initiated a literacy program (Fernández de Zamora, 1976). This so-called popular library movement was the first concerted attempt to make library services widely available to the populace. It also concentrated on the training of future librarians (Manrique de Lara, 1935). "Succeeding governments did not support library service," wrote Fernández de Zamora (1976, p. 12) and public libraries went into a period of decline with only occasional interest by and support of the Mexican government.

This downward trend ended in 1983 with the establishment of a new initiative, the Programa Nacional de Bibliotecas Públicas (Magaloni de Bustamante, 1993). As a result of this program, public libraries in Mexico grew from 351 to more than 4000 by 1992 and were located in large cities and small villages in every part of the country. This impressive effort was the result of cooperation among municipal and state governments and the Secretary of Public Education (SEP) (Magaloni, 1993). The resultant National Network of Public Libraries, the "Red Nacional de Bibliotecas Públicas" (Dirección General de Bibliotecas, 1991), is not a network in the sense of a consortia carrying out cooperative activities, although it has resulted in a vastly improved library system for the people of Mexico. Each public library now places an emphasis on children's activities and on becoming an integral part of the community it serves (Magaloni, 1993). Overviews of recent public library activity in Mexico were provided by Morales Campos (1990), Magaloni de Bustamante (1992), and Magaloni (1993).

2. School Libraries

Because of long-standing neglect and limited funds, there are precious few school libraries in Mexico, both at the elementary and secondary levels. "Although . . . the usefulness of school libraries as an indispensable aid to teachers and students is understood, these libraries have received the least support on the part of the government and educational authorities" (Fernández de Zamora, 1976, p. 18). In fact, the local public library has taken much of the responsibility for providing library materials to public school children (Magaloni de Bustamante, 1993; Morales Campos, 1990). For example, public libraries in the state of Nuevo Leon serve students in 93 different schools, from kindergarten to college (Quintanilla C., 1989). Private schools, due to requirements by SEP, are in moderately better shape in terms of library service (García Moreno, 1980).

3. Academic Libraries

Although initially slow to develop, college and university libraries in Mexico have made significant progress since the mid-1960s through increased government support and by utilizing computer technology. Within the larger universities, there are two types of libraries: one directly supports the educational mission of the institution, serving students and professors, while the other is attached to the university research institutes, serving investigators in specific subject areas (Rodríguez Gallardo, 1977). Academic libraries in Mexico may be placed in three broad categories: public universities, polytechnics, and private schools (Lau, 1993). By the end of the 1980s, there were approximately 900 academic libraries in various stages of development (Morales Campos, 1990), from small and very poor to large, well-funded library systems. Although there is no overall coordination of university libraries, SEP and ANUIES (National Association of Universities and Institutions of Higher Education) are working to improve communication and cooperation among that group (Fernández de Zamora, 1991).

Despite improvements in many sectors, a number of academic libraries still lack the human and financial resources to adequately serve their students and faculty. In particular, libraries in the provinces, i.e., outside of Mexico City, have for years been prone to chronic underfunding (Fernández de Zamora, 1990a). As a result, many are, some for the first time, entering into cooperative agreements with other academic libraries in their regions, utilizing technology to communicate and share resources (Morales Campos, 1990). In an earlier article, Morales Campos (1976) provided a general overview of Mexican academic librarianship along with detailed descriptions of several of the country's university libraries. A look at the finances of academic libraries was given by Tamez Solís (1992).

No discussion of this topic would be complete without mention of the largest and most important university system in the country, the Universidad Nacional Autónoma de México (National Autonomous University of Mexico), best known by its acronym, UNAM. Located on a sprawling campus in the southern part of Mexico City, UNAM has at least 170 libraries supporting teaching and research. Its computer catalog and database, LIBRUNAM, is not only utilized by the UNAM community, but by academic institutions and special libraries throughout Mexico (Morales Campos, 1990) and internationally (León Saavedra, 1983). Rodríguez Gallardo (1992) provided an overview of the UNAM system and its role in the development of Mexican librarianship in the past two decades.

4. Special Libraries

In Mexico, the term "special library" refers to both corporate and government libraries and information centers. The majority of these libraries are located in the Federal District (Mexico City) because that is where the majority of industries and the federal government have their headquarters (Rodríguez Gallardo, 1977). Special libraries grew rapidly in the 1970s in response to the information needs of developing industry and technology (Magaloni de Bustamante, 1993) and therefore were among the earliest users of technology for information retrieval in Mexico. Because they are well funded, special libraries and information centers provide high-quality service and possess some of the finest technical collections in the country. Libraries in private industry and business also pay more competitive salaries and thus attract some of the most qualified library school graduates (Morales Campos, 1976). Those companies that do not have their own libraries may rely on special government-sponsored information centers such as Infotec for their information needs (Morales Campos, 1990). Carrión Rodríguez (1992) provided an overview of special libraries, discussing the challenges of increased demand for technical information and rapid technological advances.

5. The National Library

Unlike the United States, Mexico has a separate Library of Congress (Biblioteca del Congreso de la Unión) and National Library (Biblioteca Nacional de México). The former, established in 1936 (Fernández de Zamora, 1976), serves the country's legislators and is a legal depository of Mexican publications. The latter, founded by presidential decree in 1867 (Brown, 1885; Rojas, 1919), is located on the campus of UNAM and is administered by UNAM's Instituto de Investigaciones Bibliográficas (Institute of Bibliographic Research). It shares a building with the National Periodicals Library (Hemeroteca Nacional de México) and also has legal depository privileges. It possesses an important rare books and manuscripts collection rich in historical source material.

With a strong emphasis on the humanities, the two national libraries serve a variety of users (Magaloni de Bustamante, 1993), especially university students due to their location. One of the library's most important responsibilities is the production of the national bibliography, the *Bibliografía Mexicana* (Carrión Rodrígues, 1981). The terminology "National Library" is perhaps a misnomer because it is not a federally funded and administered library like that of other countries, but rather a unit in the custody of a university (UNAM) since 1967 (Fernández de Zamora, 1992). As such, it only plays a minor role in developing the country's bibliographic services (Litton and Krzys, 1986).

C. Professional Activities

1. Library Organizations

Librarians in Mexico belong to a number of professional associations, most notably the Asociación Mexicana de Bibliotecarios, Asociación Civil (Mexican Association of Librarians), founded in 1954. Its two primary goals are professional development of the membership and the promotion of libraries and library service. As of 1992, AMBAC had 520 members (Magaloni de Bustamante, 1993) from a variety of types of libraries, although it is dominated by academic and special librarians. AMBAC has several regional divisions and holds an annual meeting, which alternates between Mexico City and other parts of the country.

An AMBAC affiliate group of academic and research librarians founded in 1967 is ABIESI, the Asociación de Bibliotecarios de Enseñanza Superior y de Investigación (Association of Higher Education and Research Librarians). In addition to addressing the concerns and activities of academic librarians, ABIESI is noted for the publication of an interlibrary loan code and a set of minimum standards for university libraries (Rodríguez Gallardo, 1977).

There are several other professional groups organized along subject lines: ANBAGRO (agricultural librarians), BIBAC (biomedical librarians), and ABIMAG (government librarians). In addition, there is a relatively small body dedicated to the needs of professional librarians, the Colegio Nacional de Bibliotecarios (CNB). Small in numbers because the majority of librarians in Mexico are not trained at the master's level as in the United States, the CNB came into being to elevate and maintain the status, as well as to recognize the qualifications, of the professional staff member. It also has the legal responsibility of advising the Mexican government on library matters (Aranda and Gleaves, 1981). On its 10th anniversary in 1989, the CNB sponsored a national seminar addressing issues of concern to the country's professional librarians (Verdugo Sánchez and Fernández de Zamora, 1990).

2. Library Conferences

The earliest national gatherings of librarians took place in 1927 and 1928 in Mexico City (Pan American Union, 1930). The first Jornadas (annual meeting) of AMBAC occurred in 1956 with 323 persons in attendance ("Las Primeras Jornadas," 1957). Since that time, Mexico has seen an increasing number of library meetings, in recent years sponsored by AMBAC, ABIESI, SEP, UNAM, and the National Council of Science and Technology (CONACYT). These conferences consist almost entirely of contributed papers or panel discussions. There are few committee meetings and a limited number of exhibitors, quite the opposite of the typical American library conference.

In addition to the annual AMBAC Jornadas, two other regular conferences bear mentioning. The first is the Guadalajara book fair, the Feria Internacional del Libro (FIL), held at the end of November and sponsored by the Universidad de Guadalajara (Hoffert, 1993b). Book fairs are very common and popular in Mexico but this gathering is the largest of its kind, attracting hundreds of publishers from throughout Latin America, Europe, and the United States. It includes an ambitious series of concurrent programs on books, literature, and libraries, the latter attracting participants from the United States and Central and South America.

Immediately preceding the FIL every other year is the Coloquio sobre Automatización de Bibliotecas, held in Colima near the west coast of Mexico. Dealing with library automation, this meeting is sponsored by the Universidad de Colima, a leader in the production of CD-ROM databases. Held in conjunction with a users' group meeting for SIABUC, a library software package widely used in Mexico, this conference showcases the latest developments in and applications of library automation.

D. Library Education

The most frequently cited reason for lack of library development in Mexico (indeed in most of Latin America) is a dearth of professionally trained librarians (Rodríguez Gallardo, 1977; Goldman, 1978; Macías-Chapula, 1985; Litton and Krzys, 1986). Although some libraries have formally trained staff, many are supervised by untrained personnel who were asked or "volunteered" to be the librarian. The small number of schools that offer library degrees, both master's and bachelor's, cannot keep up with demand for new professionals (Morales Campos, 1976). As a result, many of the library leaders in the country were trained abroad, mainly in the United States, Great Britain, and Canada, often with the financial support of CONACYT (Goldman, 1978).

The Escuela Nacional de Biblioteconomía y Archivonomía (National School of Librarians and Archivists), ENBA, was founded in 1945 and emphasizes the administrative side of the profession. The program at UNAM focuses on the technical aspects of library science. Other library schools are located in Guadalajara, Nuevo León, San Luis Potosí, and Guanajuato (Magaloni de Bustamante, 1993). The master's program at the Universidad de Guanajuato was initiated by CONACYT to help meet the growing demand for trained professionals (Aranda and Gleaves, 1981).

Continuing education is a major focus in Mexico and, consequently, workshops, seminars, and informal courses are offered on a regular basis to personnel at all levels. Organized informal training programs, as opposed to formal education resulting in a degree, are referred to as "diplomados," interrelated courses focusing on a given thematic area, for example, cataloging, reference work, or library automation. Recommended guidelines for diplomado programs were provided by the Colegio Nacional de Bibliotecarios (Verdugo Sánchez, 1992).

E. Library Science Research

In contrast with the United States and other nations in which university faculty are both teachers and researchers, in Mexico there are separate library science professors and researchers, although the latter occasionally teach. Most such investigators are associated with UNAM's Centro Universitario de Investigaciones Bibliotecológicas (University Center for Library Science Research). Founded in 1981, CUIB's "main goal is to carry out librarianship research to assist in solving national problems directly related to libraries and information centres in the country, and to provide indirect support to education, research, production, administration and diffusion of culture" (Morales, 1987, p. 173). In addition to conducting research, CUIB sponsors numerous training programs and conferences, works on joint projects with overseas colleagues, and publishes extensively in the field of library science (Morales Campos, 1992).

F. Obstacles to Library Development

Library progress in Mexico is complicated and hindered by periodic economic crises (Orozco-Tenorio, 1988; Fernández de Zamora, 1988, 1990a, 1991) and a change of government every 6 years. Further, library development and finances are highly centralized in the capital while the rest of the country has very limited resources (meeting with Mexican librarians, February 23, 1995). Nevertheless, steady progress is being made due to work at the local and regional level and through the efforts of individual government agencies such as CONACYT which encourages scientific and technical development and emphasizes the importance of information in a developing technological society. In addition to its role in educating Mexican librarians, CONACYT facilitates access to bibliographic databases and coordinates a union list of serials, among other projects (Goldman, 1978).

Another obstacle to library development is an absence of planning. The country lacks an overall information policy and needs "a national body to control information activities" (Lau, 1993, p. 142). Other national library problems include (1) inadequate bibliographic and authority control, (2) limited scholarly research, (3) minimal resource sharing, (4) an insufficient number of trained librarians, (5) the lack of a shared national library vision, and (6) uncoordinated development of library automation (meeting with Mexican librarians, February 23, 1995).

G. Impact of Technology

Many of these difficulties are being addressed and alleviated to some extent through automation. As in the rest of the world, microcomputers and CD-ROMs have had a significant impact on day-to-day library operations in Mexico (Fernández de Zamora, 1990a), and it was probably the first country in Latin America to have access to online databases (Lau, 1993). Currently, great strides are being made in the production of online and CD-ROM databases led by UNAM, the Universidad de Colima, CONACYT, and CICH, the Science and Humanities Information Center at UNAM. Ainsworth (1994) provided a comprehensive look at Mexican electronic resources whereas Levison and Reynel Iglesias (1993) gave an overview of its online industry. Like their counterparts in the rest of the world, Mexican librarians are increasingly using electronic mail to communicate and foster cooperation in the region (Almada de Ascencio and Pérez de Almada, 1991). Use of the Internet is on the rise, too, utilized for the same reasons as colleagues abroad: communication, discussion of issues, reference work, announcement of meetings, and so on.

H. Sources of Information on Mexican Librarianship

Perhaps the most expedient way to learn about the state of the library activity and development in a given country is through its professional literature. This process is somewhat problematic for Mexico because although the quality is high, the number and breadth of its library publications are limited. There have been several serial publications over the past half century, but most have since ceased. At present there are two established periodicals that describe professional activity and research: *Noticiero de la AMBAC*, the newsletter of the Mexican Association of Librarians, and *Investigación Bibliotecológica* (Library Research) published by CUIB at UNAM. The former provides news items on association activities, workshops, lectures, etc., whereas the latter primarily publishes scholarly research articles along with a few news notes regarding activities of CUIB researchers. A new, privately published journal, *Byblos*, attempts to fill a void in the current library journal literature. Newsletters, especially those published by university libraries, are common but generally not indexed.

The best method of keeping pace with library activity and research in Mexico is through its conference proceedings. The most well-known literature of this type are the proceedings (*Memorias*) of the annual meeting (*Jorna-*

das) of AMBAC. But memorias also result each year from a variety of other library conferences sponsored by government agencies, library organizations, and major universities. Although very useful in taking the pulse of librarianship in Mexico, they are not widely available in the United States.

Apart from conference proceedings, library science monographs are few in number. Of particular note is a recent panorama of Mexican librarianship, *La Bibliotecología en el Mexico Actual y Sus Tendencias* (Librarianship in Mexico Today and Its Trends) (Dirección General de Bibliotecas, UNAM, 1992), a comprehensive survey of all fields of library activity. A similar compilation of contributed papers was published by CUIB on the occasion of its 10th anniversary: *Edición Conmemorativa del X Aniversario del Centro Universitario de Investigaciones Bibliotecológicas* (Morales Campos and Ramírez Leyva, 1992).

III. Library Cooperation in Mexico

A. General Overview

1. Obstacles

Because many of the relationships between the United States and Mexico in the field of librarianship are in fact cooperative in nature, a brief overview of resource sharing within Mexico itself is presented in this section. While collaborative efforts are very common in the United States, they are less common and more limited in scope in Mexico and other developing nations. That does not mean that there has not been interest in library cooperation in Mexico, indeed the opposite is true (Fernández de Zamora, 1988). In fact, the subject of resource sharing has been a common theme of seminars and conferences for some years, beginning with the first Jornadas of AMBAC in 1956. At that meeting, several recommendations were made regarding the need for cooperation among the nation's libraries (Fernández de Zamora, Ansoleaga de López, García Velarde, and Saavedra Fernández, 1977).

Nevertheless, library collaboration has not had tremendous success in Mexico. Projects are more difficult to get started and when they do, they often are doomed to failure at the outset because one of two key ingredients is missing: something to share and a true willingness to do so (Orozco Tenorio, 1992). Further, cooperative efforts in Mexico are often informal and depend too much on one person's goodwill or on personal friendships, neither of which can be the basis for long-term success (Orozco Tenorio, 1992). Fortunately, many cooperative endeavors are now being given more weight by the use of written agreements called "convenios" or "acuerdos."

A number of obstacles to successful library cooperation in Mexico have been noted in the literature and in conversations with colleagues. These include, but are not limited to (1) minimal knowledge of library holdings in other locations due to the lack of a national bibliographic network like OCLC; (2) scant financial resources exacerbated by periodic economic crises; (3) unevenly developed and distributed collections resulting in many libraries with little to share, especially those outside Mexico City; (4) insufficiently trained numbers of staff to carry out resource sharing; (5) nonstandard computer systems, bibliographic record formats, and Spanish language subject headings, and little or no authority control, all of which hinder sharing and accessing data and limit cooperative cataloging efforts; and (6) the lack of a national resource sharing vision.

In addition to these very real barriers, there are also a number of intangible problems such as apathy and government bureaucracy, problems not unique to Mexico. Garduño (1985) pointed out that cooperation in Mexico is subject to political, technical, and organizational factors as well as "professional jealousies and institutional selfishness which impede joint action" (p. 11). He stated that a lack of planning hinders cooperative ventures, many of which are really intended to primarily benefit the institution which created the plan in the first place (Garduño, 1985).

2. A Changing Environment

Despite these obstacles, there have been many successes, especially since the early 1980s. Much of the progress has been due to work by individuals and government agencies such as CONACYT, SEP, and the Consejo Nacional para la Cultura y las Artes, as well as professional organizations such as AMBAC, ABIESI, and CNB (Orozco Tenorio, 1992). Fernández de Zamora *et al.* (1977) and Carrión (1977) also cited the importance of associations and CONACYT, respectively, in the promotion of resource sharing.

The advent of less expensive, more powerful computer technology in the past decade has contributed to the recent progress in library cooperation in Mexico. Shepard (1984) noted that throughout Latin America the application of automation to library and information services has led to centralized technical processing, a broader acceptance of standards, and an increased number of library networks. The use of fax and the Internet has helped an increasing number of libraries be more "connected" and has contributed to more cooperation, especially interlibrary loan. In addition, successful binational projects like the U.S.–Mexico Interlibrary Loan Project and the Transborder Library Forums (discussed in Sections IV,H1 and IV,D,2,b, respectively) have demonstrated the possibilities of and have spawned new resource sharing efforts in Mexico. Fernández de Zamora (1991) pointed out that Latin American librarianship in the past was characterized by individualism but now collaboration is seen as a means to work more effectively by sharing limited resources.

Indeed, a new environment favorable to cooperation seems to be emerging in Mexico. This trend is apparent from the Mexican library literature, which includes an increasing number of papers and articles focusing on the need for and importance of resource sharing. This is especially true for conference proceedings which present both theoretical papers and descriptions of specific projects (Bernal Flores *et al.*, 1982; "Seminario de Cooperación," 1977; "Segundo seminario de Cooperación," 1983; "Reunión de Trabajo," 1988).

Fernández de Zamora *et al.* (1977) described several areas in which Mexican libraries could and should work together, whereas Robles Zafra (1983) gave a brief history of library collaboration worldwide and in Mexico. Types of cooperation and the elements necessary for success were reviewed by Ramírez Escárcega (1984); Thomas Giraud and Barberena Blásquez (1986); and Fernández de Zamora (1988). Ladrón de Guevara Cox (1990) made several recommendations for improving cooperation, both among Latin American nations and within Mexico. She emphasized the need for AMBAC to take a central role and for conference programs to include presentations on collaboration.

Much of the existing cooperation takes place among academic institutions, and Orozco Tenorio (1977) provided a theoretical look at shared resources for university libraries. Like many of his colleagues, Orozco Tenorio emphasized the economic necessity for and benefit of sharing collections and other resources.

One of the most useful sources of information on networking in Mexico was done in 1987 under the auspices of the Programa Integral para el Desarrollo de la Educación Superior (Complete Program for the Development of Higher Education). The report provided an overview of networking concepts, and listed and analyzed 11 national, regional, and local library systems, past and present. It also outlined obstacles to systems of shared resources and made several specific recommendations for future action. The document's authors concluded that only with great difficulty can Mexico's academic libraries advance if they work alone and that new resource sharing efforts are to be encouraged to help libraries support the advance of teaching and research (Voutssás, Rodríguez, Ladrón de Guevara, Feria, and González Arteaga, 1989).

B. Examples of Resource Sharing in Mexico

Fernández de Zamora (1990b) described the cooperative efforts of Mexico City libraries to help colleagues after the September 1985 earthquake. Other similar ad hoc efforts could also be cited. Long-term, ongoing library cooperation in Mexico can be grouped into three major categories: consortia and networks, interlibrary loan, and union lists of serials. The following projects are examples only and should not be construed as the total extent of such activity in Mexico.

1. Consortia and Networks

While a national bibliographic network would be highly desirable for Mexico, cooperation might best be done at first on a regional basis (Enciso Carbajal and Gallardo Gómez, 1984) and indeed there have been several such successful endeavors in cities, states, and regions. One of the most often cited achievements is a network of academic, government, and special libraries in the Northeast known as ARDUSI (Acuerdo Regional de Universidades para el Desarrollo de Sistemas Bibliotecarios), founded with the signing of a formal "acuerdo" in 1984. Sáenz (1983) described the origins and goals of this group located in the states of Nuevo Leon and Coahuila, whereas Arteaga Carlebach (1990) reviewed the network's progress after 4 years, discussing its organization and bases of operation. Among its goals are (1) to exchange information about each other's collections, (2) to undertake projects to establish databases, and (3) to plan new user services. Other such regional consortia have also been created with varying success (Fernández de Zamora, 1988).

There are also consortia established along the lines of type of library. These include the Consejo Nacional para Bibliotecas, CONPAB, the state university librarians group, and RENABIT (Red Nacional Bibliotecaria de los Institutos Tecnológicos), a consortium of technical school libraries. The latter, created in 1987, is divided into nine geographic zones. Arjón Castro (1991) described the workings of zone 3 in the southern part of the country.

An active consortium of 21 biomedical libraries known as RENCIS (Red Nacional de Información y Documentación en Salud) has created union catalogs and a CD-ROM of the full text of more than 19 Mexican medical journals. Established in 1992, the network consists mainly of biomedical libraries at universities, but also includes several which are connected with the federal research institutes. Other RENCIS projects include creating databases of tables of contents of journals and document delivery utilizing Ariel (G. Arteaga, personal communication, November 17, 1995).

An outgrowth of the U.S.–Mexico Interlibrary Loan Project (described in Section IV,H,1) is the Grupo AMIGOS consisting of several academic libraries in the Federal District and environs. Among their collaborative efforts is a union catalog of rare books titled ABIMEX, the Antigua Bibliografia Mexicana, of which a CD-ROM version was expected in late 1995 or early 1996. The group is also working to develop a common data format to be used in sharing catalog records (P. Verdejo, personal communication, September 28, 1995). The members of that group are convinced that resource sharing in Mexico is advancing, although there are challenges and obstacles that must be overcome (meeting with Mexican librarians, February 23, 1995).

2. Interlibrary Loan

There has long been interest in interlibrary loan in Mexico with the earliest formal activity occurring in the late 1940s (Fernández de Zamora *et al.*, 1977)

T. de Zubarán (1956), noted that the Benjamin Franklin Library (see Section IV,B,1) had been requesting loans from the United States since 1943, the year after its founding. This service was discontinued in 1975 (Pérez Monroy, 1991). Special libraries have engaged in cooperative activities, including interlibrary loan (Fernández de Zamora, 1976), whereas the larger university libraries such as UNAM have been obtaining materials from abroad for quite some time. Lau (1982) rviewed the state of interlibrary loan in Mexico, noting that there is sufficient demand and resources to justify its use. In another paper, he presented a series of recommendations to improve ILL service (Lau, 1983).

Despite the fact that interlibrary loan is the most common form of resource sharing internationally, it is conducted on a very limited basis internally in Mexico. There is no national interlibrary loan code or guidelines, although there is an ILL code for academic libraries developed by ABIESI (see Section II,C,1). The borrowing and lending process itself is hindered by (1) limited bibliographic and location tools; (2) a slow and unreliable postal system; and, in some quarters, (3) an unwillingness to participate (Lau, 1982).

That does not mean that ILL does not take place, because it does, but mainly in small groups or within regional consortia. (Ainsworth (1994) noted that ILL agreements in Mexico are traditionally made "library to library" resulting in many individual "acuerdos." To cite just one example of recent progress, the Library of the Querétaro campus of Monterrey Tech (ITESM) has developed detailed procedures and formal request forms for carrying out interlibrary loan. It follows the ABIESI code and has entered into a number of agreements with other libraries to exchange materials (A. Belandria, personal communication, February 1995). The ITESM-Querétaro program could be a model for other libraries in Mexico.

Interlibrary loan is gradually on the increase in Mexico as computer technology aids in the location and transmission of materials, as demand by users increase, as a new resource sharing attitude emerges, and as the economic situation in Mexico makes it more attractive, indeed necessary, for libraries to consider resource sharing as a viable means of supplying their patrons with information. Lau (1983), in reviewing the Mexican economic crisis of the early 1980s, recognized that interlibrary loan is a necessity in good times, but even more so in bad.

3. Union Lists

Union lists are seen as important in Mexico for making selection and deselection decisions and as a basis for library collaboration (Arista and Yáñez, 1983), and a number of such compilations have been issued since the mid-1970s. In fact, some of the earliest successful efforts at cooperation were union lists of serials. Fernández de Zamora *et al.* (1977) cited a 1949 union list of medical and biology journals ("Catálogo Colectivo de Publicaciones Periódicas en la Ciudad de México, sección de medicina y ciencias biológicas") as the first instance of cooperation in Mexico. In 1968, the first national union list serials was issued; it included 13,035 serial titles in 134 libraries (Fernández de Zamora *et al.*, 1977). CONACYT took this project over in 1971 and in 1976 issued the second edition as a computer database. The country's largest academic library, the UNAM system, published its first union list in 1976 (Arista and Yáñez, 1983).

Union lists and other collective catalogs remain among the most successful cooperative ventures in Mexico. The most recent developments (and successes) in this area emanate from UNAM and the Universidad de Colima. The former provides online databases and CD-ROMs of its serials, theses, and book collections, all of which are heavily used throughout the country for reference work and resource sharing. The UNAM serials database, SERIUNAM, not only includes the holdings of the very large UNAM system, but of 62 other academic libraries as well. It updates, but does not replace, the most recent edition (1988) of CONACYT's union list cited earlier (Ainsworth, 1994). The Universidad de Colima, mentioned elsewhere as a leader in Mexican library technology, also plays an important role in resource sharing by publishing union catalogs and other bibliographic tools on CD-ROM.

IV. U.S.–Mexico Library Interaction

A. Background: United States Involvement in Latin America

1. Introduction

As noted earlier, librarians from the United States have long had ties with their counterparts in Mexico, Central America, and South America. Led by visionaries like Marietta Daniels Shepard who espoused the importance of the international dimension of librarianship, they have been involved in a variety of ways with their Latin American colleagues. Indeed, the United States has greatly influenced library development south of its borders in a variety of ways (Litton and Krzys, 1986; Fernández de Zamora, 1991). Latin American librarians have studied in the United States; Library of Congress and Dewey classifications and the *Anglo-American Cataloging Rules* are commonly used in Latin American libraries; and MARC and various other technological advances have influenced library automation (Fernández de Zamora, 1991). While librarianship in the United States has indeed at times been a model imitated by others, Thomas Galvin, the first ALA president to attend an AMBAC conference, warned against the idea that our way is the *only* way. He also urged stronger ties between Mexican and American librarians (Galvin, 1985).

2. The United States Information Agency (USIA)

The USIA, through its library and book programs, has also had a significant impact on library development in Latin America. Known abroad as the United States Information Service (USIS), the agency operated 146 special purpose libraries in 88 countries in 1986 including the Benjamin Franklin Library in Mexico City. Fitz (1986) noted that while its primary function is to provide U.S. imprints and library service to foreign nationals, "the USIA library network functions increasingly as an intermediary between foreign leaders in government, politics, the media, business, and academic life and the wealth of information in American government and private-sector collections, including commercial American databases" (p. 126). Fitz (1986) also stressed the USIA role in supporting visits by foreign and U.S. library specialists for the purpose of international exchange and mutual understanding. Sussman (1973) provided another look at the USIS library program, examining its role within the information dissemination role of the U.S. government. Finally, the USIA libraries have an important role in the achievement of the United States foreign policy objective of influencing public attitudes overseas (White, 1970).

3. The Organization of American States (OAS)

One of the greatest influences on the overall development of library services, collections, and education in Latin America has been the Organization of American States, formerly the Pan American Union and the Bureau of American Republics (Wilson and Shepard, 1977). While not a U.S. organization per se, the OAS headquarters is located in Washington, and the United States plays a major role in the formulation and execution of its programs. The history of the OAS Library Development Program, founded in 1956, was provided by Wilson and Shepard (1977) who noted that prior to that time the library interests of the OAS were limited to collecting publications from and about member states for its Columbus Memorial Library.

The OAS Library Development Program was founded in response to the recognition that "access to information and knowledge in printed form is essential for economic and technical progress" (Daniels, 1960). To this end, the primary goals of the OAS program were (1) to improve library education and (2) to create bibliographic tools so that the nations of Latin America could make progress on their own. A variety of activities were undertaken, including training of librarians and bibliographers, creation of manuals for library staff, development of standards, and the exchange of publications. In addition to improving library service, a parallel goal of the OAS was to reduce illiteracy by providing sufficient numbers of books and promoting reading (Pan American Union, 1962). Mexico benefited from these programs, especially in the area of library education. The OAS provided four to five scholarships annually to study in the United States (Benson, 1990).

In recent years, the OAS has been instrumental in supporting and promoting library cooperation among and within the countries of Latin America (Benson, 1990). Two programs in particular deserve mention: the OAS and UNESCO projects for centralized cataloging (CATACEN) and machine readable cataloging for Latin America (MARCAL) (Litton and Krzys, 1986). Benson (1990) described numerous collaborative projects supported by the OAS library program, including several in which Mexico has assisted its Latin American colleagues.

Specific OAS-funded programs involving Mexico in recent years have included

1. support for the development of the CUIB's "Infobila" database of library science research in Latin America.
2. support for several CUIB courses in the late 1980s and early 1990s to teach research methods to Latin American library science professors.
3. support for Central American librarians to attend the Guadalajara Book Fair (FIL) to participate in pre- and postconference library science programs as well as the reimbursement of speakers' expenses.
4. support of Mexico's national network of public libraries (S. Benson, personal communication, October 2, 1995).

B. Overview and Brief History of Interaction with Mexico

Although the United States has long had relations with libraries throughout Latin America, the most frequent, and often most fruitful, interactions have been with Mexico. As will be seen later, many contacts have been personal, through conference attendance and excursions to individual libraries. In terms of resource sharing and library development, the most beneficial interactions have been at the institutional level, carried out by dedicated persons from both sides of the border. The three most important players in initiating and developing library relations with Mexico have been the Benjamin Franklin Library in Mexico City, the Library of Congress, and the American Library Association (ALA). In both countries, however, universities and library organizations such as AMBAC and SALALM have also played key roles, as have international organizations such as the OAS.

1. The Benjamin Franklin Library

Possibly the single most influential player in fostering relations between libraries and librarians in the United States and Mexico has been the Benjamin

Franklin Library, founded in 1942 by ALA with the support of the U.S. Office of International Affairs (Thigpen, 1969). The Biblioteca Benjamin Franklin, or the BBF as it is known throughout Mexico, was the first of four Latin American libraries founded in the early 1940s (Sussman, 1973). Presented by the United States as a gift to the Mexican people, "the library promised free circulation of books . . . and aspired through materials and supplementary programs to improve, mutually, international understanding while presenting distinguished American works of all types" (Thigpen, 1969, p. 453). In 1953, the Franklin Library became part of the United States Information Service (USIS).

Pérez Monroy (1991), in her history of the Benjamin Franklin Library, noted that the BBF had many purposes, the most important of which was the provision of books and other cultural materials about the United States. It also offered traditional library services and, in fact to this day, acts as a public library for the Mexican people. But those were, and are, only part of its mission. Among its many functions are two very important ancillary roles: (1) serving as a center for U.S. cultural activities and (2) maintaining and strengthening relations between libraries in both countries (Pérez Monroy, 1991). With regard to the former, the Franklin Library has hosted numerous art exhibits, conferences, and visiting scholars and lecturers, many of whom are librarians or library science educators sponsored by the U.S. government as part of cultural exchange programs.

The Franklin is also the site of frequent meetings of local librarians as well as training workshops sponsored by USIS and area institutions. It plays a central role in an ongoing program of interlibrary loan between Mexico and the United States, a program it helped initiate. Mexican librarians are uniformly supportive and appreciative of the BBF for its role in strengthening U.S.–Mexico library ties. They particularly benefit from the continuing education programs which bring visiting lecturers and provide training for staff, and they are enthusiastic about the ILL program (meeting with Mexican librarians, February 23, 1995). Finally, the BBF has served as a training ground for many Mexican librarians, a number of whom now occupy key positions in major libraries (Pérez Monroy, 1991). In short, the role of the Franklin Library in U.S.–Mexico relations cannot be overemphasized.

2. The Library of Congress

Strictly speaking, the Library of Congress (LC) has as its primary mission the provision of the information needs of the legislative branch of government. It is, of course, also the *de facto* national library of the United States of America. In this role, LC has originated or influenced several important developments in the field of library science in the United States, particularly in the areas of standards, preservation, and resource sharing. In addition to its domestic role, LC has had a major presence abroad with very active and highly successful international programs. Lorenz *et al.* (1972) described those activities in some detail: a well-developed foreign acquisitions program, centralized cataloging of foreign research materials, production of machine readable cataloging copy, and much more. The Library of Congress also has had an international focus in the areas of reference service, bibliography, special formats collections (music and maps), copyright, and preservation.

Latin America, including Mexico, has been a major focus of these programs for several decades. The Hispanic Division (formerly Foundation) "serves as a center for the pursuit of studies in Spanish, Portuguese, and Latin American culture," and publishes the *Handbook of Latin American Studies*, the oldest continuous Latin American bibliography (Lorenz *et al.*, 1972, p. 562). In addition to regular buying trips to Mexico, LC staff are also involved in a variety of cooperative programs. In recent years they have conducted automation workshops, invited Mexican librarians to serve as interns at LC, and assisted with the microfilming of official Mexican documents held by the Library of Congress. Staff at LC were also instrumental in the founding of the Latin American Data Base Interest Group (LADIG), a binational effort to facilitate communication among the producers and users of data files from and about Latin America, a project now based at the Universidad de Colima (H. L. Davis, personal communication, September 15, 1995).

Library of Congress' librarians also regularly visit Mexico and are frequent speakers at conferences there. Likewise, Mexican library professionals often travel to Washington to consult with LC staff. In short, our national library has been actively involved in collaborative efforts with Mexican colleagues on several fronts.

3. The American Library Association

The American Library Association has long played an active role in international relations (Sullivan, 1972) and has worked in Latin America for several decades. Around 1920, it created the Committee on Library Co-operation with Hispanic Peoples which made its first report in 1921 at the ALA conference in Swampscott, Massachusetts. The 1923–1924 annual report of the Committee commended member Mrs. Maud Sullivan of the El Paso Public Library for her work with Mexican libraries. The report stated that "Mrs. Sullivan is of the opinion that the American Library Association might render service by aiding libraries of Hispanic–American countries, and especially those of Mexico, in securing a more effective organization" ("Annual Reports," 1924, pp. 233 and 234).

"In May, 1928, Mexican librarians entered into closer relations with their American colleagues when the Mexican government sent a delegation to the annual meeting of the American Library Association in West Baden, Indiana. . . . Though an extensive program of library co-operation with the United States was agreed upon, unfortunately it has borne little fruit . . ." (Peñalosa, 1953). In the early 1930s, due to the Depression, little activity took place. By 1933 the Committee had changed its name to Library Cooperation with Latin America (Brief Board and Committee Reports, 1933) and work with Mexico continued. The committee had funding from the Rockefeller Foundation for 4 years beginning in 1939. Among its successful efforts were (1) research and publication; (2) exchanges with Latin American librarians; (3) donations of books and periodicals on library topics; (4) arranging exhibits of Latin American books in the United States; (5) initiating and strengthening relations with libraries; (6) consulation; (7) direct grants; and more (Shaw, 1947).

The next major appearance of ALA in Mexico was its sponsorship in 1942 of the Benjamin Franklin Library (see Section IV,B,1). In the mid-1940s, the International Relations Office carried out a number of projects which aided libraries in Latin America, including (1) the promotion of translating library literature into Spanish; (2) the distribution of bibliographies such as the *Handbook of Latin American Studies;* and (3) the administration of library schools (Shaw, 1947). A report to the ALA Board on international activities cited several interactions with Mexico during the previous five years (Shaw, 1947). These included (1) a grant to the Jalisco State Library in Guadalajara for cataloging, (2) support for the U.S. government's cultural relations program through the Books for Latin America Project, (3) grants for books and equipment for Mexican libraries, and (4) various projects in support of the Benjamin Franklin Library. Most of the aforementioned were supported by funds from the Rockefeller Foundation.

Relations between ALA and Mexico continued intermittently until 1990 when the International Relations Committee of ALA created a new subcommittee on U.S.–Mexico libraries. The purpose of this body was to coordinate efforts by individuals and groups in the United States who were already working with Mexican colleagues, as well as to provide an opportunity for new projects and interactions. The subcommittee's mission statement expressed "the need for reciprocal respect for cultural values, greater knowledge, better communication and ready sources of accurate information." Among the issues to be addressed were (1) cooperative resource sharing, (2) identification of and access to research and archival collections, especially those in Mexico, (3) training and continuing education, (4) librarian exchanges, (5) binational meetings, (6) funding for projects, and more (Seal, 1992b).

During its 4-year existence, the U.S.–Mexico Libraries Subcommittee (1) assisted with the donation of college textbooks to Mexican academic libraries; (2) cosponsored binational meetings such as the Transborder Library Forums; (3) developed links with AMBAC; (4) encouraged interlibrary loan; (5) promoted exchanges of librarians; and (6) worked with Reed Publishing, the parent company of R. R. Bowker, to expand the *American Library Directory* to include Mexican libraries (Seal, 1993). It also cosponsored a meeting with Mexican colleagues at the 1991 Guadalajara Book Fair and drafted a resolution recognizing the 50th anniversary of the Benjamin Franklin Library ("Annual Report," 1992).

The subcommittee continued until the summer of 1994 when it was incorporated into a new Subcommittee on Relations with Libraries in Latin America and the Carribbean as part of a reorganization of the International Relations Committee. The new Latin America and Caribbean Subcommittee continued several programs started by the U.S.–Mexico group, for example, exchanges, and also began to branch out into other areas such as establishing links with related library organizations interested in Latin America.

C. Interactions Involving Individual Librarians

The most common, and least documented, form of interaction between the library professions of Mexico and the United States involves individual librarians making visits, doing consulting, lecturing, and even working in the neighboring country. In addition, today there is much ongoing interaction among colleagues via phone, fax, and now electronic mail for the purposes of carrying out research, exchanging ideas and information, coauthoring articles, and so on.

1. Travel, Training, Research, and Employment

A frequent and potentially beneficial component of international librarianship involves travel to a foreign country. For years, librarians from the United States have gone to Mexico, and vice versa, for just that purpose. Rivera (1941) noted that there are obvious benefits to such activity between the United States and Latin America, i.e., improved cultural awareness and understanding, the establishment of personal contacts, and, in some cases, the acquisition of technical training. This was echoed by Milam (1944a) who wrote "the importance of increasing the interchange of librarians between the United States and the other American countries cannot be overemphasized (p. 299)."

A number of American librarians have traveled to Mexico and published accounts of their visits. Greer (1919) wrote of a trip to reorganize a women's college library in Puebla. Coleman (1934) described several public libraries she toured on a personal visit to Mexico. On a trip to "increase the general effectiveness of the relations between the libraries of the United States and those of Latin American countries," Milam (1944b, p. 229) visited the Franklin

Library in Mexico City. Cluff (1991) gave an account of a visit to Colima where he and a colleague presented a seminar on current library issues and attended a library automation conference. What does not appear in the literature are accounts of U.S. librarians employed in Mexico and vice versa. This includes work as professional staff, library science professors, teachers, and interns, some short term, others on an indefinite basis.

Mexico has for some time sent its librarians to the United States and other countries to learn more about our methods and to conduct research. The leader in coordinating and promoting such activity for Mexico is CUIB, the library science research institute of UNAM (see Section II,E). One of its principle tasks is to sponsor academic exchanges with other institutions, both internally and outside of Mexico ("Estancias en el CUIB," 1991). This very successful program has supported both short- and long-term visits by library school professors, researchers, and practicing librarians for the purposes of observation, study, and teaching both in Latin America countries and in the United States.

2. Consultants

Like individual interactions, the majority of work done by library consultants is not well documented in the literature. Such activity may include an informal visit to help with automation planning or to share expertise on collection building; a government-sponsored fact-finding trip; or a full-scale library review and upgrade. In most cases, the movement of consultants is one way, from the United States to Mexico. Two such examples are presented below.

One of the best-known such consulting activities occurred in the fall of 1966 when Carl White and Paul Bixler visited Mexico with the goal of making recommendations on library development, both to the Mexican government and to the Ford Foundation, the latter desiring better information for making decisions on grants. The consultants paid special attention to "university libraries where opportunities for further development are agreed to be singularly important" (White, 1969, pp. viii–ix). White (1969) and Bixler (1969) gathered voluminous data through extensive research and personal interviews on the current state of Mexican libraries before making their final recommendations.

A more recent example of U.S. consultants in Mexico is the work undertaken by the Academy for Educational Development at the Benémerita Universidad Autónoma de Puebla (BUAP) in 1994–1996. The new administration of this public institution of 66,000 students decided to upgrade and modernize all parts of the university, including the library. Following an initial survey by another firm, the AED team was brought in to finalize plans and to implement, with the help of the library's staff, improvements in reference service, the book collection, and automation. Among the enhancements were (1) the installation of the Innovative Interfaces integrated library system; (2) approval plans from Blackwell North America; (3) cataloging on OCLC; and (4) OCLC FirstSearch (A. Mathews, personal communication, August 1995). The BUAP library was the first in Latin America to utilize the First-Search databases ("Mexican library first in Latin America," 1995).

D. Interaction at the Association Level

1. Overview

"Professional associations have an influential and dynamic role in the field of international librarianship and the internationalization of the library profession" wrote Bliss (1995, p. 219), who noted that such activity varies depending on the goals of the groups involved. Indeed, much of the interaction between Mexico and the United States is fostered by and occurs within the framework of professional library organizations. These groups over the years have conducted such work in varying intensities depending on member interest, finances, and other factors. Attendance at and participation in conferences, workshops, and seminars, as well as membership in professional organizations, have all provided a forum for the establishment of links and exchange of ideas with very positive results.

In the early 1920s, the Texas State Library invited the newly created Library Department of Mexico's Education Bureau to attend meetings to organize the Southwestern Library Association. This was apparently not the first time that librarians from the two countries had collaborated because in describing that meeting, Heliodoro Valle (1923) wrote "This is another proof that American and Mexican scholars are doing their utmost to cement the good understanding between both peoples . . ." (p. 265). Just a few years later in 1928, librarians from the United States attended a National Librarians' Congress in Mexico City. Early on, the Library Bureau of Mexico had close relations with ALA "to promote the technical advancement of Mexican libraries," and it adopted with slight modifications the ALA cataloging rules (Pan American Union, 1930).

ALA conferences have long been attended by a number of international librarians, many supported at one time by the Carnegie Corporation and the Rockefeller Foundation (Severance, 1938). Although today Mexican librarians do not participate in large numbers due to limited financial resources, there is usually at least one representative at the major conferences. At the same time, American librarians frequently travel to Mexico to take part in the Guadalajara Book Fair, to participate in the AMBAC Jornadas, and to attend special meetings such as the Latin American Seminar on Official Publications ("Latin American seminar," 1991). American and Mexican delegates alike often make speeches and participate in panel discussions, especially those focusing on binational cooperation.

The Texas Library Association (TLA) also maintains contacts with Mexican colleagues who have on occasion attended TLA conferences. At one such meeting, delegates from both countries explored possible collaborative projects ("Minutes of Meeting," 1992). Before its demise, the Southwestern Library Association had a subcommittee that was actively involved in working with colleagues from Mexico, arranging vists to Mexico for its members, and bringing Mexican librarians to the United States to attend the biannual SWLA conference (Sheldon, 1985). The Public Library Association conference in San Diego in March 1991 included a program on U.S.–Mexico library cooperation sponsored by the U.S.–Mexico Libraries Subcommittee of ALA's International Relations Committee.

AMBAC, which has been invited to participate in various library meetings such as American Library Association and the Transborder Library Forums, in 1992 formed its own Comisión de Relaciones Internacionales de la Asociación (International Relations Commission) to work with American and other international library groups (Comisión de Relaciones Internacionales, 1992). Its first task was to organize a colloquium on Mexico–U.S. cooperation at the 1992 Guadalajara Book Fair.

2. Binational Meetings

a. The California Conferences.   One of the most productive types of cooperation in recent years has been library meetings jointly sponsored by the United States and Mexico. One such gathering, the First Binational Conference on Libraries in California and Baja California, took place in Tijuana, Baja California, January 13 and 14, 1984. With the theme of public library service, it included round table discussions and several formal presentations by librarians from both countries (Ayala, 1984). This was followed by the Second Binational Conference on Libraries of the Californias, November 11 and 12, 1985, in which the scope was broadened to cooperation between libraries in the United States and Mexico. The use of technology to enhance information sharing, personnel exchanges, and serving border populations were just a few of the topics explored ("Hands across the border," 1986). The goal of this second conference was the improvement of library and information services for the Spanish-speaking populations on both sides of the border (Sheldon, 1985).

b. The Transborder Library Forums.   The importance of binational meetings was stressed by Gutiérrez-Witt (1985) who noted that such events open channels of communication and provide an opportunity for the discussion of common problems. Thanks to the grass-roots efforts of librarians in the states of Arizona and Sonora, linkages between the United States and Mexico were firmly established with the first Transborder Library Forum (Foro Binacional de Bibliotecas). The FORO, as that meeting came to be known, turned out to be the just the beginning of a series of binational conferences at which Mexican and U.S. librarians would meet to discuss mutual problems and work cooperatively to solve them.

The first FORO was held in Río Rico, Arizona, not far from the Mexican border, in February 1991. The focus of the conference was the exchange of information and the establishment of contacts among the librarians of both countries. The conference moved into Mexico in February 1992 to Hermosillo, Sonora, attended by an larger contingent of Mexican librarians, including several invited speakers from Mexico City. The central theme of the conference was NAFTA and its potential impact on libraries (Neugebauer, 1992). Other topics included copyright, the exchange of technical information between the United States and Mexico, and library cooperation.

El Paso, Texas, was the site of the Third Transborder Library Forum in February 1993 with the theme of "Libraries and Education in the Americas." In addition to keynote speeches on the importance of libraries in the educational process, U.S. and Mexican colleagues continued discussions of resource sharing, NAFTA, technology, collection development, and preservation. The February 1994 conference in Monterrey, Nuevo Leon, Mexico, became the *Trinational* Library Forum as Canadian librarians were invited to explore issues related to NAFTA, information technology, public libraries, the exchange of information, and other topics of interest to librarians throughout North America. Although Canadian librarians are now regularly invited, to date their participation has been limited and the focus is still decidedly on U.S.–Mexico library relations.

The Fifth Trinational Library Forum took place in Mexico City in February 1995 amidst an atmosphere of anxiety and concern due to the most recent economic crisis in that country. Although attendance was down, enthusiasm and interest remained high and lively discussions occurred on a variety of topics. Formal presentations were made on library cooperation, international exchange, copyright, and library education, among others. Tucson, Arizona, was the location of the sixth FORO in February 1996. Titled "Coming Full Circle," it took a retrospective look at the first five Transborder Library Forums. FORO VI's topics included binational cooperation, cross-cultural understanding, information technology, business resources, NAFTA, and library education from an international perspective.

While each of the six conferences included formal keynote speeches, the heart of the meetings were the discussion sessions where, despite occasional language differences, colleagues from North America have not only collaborated to achieve common goals but have gained a better understanding of another culture and other ways of providing library service. Each of these meetings was planned and executed totally by volunteers, without any formal organization to support or hinder its work.

The impact and importance of the FOROs in promoting transborder cooperation and improving library service in the region cannot be stressed enough. Hoffert (1993a) presented an overview of the first three FOROs, describing their origin and goals. An updated view of the Trinational Library Forum phenomena was provided by Gregory (1995) who noted that "over its 6-year existence, the FORO has taken giant steps toward becoming a permanent vehicle for international cooperation" (p. 508). Indeed, they are a model for future activity between librarians in Mexico and the United States.

3. Exchange Programs

a. Overview.   One of the most useful forms of international cooperation is the exchange, i.e., visits to the libraries of other countries to gain work experience, update skills, or obtain a better understanding of methods and philosophy. The word "exchange" is somewhat misleading, however, since it rarely involves a simultaneous, if any, trade of personnel. In addition to or in lieu of observing local practice, the visiting librarian may carry out a project, say the cataloging of an archive, the implementation of an automation program, or training staff in reference work. Although there is not a one-to-one exchange of staff, there is a beneficial exchange of ideas and cultural viewpoints benefiting all participants.

b. Library Fellows Program.   Over the past four decades, there have been a number of international library exchange programs, both formal and informal. Perhaps the best know such activity today is the Library Fellows Program, funded by the United States Information Agency and administered by ALA. In this program, U.S. specialists spend up to 1 year working in libraries overseas, and since its inception in 1986, 133 librarians have participated (B. Doyle, personal communication, August 16, 1995). The Library Fellows Program is a combination goodwill effort and library consultants program in which U.S. librarians assist colleagues in a variety of special projects. Assignments are broadly based: the 1995–1996 fellows were assigned to Zimbabwe, South Africa, Germany, Switzerland, Burma, and several other nations. Participants are required to submit a final report summarizing their accomplishments and explaining how the experience will help them in future endeavors. Since the program's beginning, two American librarians have worked in Mexico, one in Monterrey and another in Puebla, both at private universities. A request for a Library Fellow to work in northern Mexico in 1995–1996 went unfilled due to the lack of a qualified applicant.

In 1993, the program was reversed and a pilot project was initiated by ALA and the USIA to bring international librarians to the United States. The first class of International Library Fellows consisted of 10 librarians from Poland, Kenya, Romania, Laos, Morocco, and five other nations, including Mexico. Designed for midlevel librarians with potential for leadership in the profession in their own countries, the International Library Fellows "work in the U.S. for 3 to 10 months to enhance their understanding of contemporary librarianship as practiced in the United States, develop new areas of expertise and establish contacts that will lead to enduring professional and institutional relationships" ("First International Library Fellows," 1993, p. 6).

c. IRC/IRRT Subcommittee on International Exchanges.   In addition to the Library Fellows Programs, ALA members have been involved in international exchanges in other ways. A continuing effort is the International Relations Committee/International Relations Round Table Subcommittee on International Exchanges. Initiated in 1985, the joint IRC/IRRT Subcommittee attempts to facilitate librarian exchanges worldwide by (1) collecting information on librarians and libraries with an interest in study visits and exchange programs; (2) disseminating that information to librarians in the United States and overseas; and (3) promoting professional development and fostering friendly and peaceful relationships with countries around the world. Because of the enormity of this task, the subcommittee picks one area of the world to concentrate on every 2 years. Although Latin America was the official focus of 1994–1996, it will continue to be a vital part of the program on an ongoing basis (L. Covert-Vail, personal communication, November 14, 1995).

In addition to creating a database of potential hosts, the subcommittee's projects have included the creation and maintenance of a Directory of Funding Sources and a Directory of Sponsoring Agencies, now merged into a single resource available both electronically and in print. Two other documents are also being created: "Guidelines for Short-Term Visits to the U.S. by Foreign Librarians" and a "Checklist for Preparing for an International Exchange" (S. Milam, personal communication, April 20, 1995).

d. SALALM Exchange Activities.   The Seminar on the Acquisition of Latin American Library Materials has actively supported international exchanges involving Latin American libraries. The SALALM Outreach/ Enlace Committee originated in 1985 as an ad hoc group aimed at (1) promoting communication between SALALM and Latin American individuals and institutions concerned with books and information; (2) facilitating participation by this group in SALALM; and (3) promoting exchanges between libraries in Latin America and the United States. The committee became permanent in 1989 and continues with the same purposes (S. Milam, personal communication, April 19, 1995).

Enlace made 31 travel awards to bring Latin American librarians to the United States between 1986 and 1995, including several from Mexico. Supported by SALALM funds, miscellaneous grants, and contributions from book dealers, these awards have made possible conference attendance as well as library visits, work experience, and research. Five Mexican librarians served internships in Texas, California, Arizona, and New Mexico in 1994 thanks to an Enlace proposal funded by the U.S.–Mexico Fund for Culture (Fideicomiso para la Cultura México/USA). In 1995, the ALA/IRC Subcommittee on Relations with Libraries in Latin America and the Caribbean announced its intent to work with SALALM Enlace to cosponsor a future internship project involving Latin American and Caribbean librarians.

e. The Mortenson Center. Another opportunity for Mexican librarians to visit the United States is through the Mortenson Center for International Librarianship located at the University of Illinois at Urbana–Champaign. Founded in 1988 with a gift by Dr. C. Walter Mortenson, a retired chemist and lawyer, the center's purpose is "to foster international tolerance and peace by strengthening ties among the world's research libraries and librarians in an effort to ensure access to knowledge throughout the world." It does this through an international exchange program and an annual distinguished lecture series ("Mortenson Center," 1993). The exchange program, initiated in 1989, aims to increase the skills and knowledge of working professionals through work experience in a major U.S. academic library (Bliss, 1995).

f. Texas Library Association Exchange Program. A small but successful program of U.S.–Mexico library exchanges was initiated in 1994 by the Texas–Mexico Relations Subcommittee of the College & University Library Division of the Texas Library Association. This effort brought two librarians from Mexico City to visit Texas libraries in the summer of 1994 and three more from other parts of Mexico to Texas in 1995. The exchanges are short in duration, between 1 and 2 weeks, but very beneficial: participants visited several libraries and attended workshops. Future plans involve sending American librarians to Mexico (C. Felsted, personal communications, 1994–1995).

E. Acquisition of Library Materials

1. Overview

An activity that has long afforded an opportunity for meaningful contact among library colleagues in Mexico and the United States has been the acquisition and bibliography of books, periodicals, documents, and other materials from Latin America. Because this topic is covered so well elsewhere in the literature, only brief mention is made here of (1) national cooperative U.S. programs for Latin American acquisitions including Mexico, and (2) SALALM, a group that has been extremely active in this field and that has fostered many relationships, cooperative and otherwise, among U.S. and Mexican librarians.

The acquisition of Latin American library materials has always been problematic, even for librarians in Latin America. Shepard (1968) summarized very well these difficulties when she wrote "the principal problem in the acquisition process has been the bibliographic one—finding out what is being or has been published in Latin America and determining which are the most important of these works . . . " (p. 705). She pointed out that cooperative programs are required to obtain materials from "developing countries whose booktrade is also underdeveloped" (Shepard, 1968, p. 703).

2. Formal Cooperative Acquisition Programs

For years, librarians, government, and professional associations in the United States have been working together to acquire materials from developing countries. An excellent overview of early cooperative acquisitions efforts for Latin America can be found in the introduction to the conference proceedings of the first SALALM meeting (Hixson, 1956). The Farmington Plan, established by former Librarian of Congress Archibald MacLeish in 1942, was the largest acquisitions program ever implemented. Although its original focus was collecting publications from Europe, it added Mexico from 1948, and three other Latin American countries soon after. By the early 1960s it was a worldwide effort (Savary, 1975).

At the urging of the members of SALALM, the Farmington Plan was extended full-scale to Latin America, resulting in 1960 in the birth of LACAP, the Latin American Cooperative Acquisitions Program. Unlike Farmington, it was a commerical venture, sponsored by an international book company, Stechert-Hafner, in cooperation with three research libraries. New York Public, the University of Texas, and the Library of Congress. For the first time, books were brought to the United States on a regular basis and in large numbers from nearly every Latin American country. Dozens of collections were enriched and the cost and logistical problems of acquiring such items were significantly reduced. Savary (1975), who provided a detailed and useful history of LACAP, called it "a milestone in library cooperation." For a variety of reasons, however, including rising costs, declining sales, and changes inherent in the Latin American book trade, the program was suspended at the end of 1972.

3. Seminar on the Acquisition of Latin American Library Materials

Before, during, and since LACAP, SALALM has played a key role in helping U.S. libraries carry out the sometimes difficult tasks of the bibliography, acquisition, and cataloging of library materials from North, Central, and South America, and from the Caribbean. The first Seminar on the Acquisition of Latin American Library Materials was held in Florida in June 1956, sponsored by the University of Florida Libraries and the Columbus Memorial Library of the Pan American Union (later the Organization of American States). That gathering of librarians, bibliographers, scholars, book dealers, and others was seen as "the latest link in the chain of cooperative efforts to resolve mutual acquisitions problems" (Hixson, 1956, p. iv).

SALALM eventually evolved into an independent organization separate from OAS with its headquarters rotating among several different universities with major Latin American collections. The Secretariat currently resides at the University of Texas at Austin. Savary (1975) provided a brief history of SALALM's first two decades, describing its role in cooperative acquisitions ventures, especially the founding and operation of LACAP. During those 20 years, the organization saw many accomplishments which benefited libraries in the United States and throughout Latin America. Among these achievements were several pertaining to Mexico: "the rebirth of a current Mexican bibliography; . . . the publication of the *Directorio de publicaciones periódicas mexicanas* . . .; the improvement of bibliographic lists in a number of trade bibliographics in Mexico . . ." (Wilson and Shepard, 1977, p. 30). The past two decades have seen a number of other bibliographic works from SALALM focusing on Mexico. The organization also presents an annual prize for the best reference book or bibliography on Latin American studies, the José Toribio Medina award, and it plays a major role in the production of HAPI, the Hispanic American Periodicals Index (S. Milam, personal communication, November 14, 1995). Mexican librarians volunteer their time to assist with HAPI, indexing all issues of several journals each year (B. Valk, personal communication, May 10, 1995).

SALALM continues to hold annual conferences to explore issues related to Latin American bibliography and librarianship. The resulting working papers, in addition to providing a historical record of the organization's programs, are an invaluable resource for Latin American librarians, scholars, and other specialists. Its support of exchanges through the Enlace program, mentioned earlier, is just another example of its many cooperative activities and the scope of its influence.

4. Other Programs

Apart from the formal programs like LACAP and the activity of professional associations such as SALALM there are, of course, many examples of individual libraries and acquisitions librarians working in Mexico and other Latin American nations. These include the Library of Congress as well as university libraries with significant Latin American collections, such as the Benson at the University of Texas, Austin. Their activities range from buying trips to the exchange of materials to the creation of bibliographies, and much more. Latin Americanists are also concerned with and involved in matters of preservation (Hazen, 1995) and in helping Latin American librarians, including those from Mexico, to more easily acquire U.S. publications.

F. U.S. Library Education and Mexican Librarianship

1. Overview

One way in which the United States has affected library development in Mexico and other parts of Latin America is through its formal graduate program of library and information science. Many Mexican librarians have been trained in our library schools, with the support of their government, ALA, and international organizations such as the OAS. As noted earlier, the Benjamin Franklin Library has also had a great deal of influence because many Mexican professionals got their start there and often went on to study library science in the United States.

Morales Campos (1990) noted that the United States has also influenced Mexican library education, and thus its librarianship, primarily in its technical aspects, i.e., the organization of collections and classification schemes, and by its emphasis on reference and children's services. Other countries such as Great Britain and France have also been factors in library development in Mexico. Despite foreign influence, Mexico must ultimately have its own identity in terms of how its libraries are organized and operated. Indeed, this appears to be happening with the emergence of a "bibliotecología mexicana" in the 1980s after decades of accumulated effort and development (Morales Campos, 1990). Morales Campos (1990), in an insightful paper on the Mexican library system, concluded that the combination of external influence and internal developments has resulted in a number of advances in the field and sustained growth that will soon achieve a level of excellence.

With the help of a number of foundations, ALA formerly provided fellowships for Latin Americans to study in our library schools and for American students to survey and study Latin American libraries (Severance, 1938). The OAS has long had as goals to (1) assist in the training of library professionals and (2) train library school professors in Latin America. In the past, the OAS also provided a small number of graduate fellowships to study in the United States and sponsored a variety of courses at the regional and national level "ranging from orientation courses to specialized graduate-level studies" (Wilson and Shepard, 1977). All these programs have benefited librarians from Mexico.

2. Recent U.S. Library School Activity

Mexican librarians have studied at a number of U.S. library schools over the past half-century, most notably the University of Texas and the University of Denver, both of which have had special programs for Latin American students. One of the most successful recent programs of American library education aimed at Mexico was that offered in the early 1990s by the School of Library and Information Science of the University of Wisconsin, Milwaukee, for the head librarians of the 26 campuses of the Instituto Tecnológico y de Estudios Superiores de Monterrey (ITESM), the largest private university system in Mexico. At the request of the ITESM administration, the 2-year program had a particular emphasis on library administration and technology. Classes were given in Milwaukee in the summers and in Monterrey in the fall and winter semesters with UWM faculty traveling to Mexico to teach. An intensive English program was offered for those who needed to improve their language skills. Students and faculty kept in touch by mail, phone, e-mail, and fax, and ultimately, 21 members of the class graduated in 1993 with their MLIS degrees. A second program for another group of ITESM librarians had to be postponed due to the 1995 economic downturn (M. Aman, personal communication, August 14, 1995). The success of the UWM-ITESM program demonstrated the possibilities of cooperative library education between the United States and Mexico.

The University of Arizona offers a Masters of Arts degree with an emphasis in Library Science through its distance education program, serving students all over the United States "through virtual and established regional sites." Beginning in the summer of 1995, the School of Library Science initiated a partnership with the Universidad de las Americas in Puebla to offer the program's courses to librarians in Mexico and throughout Latin America. Students view videotapes of class lectures and receive assignments via the Internet. Future plans include the exchange of faculty and students between University of Arizona and UDLA (C. D. Hurt, personal communication, October 24, 1995).

Interaction between library schools has also occurred on a less formal basis with the exchange of faculty for both long and short visits. A recent example is an interchange involving the University of North Texas School of Library and Information Sciences and the Escuela Nacional de Biblioteconomía y Archivonomía (National School of Library and Archival Science), ENBA, which took place in 1994. Following a visit to Denton, Texas by the Dean of ENBA, a delegation from the UNT SLIS was invited to Mexico City to participate in a symposium on the "Education of the Librarian of the Future." Several presentations were made by the faculty and doctoral students at the conference ("SLIS Faculty and Students," 1995).

G. Border Relations

1. Overview

The most frequent and intensive interaction between libraries in the United States and Mexico occurs, not surprisingly, in the region encompassing the international border between our two nations. This area, as Gutiérrez-Witt (1985) so aptly pointed out, is a special place with its own history, people, and culture, even though it is arbitrarily divided into two political entities. The border region, she wrote, is neither an American nor Mexican culture but rather a combination of the influences of both peoples and libraries in that region must take this into account when building collections and planning services. The following examples of transborder library cooperation illustrate a strong willingness to work together to achieve common goals despite disparities in resources (collections and personnel) and differing needs and expectations of local users.

2. Arizona–Sonora Cooperation

The most prominent example of two bordering states successfully cooperating in the library sphere is that of Arizona and Sonora, an overview of which was provided by Milam and Salas (1990). Collaborative activities have included (1) the exchange of state publications, (2) gifts of scientific and technical books to Mexico, (3) jointly sponsored conferences such as the first Transborder Library Forum, and (4) participation on binational commissions. The original impetus for these successful endeavors was an invitation to Sonoran librarians to attend the 1989 Arizona Library Association (AzLA) conference in Tucson. A direct result of that meeting was the creation of the Asociación Bibliotecaria de Sonora, A.C. (the Sonoran Library Association), the first such group of its kind in that Mexican state (Baldwin, 1991).

Since that time, much of the Arizona–Sonora collaboration has been initiated by AzLA's International Librarianship Round Table (ILRT), which has a standing committee, the Arizona/Mexico Area Committee (AMAC), that coordinates several cooperative ventures. These have involved the exchange of personnel, a reciprocal state document exchange agreement, interlibrary loan, and more (Baldwin, 1991). The AzLA ILRT also collaborated with the Arizona Chapter of the Special Libraries Association to sponsor an International Special Librarians Day in April 1994. That program provided a forum for the exchange of information, planning of cooperative ventures, and further strengthening of ties among librarians (C. Elliott, personal communication, May 16, 1995). The Arizona–Sonora relationship, in all its manifestations, is a model for other border states to emulate.

3. Collaboration between the Californias

There has also been an ongoing relationship between California and Baja California, although that interaction might more aptly be described as a San Diego–Tijuana connection because of the close ties between librarians in those two cities. The San Diego Chapter of Special Libraries Association, like its counterpart in Arizona, has also sponsored an International Librarians Day, which involved meetings with Mexican colleagues. LIBROS, the San Diego chapter of REFORMA, invited librarians from Baja California to the California Library Association meeting in 1990 (M. MacPhail, personal communication, May 24, 1995). The California State Library has supported a number of binational meetings with Mexico and has participated in a working group on interlibrary connections among Pacific nations (Ruby, 1985).

4. Texas–Mexico Interaction

Public and college libraries located on the border frequently find themselves serving patrons from both countries. Quintanilla C. (1989) described the use of the Piedras Negras (Mexico) public library by Texas citizens, while Garmon (1990) noted that Texas Southmost College in Brownsville routinely serves both U.S. and Mexican patrons. Indeed, public and college libraries from San Diego to the Gulf of Mexico have long welcomed users from both sides of the border. In-house reading and reference help are the most common services offered; loans are less common.

A strong university library connection has developed in the El Paso–Ciudad Juárez metropolitan area involving the University of Texas at El Paso and the El Paso Community College working in tandem with the Universidad Autónoma de Ciudad Juárez, the Instituto Tecnológico de Ciudad Juárez, and the Instituto Tecnológico y de Estudios Superiores de Monterrey, Ciudad Juárez campus. UTEP has been particularly active, signing several "convenios" to work with Mexican libraries. Under these agreements, students from the Ciudad Juárez schools may use the UTEP Library, borrow books, and obtain database searches (Seal, 1992b). Librarians from Ciudad Juárez also participated in the planning of FORO III. The UTEP Library was involved in the project to microfilm Mexican archival records (see Section IV,H,4) along with other Texas libraries (Seal, 1989).

H. Other Forms of Cooperation

1. Interlibrary Loan

As noted earlier in Section III,B,2, Mexico has for some years conducted foreign interlibrary loan, most notably through the Benjamin Franklin Library. The national university, UNAM, treats international requests for photocopies as "document delivery" and therefore changes for such service (E. R. Hernández, personal communication, March 29, 1995). For the most part, Mexican universities carry out some foreign interlibrary loan as the need arises. Informal agreements, such as the one between the Instituto Tecnológico de Chihuahua (ITdeC) and the University of Texas at El Paso (UTEP), are sometimes utilized. In this case, a Mexican librarian searches the UTEP catalog via the Internet and faxes requests to their interlibrary loan office (Kahl, 1993). He then travels 250 miles from Chihuahua City to El Paso to pick up the materials that he also personally returns. A similar arrangement involves the ITdeC and the University of New Mexico (D. Warren, personal communication, May 9, 1995).

An exception to the normally infrequent ILL activity between the United States and Mexico is a highly successful formal program of interlending established in 1989 involving academic libraries in Mexico City and the southwestern United States (Seal, 1990b, 1991; Kahl, 1993; Morales Campos, 1994). The so-called U.S.–Mexico Interlibrary Loan Project is a joint effort of the Benjamin Franklin Library (USIS), the University of Texas at El Paso, and the Colegio de México. Requests from Mexico are directed to UTEP, which uses the OCLC ILL system to locate and request items from 1 of 27 AMIGOS member libraries or 2 non-AMIGOS libraries. The U.S. requests are directed to the Colegio de México, which uses various bibliographic tools and the telephone to locate the item in question among the ten participating Mexico City libraries and, more recently, the main campus of Monterrey Tech (ITESM). For the first 5 years of the project, this work was carried out by the Instituto Tecnológico Autónomo de México (ITAM).

In the planning stages, a perceived obstacle to the success of this project, now an ongoing service, was the unreliability of the Mexican postal system, which discourages the internal and external interlibrary loan of books and microforms. This was overcome by utilizing the U.S. Embassy courier, which makes regular deliveries between Mexico City and Laredo, Texas. By the end of FY1994–1995, 7439 requests from Mexico had been filled by the participating U.S. libraries. While no firm figures are available for U.S. requests filled by Mexico, the number is only a fraction of the traffic from Mexico to the United States. Numbers are less important, however, than the accessibility to certain Mexican publications that are not available in the United States, e.g., theses and dissertations, statistical data, government publications, and monographs. Scholars in both countries have benefited from this model program, which received the "Project of the Year" award for 1991 from the Texas Library Association (Kahl, 1993). The project "met its original goals of facilitating the exchange of scholarly information; promoting and enhancing scholarly research; and improving ties between the library and research communities in our two countries" (Seal, 1990b, p. 12).

2. Book Donation Programs

Worldwide, book donation programs are a very common form of library assistance and cooperation, undertaken with varying degrees of success (Bliss, 1995). Although such gifts can be very beneficial, there are associated risks and problems that cannot be ignored. Without careful planning and adequate support on the receiving end, "books that are either not needed or dated are sent at great financial cost" (Bliss, 1995). Bixler (1969) discussed the pros and cons of book donation programs in the context of foundation support for Latin American libraries in general and Mexican libraries in particular. Bayardo Gómez (1985) listed criteria for donation and emphasized the need for good communication to ensure that materials of interest sent will be to the receiving parties.

U.S. border libraries are in an excellent position to assist Mexican colleagues by donating duplicates and other unneeded volumes. For example, in the late 1980s and early 1990s the library of the University of Texas at El Paso collected large numbers of textbooks, duplicate periodicals, and unwanted gift books to present to academic libraries in their sister city of Ciudad Juárez. The greatest problem encountered in that program, and similar efforts, was simply getting the materials across the border through Mexican customs.

One of the more recent and ambitious book donation efforts involving the United States and Mexico was sponsored by the Mexican Project Center in Sedona, Arizona. From 1988 to 1990, more than 50,000 donated technical works were sent by the center to many of the 34 state universities in Mexico. Another several thousand volumes were shipped to several of the 60 technical colleges in 1991–1992. The books were donated by the Nebraska Book Company and the Follett Book Company and transported to the border by Pet Foods and Wyatt Cafeterias. After resolving the difficulties of moving the materials across the border, the books were shipped to various locations in Mexico, with transportation paid by the Mexican government. A highly successful program carried out with the assistance of Mexican librarians, this project resulted in several donations to university libraries in desperate need of scientific and technical books (R. Forney, personal communication, August 23, 1995).

3. Government-Sponsored Collaboration

In addition to the work described in Section IV,A,2, the U.S. Information Agency has fostered U.S.–Mexico cooperation by periodically bringing together representatives from the two countries to discuss topics of mutual interest. One such program is the Mexican/American Commission on Cultural Cooperation, initiated in 1948 and involving officials of the USIA and the Mexican Foreign Ministry. In 1990, the commission, which meets every 3 years, included for the first time, representatives from private organizations and other government agencies in five areas: libraries, publishing, museums, U.S. studies, and the performing arts.

The U.S. library delegation included six professionals representing universities, ALA, and the Library of Congress, while the Mexican group consisted of six librarians from government, public, and academic libraries. Meeting June 6–7, 1990, the Library Working Group recommended cooperative programs in three areas: human resources, materials resources, and library information services. Specific ideas included (1) the exchange of personnel and training programs; (2) closer ties between professional organizations; (3) increasing scholarships for Mexicans to study in the United States; (4) compiling information on Mexican databases; (5) expanding access to government publications; (6) increasing cooperation between the Library of Congress and the National Library of Mexico; and (7) promoting and expanding existing interlibrary loan efforts ("Mexican, American librarians, 1990). The U.S./Mexican Commission on Cultural Cooperation adopted the Working Group's recommendations in Washington in August 1990. One of the direct outcomes of the binational meetings was the creation by ALA of the U.S.–Mexico Libraries Subcommittee of the International Relations Committee (see Section IV,B,3).

4. Microfilming Projects

Two separate efforts to preserve Mexican archival records are yet another example of U.S.–Mexico collaboration. The first, the Texas Consortium to Microfilm Mexican Archival Resources, was founded in 1969 and involved 15 academic libraries and the Texas State Library. Their objective was to film for preservation and research purposes as many Mexican archival collections as possible: national, state, city, and church records. Each of the Texas institutions involved chose a geographic area of Mexico and was responsible for carrying out the work in that region. The resulting microfilm was sent to the Texas institution's library with a copy being given to Mexican authorities. This project was the outgrowth of the 1967 International Conference on Mexico on Microfilm, convened to plan for a national consortium to cooperatively film Mexican archives. The Texas project was not seen as a competitor to the national group but rather a complement to it and the work of other groups (Kinney, 1971).

A second project was the Latin American Microform Project (LAMP) initiated in 1975 by 16 U.S. research libraries. Following similar programs that had preceded it, LAMP had two basic premises: first, to make more accessible to scholars important research materials heretofore unavailable except through foreign travel; and second, to preserve disintegrating or poorly stored materials. The LAMP project, initiated by SALALM, is administered through the Center for Research Libraries, which had handled similar projects for other parts of the globe. The project includes filming of newspapers, periodicals, and archical collections held in the United States as well as collections in Latin America. The first decade saw a focus on Mexico and Brazil and, by 1985, the number of participating libraries had increased to 29. The resulting microfilm is held by CRL where it is available for use by the membership (Deal, 1987). While both microfilming projects could be perceived as primarily U.S. ventures, both in fact relied heavily upon the good graces and assistance of archivists and librarians in Mexico and, in the case of LAMP, several other Latin American countries.

5. U.S. Bibliographic Utilities

In 1975, the AMIGOS Bibliographic Council began exploring the possibilities of cooperation with Mexican libraries. At that time, AMIGOS had as a major focus the brokering of OCLC cataloging services and it made several presentations in Mexico and elsewhere in an effort to bring shared cataloging to Latin America. However, low hit rates, insufficient numbers of Spanish records, and high costs initially discouraged the widespread adoption of OCLC in Mexico. Quijano Solís (1982) noted that the OCLC system was too costly and inappropriate for Mexican libraries at that time. Nevertheless, UNAM (1982–1983) and the Universidad Iberoamericana (1980–1983) became AMIGOS members for a short time in the early 1980s, committing to use the OCLC Online Union Catalog as their cataloging source. Both were forced to discontinue service due to the financial crisis of the early 1980s.

Because of the costs and time involved in marketing and the inability of Mexican libraries to pay for cataloging and other network services, AMIGOS notified OCLC on March 5, 1992, that it would no longer serve libraries in

Latin America (P. Mooney, personal communication, November 14, 1995). In 1995, OCLC began marketing its products and services in Mexico and other parts of Latin America as part of its expanding international programs. As a result, a number of Mexican libraries began conducting trials with or purchased FirstSearch. There was a great deal of interest in FirstSearch, WorldCat, and other reference products such as CD-ROMs and electronic journals, none of which require OCLC membership (N. Cop, personal communication, November 7, 1995).

In 1995, the Research Libraries Group (RLG) announced a joint venture with the Centro de Tecnología Electrónica e Informática (CETEI), a non-profit company based in Mexico City, to provide RLG products to Mexican academic libraries. Under the program, a pilot group of 10 libraries were to have access to the RLIN bibliographic data bases as well as to a number of RLG's CitaDel files. Document delivery was also available to the group, which included UNAM, the Universidad de Colima, the Universidad de Guadalajara, and seven other schools ("RLG to Serve," 1995).

V. Future Relations

A. Rationale for Continued Interaction

The cooperative endeavors just described do not occur in a vacuum but rather in the context of differing government structures, economies, educational systems, and cultural heritages. "U.S. foreign relations with Mexico are among its most important and complex. They are shaped by a mixture mutual interests, shared problems, growing interdependence, and differing national perceptions" ("Background Notes: Mexico," 1994, p. 6). For many years our two nations have cooperated in order to solve a number of border issues including immigration, drug trafficking, the environment, and many others (Background Notes: Mexico, 1994).

Where do libraries fit into this picture of binational collaboration? Milam (1939, p. 231) noted that "Libraries are . . . ideal agencies for international cooperation" because they and their patrons cannot help but benefit from the exchange of knowledge that results from working together. Because libraries are educational and cultural institutions dedicated to service, they can indeed be models for other groups seeking to establish ties with their counterparts across borders or oceans. Tocatlian (1975) reviewed the rationale for international cooperation, examined incentives for doing so, and described numerous international library and information networks. Tocatlian (1975) noted that "cooperation has long been an essential ingredient of library and information management, at both the national and international level" (p. 2).

As Section IV illustrates, there is a long history of interaction between and among libraries and librarians in the United States and Mexico. Although there have been a variety of collaborative efforts, the extent of actual direct cooperation or resource sharing has been somewhat limited, although on the increase. However, the possibilities for working in tandem are numerous and should continue to be explored.

In writing about the need for continued collaboration, Ladrón de Guevara (1990) wrote "in spite of efforts made by librarians, institutions, and other organizations that have made advances in library development in Latin America, grave problems still persist, and they need to be explored again in the search for solutions" (p. 231). Even in a highly developed country like the United States, there are library problems that can be solved through cooperative efforts with other countries.

B. U.S.–Mexico Resource Sharing

1. How U.S. Libraries Can Help Mexico

In the past half century, Mexico and other Latin American countries have developed a strong foundation of librarianship based on local efforts and assistance from abroad. In the late 1930s and early 1940s, Latin American colleagues expressed a need for help with articulating a vision of what a library should be and for developing the rules necessary for acquiring, classifying, and cataloging their collections (Milam, 1939). Rivera (1941) suggested that U.S. librarians work with Latin American libraries to help them organize and make accessible rich collections of history and literature, including manuscripts. In reference to the opportunity to train Latin Americans in library organization and administration and for us to learn more about their countries, (Rivera, 1941, p. 113) noted that there was "a unique opportunity for service and a continent ready to receive it."

Milam (1939) also reported on requests for (1) copies of our publications, (2) fellowships for study and work in the United States, (3) help with establishing library schools, and (4) a traveling exhibit of modern librarianship. Latin American librarians also asked for (1) assistance with international interlibrary loan, (2) the publication in Spanish of library publications, (3) lists of U.S. works of interest to foreign readers, and (4) the translation of important North American books into Spanish.

Interest in collaboration with the United States continues in the mid-1990s, and although a few of the previously mentioned needs of 50 years ago remain, new areas of concern have since surfaced. A survey of 32 public Mexican university libraries conducted by CONPAB in 1989 revealed a great desire to work with their counterparts in the United States. This group expressed an interest in (1) the exchange of publications; (2) training in the

United States via internships or exchanges of staff; (3) short courses and workshops taught by American librarians; and (4) donations of equipment, software, and books (R. Forney, personal communication, August 23, 1995).

In conversations with Mexican colleagues, Cluff (1991) identified three broad areas in which the United States might work cooperatively to assist Mexican colleagues: personnel, collections, and equipment. Specific needs identified by Mexican librarians included, but were not limited to, (1) exchange of personnel, (2) scholarships for study in the United States, (3) training programs for middle managers and other staff, (4) cooperative continuing education programs, (5) exchange of publications, (6) donations of duplicates and other unwanted materials, (7) document delivery between the two countries, (8) gifts of software, (9) evaluations of computer systems, and (10) information to assist in purchasing equipment, especially computers, etc.

In a meeting with Mexican librarians on February 23, 1995, the author received very similar suggestions for ways in which the United States could be of assistance: (1) development of tutorials in the use of automated systems; (2) assistance with the transfer of electronic data between disparate automated systems; (3) help with the development of bilingual, standardized subject headings; (4) exchange of library school professors and students; (5) assistance in the acquisitions process for U.S. publications, especially speeding up the receipt of materials; (6) exchange of library science researchers needed to raise the level of research in Mexico; (7) training programs through distance education from the United States; and (8) helping Mexico develop its own library science distance education program.

In summary, Mexican libraries would most appreciate help with (1) training of library staff, (2) developing and better utilizing automated systems, (3) interlibrary loan and document delivery, and (4) collection development. Such areas are either not well developed or lack the funding to achieve minimal standards.

2. How Mexican Libraries Can Help the United States

Shepard (1968) correctly noted that "cooperation is a two-way street" (p. 705). In this author's experience, there is a sincere desire on the part of Mexican librarians to work with U.S. libraries, to reciprocate, to share their ideas and expertise. Milam (1939) listed several ways in which Latin American librarians could assist their U.S. colleagues: (1) assistance in securing books and periodicals more quickly and easily (still a problem in 1996); (2) provision of current, regular bibliographies of Latin American publications; (3) access to information on libraries and their collections; (4) help with interlibrary loan; (5) translation of important works into English; and (6) opportunities for librarians to study and conduct research.

Ruby (1985) pointed out that there is a great void in terms of information on Mexico in the United States and suggested that Mexican librarians could identify and recommend sources to fill that gap. She also noted that American librarians could do the same for Mexican colleagues. In a similar vein, Mexico could offer access to historical materials and local authors reflecting the philosophy of Northern Mexico (Quintanilla C., 1989), something of potential interest to scholars and laypersons alike. Our Mexican colleagues can also share their public relations and outreach experience as well as how to create an environment attractive to and comfortable for Hispanic patrons (Ruby, 1985).

Other ways in which Mexico can offer help to librarians in the United States are (1) access to and information about special collections; (2) partnerships in international research projects; (3) videos of popular and indigenous culture; (4) cultural and language education; (5) exchange of personnel, material, and information; and (6) Spanish courses (Cluff, 1991). Additional assistance could come in the form of (1) identification of and access to archival collections, many outside of libraries, to benefit researchers; (2) opportunities for and assistance with research sabbaticals in Mexico; (3) loans of unique materials such as government publications, theses, and statistical data; (4) cataloging of unique historical and literary collections for inclusion in our national data bases; and (5) expertise with indigenous Mexican languages (meeting with Mexican librarians, February 23, 1995).

C. Obstacles to Further Cooperation

While most librarians would agree that interinstitutional cooperation is a priority, it is often difficult to put into practice, and it becomes even more difficult and complicated when it involves two different political entities such as the United States and Mexico. In Section III,A,1, several barriers to cooperation within Mexico were delineated. Many of these obstacles also hinder or slow progress on the international front. White (1982) identified five categories of barriers to library cooperation: (1) economic, (2) technological, (3) bureaucratic, (4) geographic, and (5) personal. To these can be added (1) the language barrier; (2) differing standards, say for cataloging or data format; (3) distance and communication problems; (4) the political realities of international interaction; and (5) apathy. In short, it is no easy matter to carry out collaborative efforts in the international arena.

Another very large obstacle to U.S.–Mexico collaboration is the fact that many libraries in Mexico are much less well developed than their counterparts in the United States. As noted earlier, one must have something to share for cooperation to be fruitful and many libraries in Mexico are in position of having very little to offer in the way of collections and other resources. The reality is that in Mexico there are often extraordinary needs that can only be alleviated through cooperative efforts with other Mexican or American libraries. However, Mexican librarians can offer their U.S. colleagues expertise and the intellect to solve a variety of library problems. With a long tradition of "doing more with less," they are particularly adept at managing scarce resources, something American librarians could benefit from.

D. Suggested Future Activities

A number of librarians have suggested additional ways in which the United States and Mexico could work together. In speaking of future cooperation between Arizona and Sonora libraries, Milam and Salas (1990) listed several possibilities: (1) promotion of library services; (2) increased access to information through loans, gifts, and exchanges; (3) exchange of experience and knowledge though training courses, scholarships, internships, and consulting; (4) securing gifts of furnishings and equipment for libraries in need; (5) involvement of libraries in cultural projects to benefit Hispanic communities; (6) securing discounts for books and equipment; and (7) bilateral participation in professional associations.

In reference to public library cooperation, Ruby (1985) suggested (1) interlibrary loan agreements, (2) shared public services programs, (3) exchange of personnel, (4) visits to libraries, (5) interns, and (6) joint projects for providing children's services. Other possible programs were outlined by Gutierrez-Witt (1985): (1) joint conferences to improve communication, share information, and establish personal contacts; (2) exchange of state and local government publications, especially for border libraries; (3) exchange of duplicate materials, especially those having to do with border culture and life; (4) visits to libraries for the purposes of training and keeping current; (5) projects to document border information sources; and (6) preservation of local historical sources. She also emphasized the need for libraries in the interior of Mexico, those with more resources, to assist those in the outlying regions beyond the capital to develop their collections and personnel.

Ladrón de Guevara Cox (1990) recommended the formation of an international committee, with representatives from Latin America and the United States to identify areas for cooperative endeavors among Latin America libraries and with the United States. In addition to representatives from national library associations, she stressed the need for participation by SALALM and OAS. Among the areas of critical need are (1) teaching and training in library science, (2) library research to advance the profession and produce publications, and (3) the translation of papers on library science into English and Spanish.

Seal (1992b) underlined the importance of the involvement of professional organizations in U.S.–Mexico cooperation, noting that they can provide the appropriate framework and necessary resources for bilateral activity. He also recommended (1) more interlibrary loan between the two countries; (2) the creation of a list of and guide to special collections, especially those with a focus on border topics; (3) cooperative preservation efforts, especially for manuscripts and other unique materials; and (4) the exchange of personnel, for both short- and long-term visits (Seal, 1989).

Our Mexican colleagues have also suggested the following possibilities: (1) cooperative projects among special libraries; (2) the identification and documentation of archival collections in Mexico of interest to researchers in both countries; (3) work with scholars to determine how they conduct research in order to better organize collections; and (4) cooperative distance education efforts (meeting with Mexican librarians, February 23, 1995).

Financial support for cooperative activity must be borne by individuals, institutions, and consortia, or by foundations and government agencies. Although a number of possible sources exist to finance international library cooperation, one is particularly well suited for U.S.–Mexico collaboration, the so-called Fideicomiso para la Cultura Mexico/USA. The U.S.–Mexico Fund for Culture is an independent organization founded in September 1991, to foster cultural exchange between our two countries. A joint effort of the Rockefeller Foundation, the Mexican National Council for Culture and the Arts, and the Bancomer Foundation, the foundation provides financial support for binational projects in the performing arts, defined by the fund as dance, theater, and music; museums and visual arts; media arts; cultural studies; literary and cultural publications; and *libraries*.

Headquartered in Mexico City, the Fideicomiso para la Cultura Mexico/USA began with an initial annual budget of 1 million U.S. dollars. To date it has supported exchange programs, cooperative cataloging, exhibitions of books, collaborative preservation, and other resource-sharing efforts. The union catalog of rare books, the Antigua Bibliografia Mexicana cited earlier in Section III,B,1, was also funded by this program.

E. NAFTA and U.S.–Mexico Library Relations

The potential impact of the North American Free Trade Agreement (NAFTA) on libraries and library cooperation has already been discussed at great length, but with no consensus on exactly what that impact will be. Altbach (1994) noted that unlike the European Community agreement, NAFTA has no cultural or educational provisions, "but closer economic ties will inevitably have cultural and educational implications" (p. 48). Indeed, such implications are already being seen in the area of higher education where government, foundations, and educational leaders are at work on possible cooperative strategies. At trinational conferences in Racine, Wisconsin, in

1992, and Vancouver, British Columbia, in 1993, representatives of each group worked to devise ways to improve the quality of higher education and to make the region more competitive economically.

Trilateral collaboration in the form of strategic alliances among government, business, and education is seen by many as a way to solve common problems in administration, libraries, and computing. Library linkages have been cited as having great possibilities for cooperation, and the importance of exchanges has been stressed as a way to share expertise and personnel (Maza, 1993). Although such meetings and their results are technically separate from NAFTA, they cannot be totally separate issues. Altbach (1994) noted that "one of the main lessons is that focusing on commercial relations is not enough, and that mutual understanding is an important part of any constructive relationship" (p. 43). Libraries can play a key role in that process. Educational bridges must be built to "provide the needed understanding, knowledge, and skills required to deal with more intimate trade relations, and general sensitivity to the complex cultures of North America" (Altbach, 1994, p. 49).

Looking more specifically at libraries, the Tratado de Libre Comercio (TLC), as it is called in Mexico, could affect libraries in four areas: (1) publishing, (2) education, (3) business, and (4) copyright. Some believe that NAFTA will help libraries by increasing the flow of Mexican books to the United States and Canada through the gradual elimination of tariffs on paper, ink, and printing equipment ("Book Manufacturers," 1993). Deal (1992) noted that the production costs for books in Mexico could be reduced if NAFTA leads to reduced paper costs. Figueredo (1994) contrasted the book industry of the United States with that of Mexico and Latin America in an attempt to determine the possible impact of NAFTA on publishing. Because of several complex factors, he concluded that it is too early to tell how the trade agreement will affect the book industry and ultimately libraries who must acquire Spanish language materials for their clientele.

Because more and more colleges and universities are adding courses and degrees in international business, there is an increasing demand on libraries for information about Mexico in general and NAFTA in particular. Libraries must not only strengthen collections of print resources but also provide electronic access to meet the demand for data. Likewise, as more and more American companies show an interest in investing in Mexico, there will be an impact on business reference service with particular interest in "import-export, business start-up information, directory services queries, and labor cost data." Unfortunately, there are limited numbers of information sources available to answer these reference questions (Phillips, 1991).

Finally, because NAFTA has provisions for the protection of intellectual property, libraries will be called upon to provide information on copyright issues related to trade between Mexico and the United States. In particular,

NAFTA protects computer programs, databases, sound recordings, and motion pictures, as well as other types of intellectual property such as trademarks, patents, and integrated circuits. Its goal is to increase trade and reduce losses from piracy and counterfeiting (Donahue, 1994). Whatever the impact of the TLC, libraries in the United States and Mexico should work together to share information that will help it succeed.

References

Ainsworth, S. (1994). Mexican information resources in electronic format. In *Bowker Annual*, 39th Ed., pp. 75–90. R. R. Bowker, New Providence, NJ.

Almada de Ascencio, M., and Pérez de Almada, S. (1991). Scholarly information and serials in Latin America: Shifting political sands. *Serials Librarian* **21**, 69–85.

Altbach, P. G. (1994). NAFTA and higher education: The cultural and educational dimensions of trade. *Change* **26**(4), 48–49.

Annual Report of the U.S.–Mexico Libraries Subcommittee, International Relations Committee, June 1992.

Annual Reports [ALA], 1923–1924. *ALA Bulletin* **18**, 202–256.

Aranda, J., and Gleaves, E. S. (1981). The Master's Program in Library and Information Science of the University of Guanajuato: A new step for Mexico. *Leads* **23**(2), 1–2,6.

Arista, S., and Yáñez, J. A. (1983). "La Cooperación: Alternativa de Solución a la Problemática Económica que Enfrentan las Bibliotecas." Paper presented at the XIV Jornadas de AMBAC, Zacatecas, Zacatecas, May 2–6, 1983.

Arjón Castro, R. (1991). "Red bibliotecaria de los institutos Technológicos (REBIT) zona 3: Desarrollo y tecnología." Paper presented at the XXII Jornadas de AMBAC, Tuxtla Gutiérrez, Chiapas, May 13–15, 1991.

Arteaga Carlebach, G. (1990). ARDUSI: Primera red de bibliotecas en México. In *Latin American Frontiers, Borders, and Hinterlands: Research Needs and Resources: Papers of the Thirty-Third Annual Meeting (1988) of the Seminar on the Acquisition of Latin American Library Materials* (P. Covington, ed.), pp. 257–262. University of New Mexico (SALALM Secretariat), Albuquerque, NM.

Ayala, M. S., ed. (1984). *Proceedings of the First Binational Conference on Libraries in California and Baja California*, January 13–14, 1984, Serra Cooperative Library System, San Diego, CA.

Baldwin, C. M. (1991). Arizona promotes international librarianship. *Special Libraries* **82**, 203–204.

Bayardo Gómez, P. (1985). "Protocolos de Intercambio entre bibliotecas universitarias de la frontera norte de México." Paper presented at the Second Binational Conference on Libraries of the Californias, Calexico, California and Mexicali, Baja California, November 11–12, 1985.

Benson, S. S. (1990). Pooling resources: The OAS programs for library and archives development in the 1980s. In *Latin American Frontiers, Borders, and Hinterlands: Research Needs and Resources: Papers of the Thirty-Third Annual Meeting (1988) of the Seminar on the Acquisition of Latin American Library Materials* (P. Covington, ed.), pp. 245–256. University of New Mexico (SALALM Secretariat), Albuquerque, NM.

Bernal Flores, V., Castillo de Sáinz, T., Palacios de Avalos, M., and Reyes Ramos, G., eds. (1982). *Cooperación Bibliotecaria: Estado Actual y Perspectivas*. Memorias. IV Semana de Bibliotecología, September 29–October 4, 1980. Universidad Autónoma de Guadalajara, Dirección de Bibliotecas, Guadalajara, Jalisco.

La Bibliotecologia en el México Actual y Sus Tendencias. (1992). Dirección General de Bibliotecas, UNAM, México, D.F.

Bixler, P. (1969). *The Mexican Library*. The Scarecrow Press, Inc., Metuchen, NJ.

Bliss, N. J. (1995). International Librarianship. In *Encyclopedia of Library and Information Science* (A. Kent, ed.), Vol. 56 (Suppl. 19), pp. 214–233. Dekker, New York.

Book manufacturers hail NAFTA. (1993). *Publishers Weekly* **240** (Nov. 22), 15.

Brief Board and Committee Reports [ALA]. *ALA Bulletin* **27**, 450–473.

Brown, A. N. (1885). Note on the National Library of Mexico. *Library Journal* **10**, 248–249.

Carrión, G. (1977). "Progress and Problems of Librarianship in Latin America with Emphasis on Mexico." Speech presented at the Graduate School of Library Science, The University of Texas at Austin, October 6, 1977.

Carrión Rodrígues, G. (1981). Mexico. In *International Handbook of Contemporary Developments in Librarianship* (M. M. Jackson, ed.), pp. 559–565. Greenwood Press, Westport, CT.

Carrión Rodríguez, G. (1992). Las Bibliotecas Especializadas en México. In *La Bibliotecología en el México Actual y Sus Tendencias*, pp. 59–72. Dirección General de Bibliotecas, UNAM, México, D.F.

Cluff, E. D. (1991). Libraries and librarians in Mexico. *College & Research Libraries News* **52**, 370–371.

Coleman, M. P. (1934). In search of a Mexican library. *Wilson Bulletin for Librarians* **9**, 13–16.

Comisión de Relaciones Internacionales. (1992). *Noticiero de la AMBAC* No. 92,2.

Daniels, M. (1960). The promotion of libraries in the Americas: A five-year report of activities of the Organization of American States. *Library Quarterly* **30**, 201–208.

Deal, C. W. (1987). The Latin American microform project: A model for cooperation. In *Intellectual Migrations: Transcultural Contributions of European and Latin American Émigré: Proceedings of the 31st Annual Meeting of the Seminars on the Acquisition of Latin American Library Materials* (I. L. Sonntag, ed.), pp. 277–282. University of Wisconsin–Madison (SALALM Secretariat), Madison, WI.

Deal, C. W. (1992). Academic publishing in Mexico. *ARL: A bimonthly newsletter of research library issues and actions* May 1, 1992, No. 162, 3–4.

Dirección General de Bibliotecas, Secretaria de Educación Pública. (1991). *La Red Nacional de Bibliotecas Públicas*. Consejo Nacional para la Cultura y las Artes, México, D.F.

Donahue, G. (1994). Intellectual property issues. In *Latin America: The Emerging Information Power: 1993 State-of-the-Art Institute*, pp. 1–5. Special Libraries Association, Washington, DC.

Enciso Carbajal, B., and Gallardo Gómez, H. (1984). "Cooperación e Información: bases de un sistema." Paper presented at the XV Jornadas de AMBAC, Tlaxcala, Tlaxcala, April 30–May 4, 1984.

Estancias en el CUIB durante 1991. (1991). *Investigación Bibliotecológica* **5**(11), 65–66.

Fernández, R. M. (1989). La crisis económica y los servicios bibliotecarios y de información en México. *Investigación Bibliotecológica* **3**(7), 21–26.

Fernández de Zamora, R. M. (1976). Libraries in Mexico. In *Encyclopedia of Library and Information Science* (A. Kent, ed.), Vol. 18, pp. 1–40. Dekker, New York.

Fernández de Zamora, R. M. (1987). Cronología Bibliotecaria Mexicana 1900–1988. *Investigación Bibliotecológica* **1**(3), 48–59.

Fernández de Zamora, R. M. (1988). "Reseña sobre los Programas de Cooperación en México." Paper presented at the Reunión de Trabajo sobre Cooperación Bibliotecaria, México, D.F., September 17–18, 1987.

Fernández de Zamora, R. M. (1990a). The economic crisis and the scientific, technical and cultural information services in Mexico. *International Library Review* **22**, 263–271.

Fernández de Zamora, R. M. (1990b). Libraries in the Mexico City earthquake. *Information Development* **6**, 140–143.

Fernández de Zamora, R. M. (1991). Library resources in Latin America: A general panorama. *IFLA Journal* **17**, 45–54.

Fernández de Zamora, R. M. (1992). La Biblioteca Nacional de México y la bibliografía mexicana. In *La Bibliotecología en el México Actual y Sus Tendencias*, pp. 31–45. Dirección General de Bibliotecas, UNAM, México, D.F.

Fernández de Zamora, R. M., Ansoleaga de López, I., García Velarde, R., and Saavedra Fernández, O. (1977). "Posibilidades de Cooperación en México." Paper presented at the VIII Jornadas de AMBAC, Guadalajara, Jalisco, May 1–6, 1977.

Figueredo, D. (1994). The new NAFTA world: More books for your library? *Wilson Library Bulletin* **68**(8), 32–33.

First International Library Fellows Announced. (1993). *International Leads* **7**(4), 6–7.

Fitz, R. (1986). United States Information Agency Library and Book Programs. In *Bowker Annual*, 31st ed., pp. 125–128. Bowker, New York.

Galvin, T. J. (1985). "Igualdad de Acceso a la Información: Una perspectiva transfronteriza." Paper presented at the Second Binational Conference on Libraries of the Californias, Calexico, California and Mexicali, Baja California, November 11–12, 1985.

García Moreno, C. E. (1980). Mexico. In *ALA World Encyclopedia of Library and Information Services*, pp. 369–370. American Library Association, Chicago.

Garduño, R. (1985). "Co-operation in Mexican University Libraries." Paper presented at the IFLA General Conference, Chicago, Illinois, August 1985.

Garmon, J. F. (1990). Texas Southmost serves college and community. *Library Journal* **115**(3), 143.

Goldman, M. K. (1978). Technical information services in Mexico. *Special Libraries* **69**, 355–359.

Greer, A. F. P. (1919). Library experiences in Mexico. *Library Journal* **44**, 219–221.

Gregory, G. (1995). NAFTA spurs cooperation at trinational forum in Mexico City. *American Libraries* **26**, 507–508.

Gutiérrez-Witt, L. (1985). "El Desarrollo de las Bibliotecas: El Area Fronteriza E.U.-México." Paper presented at the Second Binational Conference on Libraries of the Californias, Calexico, California and Mexicali, Baja California, November 11–12, 1985.

Hands across the border. (1986). *Library Journal* **111**, 23.

Hazen, D. C. (1995). "Preservation Priorities in Latin America." A report from the 60th IFLA General Conference, Havana, Cuba, August 1994.

Heliodoro Valle, R. (1923). Libraries in Mexico. *Library Journal* **48**, 265–268.

Hixson, I. (1956). Introduction. In *Final Report of the Seminar on the Acquisition of Latin American Library Materials* (Chinsegut Hill, Brooksville, Florida, June 14–15, 1956), pp. i–iv. University of Florida Libraries, Gainesville, FL.

Hoffert, B. (1993a). Crossing borders: U.S./Mexican forum tackles common concerns. *Library Journal* **118**(12) 32–35.

Hoffert, B. (1993b). Guadalajara primed for book buying. *Library Journal* **118**(12) 34–35.

Kahl, S. C. (1993). A first step: The U.S.–Mexico interlibrary loan project. *Journal of Interlibrary Loan, Document Delivery & Information Supply* **4**, 17–24.

Kinney, J. M. (1971). The Texas consortium to microfilm Mexican archival resources. *College & Research Libraries* **32**, 376–380.

Ladrón de Guevara Cox, H. (1990). Cooperation among libraries: A Mexican proposal. In *Latin American Frontiers, Borders, and Hinterlands: Research Needs and Resources: Papers of the Thirty-Third Annual Meeting (1988) of the Seminar on the Acquisition of Latin American Library Materials* (P. Covington, ed.), pp. 231–234. University of New Mexico (SALALM Secretariat), Albuquerque, NM.

Latin American seminar on official publications makes recommendations. (1991). *College & Research Libraries News* **52**, 583.

Lau, J. (1993). Mexican information policy: A scattered decision model. In *Latin America: The Emerging Information Power: 1993 State-of-the-Art Institute*, pp. 132–143. Special Libraries Association, Washington, DC.

Lau, J. G. (1982). "El Préstamo Interbibliotecario en México: Factores a Considerar." Paper presented at the XIII Jornadas de AMBAC, Hermosillo, Sonora, May 3–7, 1982.

Lau, J. G. (1983). "La Crisis Nos Obliga a Cooperar." Paper presented at the XIV Jornadas de AMBAC, Zacatecas, Zacatecas, May 2–6, 1983.

León Saavedra, C. (1983). "Cooperación Bibliotecaria." Paper presented at the XIV Jornadas de AMBAC, Zacatecas, Zacatecas, May 2–6, 1983.

Levinson, A., and Reynel Iglesias, H. (1993). The online industry in Mexico. *Online* **17**(3), 116–119.

Litton, G., and Krzys, R. (1986). Latin American librarianship: A area study. In *Encyclopedia of Library and Information Science* (A. Kent, ed.), Vol. 40, pp. 114–272. Dekker, New York.

Lorenz, J. G., et al. (1972). The Library of Congress abroad. *Library Trends* **20**, 548–576.

Macías-Chapula, C. A. (1985). A descriptive study of ninety-two hospital libraries in Mexico. *Bulletin of the Medical Library Association* **83**, 66–70.

Magaloni, A. M. (1993). The Mexican library revolution: Taking books to the people. *Logos* **4**, 81–83.

Magaloni de Bustamante, A. M. (1992). Red Nacional de Bibliotecas Públicas: Desarrollo, Servicios y Resultados. In *La Bibliotecología en el México Actual y Sus Tendencias*, pp. 73–80. Dirección General de Bibliotecas, UNAM, México, D.F.

Magaloni de Bustamante, A. M. (1993). Mexico. In *ALA World Encyclopedia of Library and Information Services*, 3rd ed., pp. 570–572. American Library Association, Chicago.

Manrique de Lara, J. (1935). The popular library movement in Mexico. *Wilson Bulletin for Librarians* **9**, 409–414.

Maza, E. (1993). Con base en el TLC, Canadá, Estados Unidos y México negocian ya la estandarización de su educación superior. *Proceso* September 6, 1993, No. 879, 6–9.

Mexican, American librarians recommend cooperation. (1990). *American Libraries* **21**, 1092.

Mexican library first in Latin America to use FirstSearch. (1995). *OCLC Newsletter* No. 216, 14–15.

Milam, C. (1939). Some possibilities of library cooperation with Latin America. *ALA Bulletin* **33**, 227–231.

Milam, C. H. (1944a). Notes on the visit to Latin America. *ALA Bulletin* **38**, 299–300.

Milam, C. H. (1944b). Visit to Latin America. *ALA Bulletin* **38**, 229–230.

Milam, S., and Salas, C. (1990). "Cooperación Bibliotecaria entre México y los Estados Unidos: La Experiencia Sonora-Arizona." Paper presented at the XXI Jornadas de AMBAC, México, D.F., May 2–4, 1990.

Minutes of Meeting. U.S./Mexican Relations Committee, College and University Libraries Division, Texas Library Association, Houston, Texas, April 7, 1992.

Morales, E. (1987). Librarianship Research in Mexico. In *Comparative and International Librarianship* (P. S. Kawatra, ed.), pp. 171–178. Envoy Press, New York.

Morales Campos, E. (1976). Las Bibliotecas Universitarias en México. *Bibliotecas y Archivos* **7**, 93–115.

Morales Campos, E. (1990). Breve descripción del sistema bibliotecario mexicano. *Libros de México* No. 18, 29–36.

Morales Campos, E. (1992). Ten years of library science research in Mexico. *International Journal of Information and Library Research* **4**, 81–87.

Morales Campos, E. (1994). "U.S.–Mexico Interlibrary Loan." Paper presented at the 60th IFLA General Conference, Havana, Cuba, August 1994.

Morales Campos, E., and Ramírez Leyva, E., comp. (1992). *Edición Conmemorativa del X Aniversario del Centro Universitario de Investigaciones Bibliotecológicas*, 2 v., Consejo Nacional para la Cultura y las Artes, Dirección General de Bibliotecas, and Centro Universitario de Investigaciones Bibliotecológicas, México, D.F.

Mortenson Center for International Librarianship. (1993). *International Leads* 7(1), 6–8.

Neugebauer, R. L. (1992). Second Transborder Library Forum is successful! *Against the Grain* 4(3), 14.

Orozco Tenorio, J. (1977). "Los Recursos Compartidos en las Bibliotecas Académicas." Paper presented at the VII Jornadas de AMBAC, Guadalajara, Jalisco, May 1–6, 1977.

Orozco Tenorio, J. (1988). Information crisis in Latin America. *College & Research Libraries News* 49, 79–80.

Orozco Tenorio, J. (1992). La Cooperación Bibliotecaria en México. In *La Bibliotecología en el México Actual y Sus Tendencias*, pp. 267–275. Dirección General de Bibliotecas, UNAM, México, D.F.

Pan American Union. (1930). *Books and Libraries in Mexico.* Library and Bibliography Series, No. 3. Pan American Union, Washington, DC.

Pan American Union. (1962). *The Inter-American Program of Library and Bibliographic Development of the Organization of American States: A Statement of Principles and Practice.* General Secretariat, Organization of American States, Washington, DC.

Peñalosa, F. (1953). The development of libraries in Mexico. *Library Quarterly* 23, 115–125.

Pérez Monroy, I. C. (1991). "La Biblioteca Benjamín Franklin: Información especializada." Paper presented at the XXII Jornadas de AMBAC, Tuxtla Gutiérrez, Chiapas, May 13–15, 1991.

Phillips, R. F. (1991). Nine-state survey reveals interest in business with Mexico. *Colorado Libraries* 17(1), 26–27.

Las Primeras Jornadas Mexicanas de Biblioteconomía, Bibliografía y Canje. (1957). *Boletín de la Asociación Mexicana de Bibliotecarios* 1(1), 6–15.

Quijano Solís, A. (1982). Consideraciones sobre el Sistema OCLC en Bibliotecas Mexicanas. In *Cooperación Bibliotecaria: Estado Actual y Perspectivas*, pp. 127–137. Memorias. IV Semana de Bibliotecología, September 29–October 4, 1980. Universidad Autónoma de Guadalajara, Dirección de Bibliotecas, Guadalajara, Jalisco.

Quintanilla C., M. de J. (1989). "Los servicios bibliotecarios en las zona fronteriza: México– Norteamericana hacia una mejor comprensión entre vecinos." Paper presented at the XX Jornadas de AMBAC, Saltillo, Coahuila, May 2–4, 1989.

Ramírez Escárcega, A. (1984). "Conclusions del Segundo Seminario de Cooperación en Bibliotecas y Centros de Información." Paper presented at the XV Jornadas de AMBAC, Tlaxcala, Tlaxcala, April 30–May 4, 1984.

Reunión de Trabajo sobre Cooperación Bibliotecaria. (1988). (Memoria, September 17–18, 1987, México, D.F.). Instituto Tecnológico Autónomo de México, México, D.F.

Rivera, R. O. (1941). Cooperation among the libraries of the western hemisphere. *Inter-American Bibliographical Review* 1, 112–117.

RLG to Serve Mexican Universities. (1995). *Information Retrieval & Library Automation* 31(5), 7–8.

Robles Zafra, A. (1983). "Consideraciones Básicas para la Cooperación Bibliotecaria." Paper presented at the Segundo Seminario de Cooperación en Bibliotecas y Centros de Información, Monterrey, Nuevo León, November 24–26, 1983.

Rodríguez Gallardo, A. (1977). Some Aspects of Mexican Library Development. In *Bowker Annual*, 22nd Ed., pp 423–428. Bowker, New York.

Rodríguez Gallardo, A. (1992). El Sistema Bibliotecario de la UNAM. In *La Bibliotecología en el México Actual y Sus Tendencias*, pp. 15–30. Dirección General de Bibliotecas, UNAM, México, D.F.

Rojas, L. M. (1919). The National Library of Mexico. *Library Journal* 44, 216–218.

Ruby, C. (1985). "México y los Estados Unidos: Dos Naciones del Pacífico." Paper presented at the Second Binational Conference on Libraries of the Californias, Calexico, California and Mexicali, Baja California, November 11–12, 1985.

Sáenz, V. J. (1983). "Proyecto de Cooperación entre Bibliotecas del Noreste de México." Paper presented at the XIV Jornadas de AMBAC, Zacatecas, Zacatecas, May 2–4, 1983.

Savary, J. (1975). Library Cooperation in Latin America. In *Encyclopedia of Library and Information Science* (A. Kent, ed.), Vol. 15, pp. 214–247. Dekker, New York.

Seal, R. A. (1989). "La cooperación entre bibliotecas académicas en la zona fronteriza." Paper presented at the XX Jornadas de AMBAC, Saltillo, Coahuila, May 2–4, 1989.

Seal, R. A. (1990a). El proyecto de prueba de préstamo interbibliotecario entre México y los Estados Unidos. *Investigación Bibliotecológica* 4(8), 29–30.

Seal, R. A. (1990b). "The U.S.–Mexico Interlibrary Loan Project." Paper presented at the Arizona Library Association, Phoenix, Arizona, November 16, 1990.

Seal, R. A. (1991). The U.S.–Mexico Interlibrary Loan Project. In *Advances in Library Resource Sharing* (J. Cargill and D. J. Graves, eds.), Vol. 2, pp. 165–175. Meckler Publishing, Westport, CT.

Seal, R. A. (1992a). Untitled talk presented at the Second Transborder Library Forum, Hermosillo, Sonora, Mexico, March 20, 1992.

Seal, R. A. (1992b). "Cooperation between Libraries in the U.S. and Mexico." Paper presented at the Feria Internacional del Libro, Guadalajara, Mexico, November 29, 1992.

Seal, R. A. (1993). U.S.–Mexico Libraries Subcommittee (ALA/IRC). *REFORMA Newsletter* **12**(3), 13.

Segundo Seminario de Cooperación en Bibliotecas y Centros de Información. (1983). (Memorias, November 24–26, 1983, Monterrey, Nuevo León). ABIESI, Monterrey, Nuevo León.

Seminario de Cooperación en Bibliotecas y Centros de Información. (1977). (Memorias, September 14–16, 1977, Saltillo, Coahuila). ABIESI, México, D.F.

Severance, H. O. (1938). Fields of library and bibliographical investigations open to American scholars in Latin America. *Inter-American Bibliographical and Library Association Proceedings* **1**, 175–182.

Shaw, R. R. (1947). International activities of the American Library Association. *ALA Bulletin* **41**, 199–232.

Sheldon, B. E. (1985). "Servicios Bibliotecarios en la Region Fronteriza Estados Unidos/ México—El Papel de Tres Instituciones claves: las Bibliotecas Estatales, las Asociaciones Profesionales, y los Programas de Educación Bibliotecológica." Paper presented at the Second Binational Conference on Libraries of the Californias, Calexico, California and Mexicali, Baja California, November 11–12, 1985.

Shepard, M. D. (1968). International dimensions of U.S. librarianship. *ALA Bulletin* **62**, 699–710.

Shepard, M. D. (1984). Information systems and library automation in Latin America. In *Advances in Librarianship* (W. Simonton, ed.), Vol. 13, pp. 151–184. Academic Press, Orlando, FL.

SLIS Faculty and Students at Escuela National de Biblioteconomía y Archivonomía. (1995). *Call Number* **53**(2), 4.

Sullivan, P. (1972). The international relations program of the American Library Association. *Library Trends* **20**, 577–591.

Sussman, J. (1973). *United States Information Service Libraries* (University of Illinois Graduate School of Library Science, Occasional Papers, No. 111). University of Illinois, Urbana-Champaign, IL.

T. de Zubarán, J. (1956). "Préstamo Interbibliotecario y Servicio de Fotoduplicación." Paper presented at the [first] Jornadas de AMBAC, México, D.F., December 2–7, 1956.

Tamez Solís, P. (1992). El Financiamiento de las Bibliotecas Universitarias Mexicanas. In *La Bibliotecología en el México Actual y Sus Tendencias*, pp. 229–255. Dirección General de Bibliotecas, UNAM, México, D.F.

Thigpen, W. K. (1969). Ben Franklin in Mexico. *Wilson Library Bulletin* **43**, 452–455.

Thomas Giraud, S., and Barberena Blásquez, E. (1986). "Redes de Bibliotecas: Un ejemplo de metodología para su creación y operación." Paper presented at the XVII Jornadas de AMBAC, Puebla, Puebla, April 23–May 2, 1986.

Tocatlian, J. (1975). International information systems. In *Advances in Librarianship* (M. J. Voigt, ed.), Vol. 5, pp. 1–58. Academic Press, New York.

U.S. Department of State. Bureau of Public Affairs. Office of Public Communication. (1994). *Background Notes: Mexico* 4(4), Washington, D.C.

Verdugo Sánchez, J. A. (1992). Recomendaciones sobre el diplomado como educación no formal en el área bibliotecológia (Documento preliminar CNB). *Investigación Bibliotecológica* 6(12), 45–46.

Verdugo Sánchez, J. A., and Fernández de Zamora, R. M., comp. (1990). *Primer Seminario Nacional de Bibliotecarios Titulados de México: Bibliotecología, Información y Sociedad en México, Memorias* (Oct. 9–10, 1989). Colegio Nacional de Bibliotecarios, A. C., Consejo Nacional de Ciencia y Tecnología, México, D.F.

Voutssás, J., Rodríguez, V., Ladrón de Guevara, H., Feria, L., and González Arteaga, M. (1989). *Estudio sobre las estrategias planteadas a nivel nacional acercas de las redes de bibliotecas y su posible desarrollo.* Universidad Nacional Autónoma de México (UNAM) and Asociación Nacional de Universidades e Institutos de Educación Superior (ANUIES), México, D.F.

White, C. M. (1969). *Mexico's Library and Information Services: A Survey of Present Conditions and Needs.* The Bedminster Press.

White, C. M. (1970). Acceleration of library development in developing countries. In *Advances in Librarianship* (M. J. Voigt, ed.), Vol. 1, pp. 241–285. Academic Press, New York.

White, T. (1982). La Cooperación Bibliotecaria y Como Optimizarla. In *Cooperación Bibliotecaria: Estado Actual y Perspectivas*, pp. 37–65. Memorias. IV Semana de Bibliotecología, September 29–October 4, 1980. Universidad Autónoma de Guadalajara, Dirección de Bibliotecas, Guadalajara, Jalisco.

Wilson, J., and Shepard, M. D. (1977). Organization of American States. In *Encyclopedia of Library and Information Science* (A. Kent, ed.), Vol. 21, pp. 16–35. Dekker, New York.

Developing Site Licensing with Particular Reference to the National United Kingdom Initiative

Liz Chapman*

Institute of Economics and Statistics Library
University of Oxford
Oxford OX1 3UL, United Kingdom

I. Introduction

It is no secret that libraries in universities and colleges have long been worried by the twin pressures of spiraling prices of journals and increasing numbers of new titles. Library funding has not kept up with either of these pressures. Serials have squeezed monograph purchases. Meanwhile, publishers have been squeezing serials agents with lowered discounts. From the academic library user's point of view, a diminishing service has come to be expected, at just the time when they are increasingly pressured to publish.

The vicious circle of cuts in serial subscriptions, leading to price increases by publishers to maintain revenue and so further library cuts, has become obvious. Add to this sorry equation the technological imperative of providing more and more online services in libraries and an opportunity for the licensing of publisher products is provided.

A license can be described as a legal agreement between suppliers of serials (publishers) and users of serials (libraries). The agreement can provide access to all or only part of a publisher's output. Payment may be made up front, possibly with added payment by usage, depending on how the material is to be used.

This chapter looks at some of the existing and developing licensing projects. It considers the UK Pilot Site Licensing initiative as a case study in licensing development. It looks at some of the implications for libraries and their users, as well as other players, in the new licensing environment.

* The views expressed in this paper are those of the author and not necessarily those of the Funding Councils for Higher Education in the United Kingdom.

II. Existing Licensing Projects

A. ADONIS

The Adonis Consortium was first planned in the early 1980s by four publishers: Blackwell, Elsevier, Springer, and Pergamon. Publishers in the Adonis group were concerned about photocopying and interlending between libraries, without any revenue accruing to publishers. Studies were made involving the British Library Document Supply Centre and other publishers, with the aim of developing an automated system to produce the most frequently used biomedical journal articles, on demand.

A 2-year trial of the CD-ROM service began in 1987 with some 200 journals; the full commercial service began in 1991 (Campbell, 1991). Potential subscribers were considered to be national libraries, library networks running document supply services, commercial document supply companies, universities, and research centers. Pharmaceutical companies were expected to become major clients.

The project was developed jointly between the publishers and the British Library who worked together on the technical, financial, and legal aspects. Contracts for licensing were signed by individual sites. The Adonis Consortium wanted to test the manufacturing processes and to develop a friendly user interface. Subscribers would be able to judge the quality of the service and test the provision of CD-ROM-based services in their libraries (Stern and Compier, 1990).

ADONIS is a CD-ROM-based licensed service for providing page images of journals to subscribers. Sixty-six participating publishers provide some 640 titles in the scientific, medical, and technical area. The titles primarily come from biomedicine but also include chemistry, biochemistry, bioengineering, and biotechnology (Blackwell Science, 1995).

The CD-ROMs are provided weekly with full bibliographic indexing and bit-map images. This currently runs to about 85 CD-ROMs annually. Articles can be printed out on a laser printer or used for faxing, and usage is recorded. ADONIS offices later invoice the subscribing library each quarter and provide management reports. Prices are set by individual publishers as a "publishers' copyright charge" and average around $10 per article printed.

A browsing version is available and retrospective searches can be made by the cumulative index held on the library's computer. Searches can be made by author, title words, ISSN, year of publication, volume, issue, or pages and can utilize Boolean logic. The system can be installed on a local area network for printing but display of images on remote workstation screens is not allowed. Several document supply services use the ADONIS service as a basis, such as Article Express and the British Library Document Supply Service.

The costs for a subscription in 1995 are NLG 36,000.00 with a backset 1991–1994 price of NLG 36,000.00. This is the price for on-screen viewing, whereas the simple search service is not as expensive. Printing is an extra charge. New models of total or partial subscription are being developed whereby there is a basic subscription charge, a charge for titles likely to be heavily used, and a usage charge for articles printed from other titles. The whole package is governed by a license called a "Journal Delivery and User Agreement."

B. TULIP

The TULIP project (The University Licensing Program) was first discussed and planned in 1991 in order to find a way to accelerate the electronic distribution of traditional print journals. University librarians and systems staff wanted to improve the dissemination of electronic information whereas the publisher Elsevier had been considering the same question (Hunter and Zijlstra, 1994). The pilot license project was proposed to last 3 years from 1992, but initial connections were delayed somewhat.

Fifteen large universities in the United States originally agreed that they would become the test bed for the research project with Elsevier and they outlined three groups of objectives.

1. Technical Objectives

The project would consider the technical feasibility of a networked distribution directly to and between institutions. Such distribution would include Internet and local area network use with obviously varying levels of sophistication. Elsevier agreed to provide the information and the universities would test a variety of delivery modes, retrieval systems, and print-on-demand capabilities.

2. Organizational and Economic Objectives

The use of alternative costing, pricing, and subscription models associated with electronic distribution would be compared with the conventional methods of printing and distribution. The overall economic aim was to reduce the unit cost of information. Added to this the project would test the different campus organizations involved in delivery. The outcome should be an economically and functionally viable model.

3. Study of User Behavior Objective

User behavior would be studied under the different situations at different campuses and improvement in the functionality of the information in terms of structure and retrieval would also be considered. Data were collected in a review process so that useful comparisons could be made between sites.

The files provided were initially 42 (increasing to 60 in 1995) Elsevier and Pergamon journals in materials science and engineering. This subject spread was chosen as an area where researchers already had computer skills and, of course, suited the available titles from the publisher. Elsevier creates the files and exports them to Engineering Information (Ei), which acts as the Internet host and will maintain the archive. Ei then acts as the distributor (Elsevier Science, 1995).

Each of the universities receives the electronic full text (bit-mapped and ASCII) biweekly for the journals to which they subscribe in paper. PostScript and/or SGML were promised when they became available. Universities also receive bibliographic information for all 42 titles in the project and can have on-demand paid access if they want to use journals to which they do not subscribe. It was anticipated that universities would mount the full-text files locally on their own servers, although some would use network on-demand access from Ei. One goal was to provide local autonomy as far as possible within the confines of licenses signed at each site. From the outset it was envisaged that the number of titles might be increased once the operation was well established, even to include titles from other publishers.

By August 1993, nine U.S. universities were receiving the raw ASCII full text of 43 Elsevier and Pergamon journals and had access to more than 152,500 bit-mapped journal page images. This last represented the whole output for 1992 and around half of that for 1993. The University of Michigan was the first site to become operational in 1993, with the remainder coming on stream by January 1994 (University of Michigan, 1995). The technical approaches at each site were very different and allowed the exploration of separate models. The University of California, which itself has nine campuses, provides a complex TULIP site, which allowed access through MELVYL, the university libraries' online public access system.

The situation for the publisher is no less complex, in that it has to provide output in one electronic format from several different publishing houses, in some four countries, using 18 different typesetting companies. This leaves aside the question of individual journal layout, typeface, and size. The reality of electronic production initially meant scanning the paper versions. Ei has to customize the output according to the subscription or license of each of the participants.

The technical and organizational objectives are therefore being addressed and users are being surveyed both before and after exposure to TULIP. Research is being done to find out who uses TULIP and how they gain access to it. Comparisons will be made between different delivery modes at different sites. The economic models will be considered once the technical aspects become routine. In 1994, it was anticipated that expansion of the project in 1995 would be on a commercial basis, with a change for files. Elsevier claims to price to encourage use.

Because this site licensing scheme is now well established, it will be interesting to discover its effects and to see emerge some of the results of the user surveys. Early indications from the University of Michigan are that print on demand is not as popular as anticipated (Willis *et al.*, 1994). Although some of this may be attributable to delay and waiting time, it may also be that researchers are more willing to read on-screen than previously realized. There is no doubt too that other products such as UMI full text are competing with TULIP.

In 1995, the University of California decided not to meet Elsevier's terms for continuing TULIP (Gelfand and Needleman, 1995). Library reactions to the experiment were that it was interesting but difficult. The choice of journals in materials science did not necessarily represent the core resources for the discipline; however, if users were able to find the article they wanted, in a library that did not subscribe to the printed version, the service was considered excellent.

C. EASE

TULIP migrated to Europe to take root in the Netherlands at Tilburg University in December 1993 (Geleijnse, 1994). The newly formed project was called EASE (Elsevier Articles Supplied Electronically). In this pilot project, Tilburg University, which specializes in social sciences and the humanities, has a license to work on some 100 Elsevier journals to which the library subscribes. The journals can be distributed electronically on campus from scanned images provided by the publisher. The images include full text with illustrations and figures and represent approximately 15,000 articles per year.

The intention of the project is to allow researchers to print out articles on printers in their own departments and also to browse full-text images and receive them at their own workstations (Dijkstra, 1994). The library intends to improve service to users and to study their reactions. Greater use should be made of expensive material, and information about usage will be used to inform collection development decisions. The partners want to test an economic model that respects the legal rights of publishers, while examining the cost effectiveness of licensed electronic journals. It is intended to run the pilot for 3 years.

Issues that are being addressed by this pilot, in a university library that already has many innovatory electronic services, include that of copyright and further copying beyond first printout. Elsevier is also looking at payments beyond initial electronic subscriptions, which may be charged for browsing or printing (Dijkstra, 1994).

D. Red Sage

The Red Sage project (named after a restaurant in Washington, D.C., where the initial partners met) was planned in late 1991 and early 1992. This is an experimental licensing project set up originally with Springer-Verlag, but now includes some 20 publishers. By April 1995, 70 clinical science and molecular biology titles were available on the project. The work being carried out links the University of California at San Francisco (UCSF), publishers, and AT&T to test the "Right Pages" software for full-text networked journal delivery (University of California, San Francisco, 1995).

The development of the project came from common goals recognized at a Coalition for Networked Information meeting, where discussions were held between Springer-Verlag (New York) and the librarian of UCSF. Springer had already seen a demonstration of "Right Pages" software in 1990 at AT&T Bell Laboratories and AT&T subsequently joined the group. After an initial discussion phase, a 3-year test was proposed in August 1992, with 24 journals. The project began in earnest in 1994.

The objectives of the project are to test the "economic, legal, technical, human factors and business issues in the distribution of scientific and medical information in a networked environment" (Butter, 1994). UCSF has developed the infrastructure for delivery, and AT&T scans the journals that are provided by Springer and the other publishers. The publishers are economically protected during the experimental period by the library continuing its paper subscriptions.

Following the acknowledged strengths of UCSF, the experiment was first set up in the radiology field, but microbiology and clinical science were added later. Library staff are carefully evaluating the project, adding to the performance statistics available on the system. Users will have pre- and post-Red Sage interviews. Information for evaluation will also be taken from reference and public service staff who have helped users with Red Sage access.

Red Sage is innovative in that it brings references direct to users in their libraries, offices, laboratories, or at home. Electronic access can bring information more quickly than paper, 24 hr per day. Although potentially bypassing libraries, the interface is modeled on print library use by allowing skimming of tables of contents, browsing page by page, selecting current or back issues, and printing individual articles (DeLoughry, 1993). The system can also provide automatic searching according to a user profile, which alerts the user at log in to anything relevant which has been found (Lucier, 1992). Library staff expect this to be the most popular feature of Red Sage.

The appearance of a print journal is preserved, and it will be interesting to see whether this is preferred by researchers to the searchability of an ASCII-based file of the text of a journal. The team at UCSF intend to explore links between the Red Sage project and other services such as MEDLINE and library online categories. Red Sage is now expanding to Europe from the United States, although concentration in the expansion does not seem to be on academic libraries as recipients, but more on the business sector.

The experiment was originally set up in the UCSF libraries and, by summer 1995, was made available to academic offices, with a PC or MAC interface. The University of California at Los Angeles also joined the project and is giving similar high usage feedback to that of UCSF. Five thousand to 6000 articles per month are being accessed through Red Sage. All partners are convinced that the science research community will want to continue the service. In early 1996, discussions were held to work out a commercial model for continuing and increasing the number of journals available (R. Badger, personal communication, 1996).

E. WebDOC

WebDOC is a licensed service that provides access to electronic documents from international publishers, to 13 libraries in Germany, The Netherlands, and the United Kingdom. The project started in 1995 and is more of a partnership between libraries and publishers than some of the other schemes described. It was initiated by the Dutch Centre for Library Automation Pica, in Leiden, The Netherlands (Pica, 1995).

The service uses World Wide Web (WWW) technology for access to WebCAT, hosted by Pica, which is a central database of electronically available documents. The participating libraries contribute titles and abstracts of journal articles and other relevant material, to what is effectively an electronic union catalogue. Library users can search the WebCAT with a browser and, when they find the document they require, they can click on the relevant Uniform Resource Locator (URL). On choosing the URL, the user will see an accounting form and will have to enter a PIN number. This preallocated number represents a prepaid account for the library from which they are operating and is a commonly used procedure in The Netherlands for end user-initiated interlibrary loans. After account checking, a secure URL is provided.

The secure URL or Golden URL (GURL) is a multifunction locator. It locates the required document, providing an identifier, a time stamp, and a user identifier string. The GURL is valid for a period of time in case there are network connection problems. The stability of network connections is monitored as part of the project.

Most publications are provided via licensing agreements with publishers. When there is no license, access is paid for by users on a per-transaction basis. The suppliers of documents send invoices to the universities. The licensing agreements cover access from all users at each licensed university. Some material on WebDOC is provided free of charge. These free materials may be publicly available documents, local research output, or other gray literature.

The project began in February 1995, and has a planned 2-year pilot phase lasting from October 1, 1995 to July 31, 1997, although this may be extended. User surveys and evaluations of the service will be made in order to bring forward recommendations for a fully operational service in August 1997.

F. Other Licensing Projects

Apart from the five major licensing projects just outlined, there are several others in various states of development. OCLC has a pilot licensing project with Elsevier called Elsevier Electronic Subscriptions (OCLC, 1995). BioMedNet is a worldwide club for biomedical scientists, which in 1995 offered a free trial to libraries (BioMedNet, 1995). Wiley publishers have worked with Computer Associates, a software company, to license use of its own publications. Wiley is also working on a local licensing project with University College, London. Various publishers such as Chapman and Hall are beginning to offer full-text online versions of their journals. There are also licensing schemes in the area of images such as Designers and Artists Collecting Society in the United Kingdom, which allow libraries to take up a blanket license for copying artistic works on slides (Designers and Artists Collecting Society, 1995). The combined university libraries in Manchester, United Kingdom, are also involved in a common electronic licensing project with publishers, to be provided via a system called Infobike, using a Fujitsu full-text online distribution utility for publishers called STEAMLINE. All these projects must of course be set against the background of the possibility of an outright purchase of journal texts in CD-ROM format such as the ProQuest service from UMI.

The paradigm for library licensing outlined in this section is one largely dependent on the publishers and is subject to their control. The Internet is frequently seen as the medium for communication, thereby potentially bypassing libraries. Projects are centered on one, or a small group of libraries, or one, or a group of publishers. However, the pilot scheme being set up in the United Kingdom, for higher education libraries, is somewhat more ambitious since the intention is to provide a truly national site license for periodicals.

III. The UK Pilot Site License Initiative

A. UK Higher Education

There are 162 universities and colleges of higher education in the United Kingdom. The university sector increased overnight in the early 1990s as institutions previously known as polytechnics were redesignated universities. There is only one private university in the United Kingdom.

Public funding for these institutions is provided by four separate bodies working in the four countries of the United Kingdom. The largest of these, funding 128 universities and 75 further education colleges, is the Higher Education Funding Council for England (HEFCE). The equivalent bodies for Scotland and Wales are the Scottish Higher Education Funding Council (SHEFC) and the Higher Education Funding Council for Wales (HEFCW). Higher Education in Northern Ireland is funded by the Department of Education for Northern Ireland (DENI). The four funding bodies often cooperate, and the recent initiatives in libraries, of which the pilot site license is only a part, are examples of their working together. This pilot project began as a HEFCE initiative, but soon became a joint project. This did throw up some legal problems, as Scotland in particular has its own legal system.

The amount of funding allocated to universities in 1993–1994 was in the region of £4 billion. Funds for teaching and research, based on a formula, are allocated as a "block grant." This means any university can allocate the one-line budget as they see fit.

There are of course mechanisms for accountability for universities. Regular research assessment exercises are run to monitor and evaluate research output. These look at published output according to certain criteria, and each institution is ranked. This ranking effectively decides the university's portion of national funds. The research selectivity exercise has undoubtedly put pressure on academics to publish more, not always to the advantage of scholarship, or even of libraries. At the same time, teaching is monitored through a teaching quality assessment. Approximately one half of the recurrent funds provided to UK universities are intended for the support of teaching. Approximately £400 million is provided in nonformula funding that can go toward special activities, including library initiatives.

There are approximately 1.1 million full-time equivalent researchers and students in UK higher education, but this belies the increases over recent years (UK Higher Education Statistics Agency, 1995). In the 1960s, there were approximately 40 universities and 30 newly established polytechnics. The UK system of higher education catered to only 12% of 18 year olds, whereas now it caters for 30%. Higher education has become more of a "mass" rather than "elite" system. There has been a shift because of student numbers from teaching to learning. Students are expected to do more for themselves with a consequent increase in pressure on libraries. It is against this background of expansion and change that a review of university libraries was made.

B. The Follett Report—Joint Funding Councils' Libraries Review Group

In December 1993, a report on academic libraries in the United Kingdom was published jointly by the four funding councils (UK Joint Funding Councils' Libraries Review Group, 1993). The review group was chaired by Professor Sir Brian Follett, Vice-Chancellor of Warwick University, and was well received in university libraries, not least because it promised money to support library services. Indeed, perhaps for this very reason, there was precious little debate on its findings.

The review started from the point where pressure was mounting on libraries, in terms of space and materials. There was an acknowledged need to capitalize on new technology, and the pressure on book funds by periodicals (the "periodicals squeeze") was becoming all too obvious (Chapman, 1991).

The Follett report estimated that £140 million would be needed to alleviate space problems—in other words build more libraries. An extra £20 million was considered necessary to incorporate IT to help both users of libraries and their staff. The IT aspects were brought together under the heading of FIGIT (Follett Implementation Group on Information Technology), as part of the electronic libraries program known as Elib.

A further conclusion of the Follett report was that academic libraries were involved in a vicious circle as far as periodicals were concerned. Libraries were cutting subscriptions because prices were rising way above inflation, and they also needed money to be able to take on new subscriptions. As libraries made cancellations, publishers put up prices to maintain their income. Investigation was recommended into the question of copyright in the hope that the vicious circle could be broken and some influence could be brought to bear on publishers.

This question of copyright is a very complex one, as all authors and librarians know. To some extent there are publisher controls in the United Kingdom, exercised by the copyright licensing authority (CLA), but these in themselves are by no means straightforward as not all publishers are part of the CLA. As student numbers increase, and therefore class sizes increase, class packs of recommended readings are being put together. Copyright clearance and charging are required for these. It was hoped that site licensing would overcome some of these problems and allow freer usage on a wider basis, both for teaching and for research.

C. Technical Infrastructure for UK Higher Education Libraries

In the context of the site license initiative for periodicals, many of which are provided electronically, the technical infrastructure for UK higher education is key. HEFCE provided information to publishers about possible technical connections to academic institutions for the pilot, a brief summary of which follows.

1. JANET

JANET is the Joint Academic Network, which is managed by the UK Educational and Research Networking Associations (UKERNA) on behalf of the Joint Information Systems Committee (JISC) of the Higher Education Funding Councils of England, Wales, and Scotland. Developed as a private network, it links 200 different sites and more than 50,000 computers. It has become a crucial part of higher education's research effort and interuniversity communications. It works as a link between the various local area networks on campus (UK Educational and Research Networking Associations, 1995). JANET is compatible with TCP/IP protocols and is therefore accessible to the Internet. There are links into other European networks and to the United States through the so-called "fat pipe." Originally intended only for higher education, some publishers and library suppliers (vendors) now use JANET. As the network is enhanced to become SuperJANET, publishers intend to deliver full-text article pages.

SuperJANET is gradually becoming available throughout the United Kingdom and more than 50 sites are linked up. This figure is expected to double in the next 2 years. The operation of a 156-Mbits per second backbone has encouraged connection, although SuperJANET cabling is expensive.

The UK networking structure can allow access to electronic material from publishers in different ways, such as coded SGML or Adobe Acrobat files. Some aspects of multimedia combining sound and images are possible. SuperJANET will allow the equivalent of a 5500-page report to be transmitted in under a second.

2. CHEST

The Combined Higher Education Software Team (CHEST) funded by the Higher Education Funding Councils has been involved both in the purchase of and in the licensing of software to universities and notably in the innovative BIDS service in the United Kingdom. The BIDS service (Bath Information and Data Services) began in early 1991 to provide online access to the four major ISI databases to universities (Law, 1994). Each university that wishes to subscribe pays a fixed sum each year, and an undisclosed capital payment was made centrally to start the service. By mid-1993, this had become the largest ISI service in the world, and licenses have extended now to include *Compendex, Embase,* and *Inside Information* (from the British Library). Newly added databases are *Ecoflora, Kew Record, International Bibliography of the Social Sciences,* and *Uncover,* the document delivery service. Institutions that subscribe can offer unlimited access to the service without the constraint of connect or usage charges (University of Bath, 1995). By the end of 1995, there were 9000 uses per day recorded.

The fact that the BIDS service is a national one, free at the point of use, and not tied to a single campus or group of universities forms an important background to the national periodical licensing pilot. The experience of CHEST in purchasing software and database access for the higher education community is also a crucial contributing factor.

D. Development Work for a UK Site License

Within the framework of various initiatives following the Follett report (UK Joint Funding Councils' Libraries Review Group, 1993), HEFCE set up an advisory group on a pilot site license initiative in early 1995. The first meeting of the group took place on March 1, 1995. The group was chaired by the director of policy at HEFCE and its members are drawn from various areas. There were observers from the funding councils for Wales, Scotland, and Northern Ireland, a legal advisor to the initiative, an academic member of the Science Policy Research Unit at Sussex University, the director of FIGIT, and the head of a university computing service. There were three librarians: the head of a large university library service, the secretary of the Standing Conference on National and University Libraries (SCONUL), and the author of this chapter. The group was later afforced by members from CHEST and by a professional consultant with expertise in publishing. With secretarial support, the group comprised 16 members.

The terms of reference for the group, established from the outset and taking into account HEFCE's plan for a pilot site license initiative, were to advise the executive of HEFCE on the development of a pilot site license initiative, including the overall conduct of a pilot site license, negotiations to be held with publishers on the price and terms of a site license to be purchased by HEFCE, the management arrangements for such an initiative, and the transition from a pilot to a full-scale site licensing model, and to report to HEFCE as required by the project plan.

The purpose of the group during 1995 was to reach an agreement with publishers to provide, under license, all or some of the research periodical material they produced to any higher education library participating in the project. It was intended to run a pilot project for 3 years from January 1996. The project was to test different modes of delivery as well as the overall viability of such a blanket-type supply.

1. Timetable

From the first meeting of the advisory group, two things became clear: (1) the funding council, initially HEFCE, was clearly determined to set up such an initiative by 1996, and (2) therefore that the timetable as regarding libraries was very tight. Librarians on the group pointed out that libraries began considering periodical renewals and subscriptions in the early summer and would need information on what was happening and which publishers had been chosen as soon as possible.

An initial optimistic project timetable was drawn up for 1995 with major steps defined as

January to April:	Define scope of project/selection methods/pricing models.
April 30:	Invite expressions of interest.
May 31:	Receive expressions of interest.
June to July:	Evaluate expressions of interest, make recommendations on charging, and make recommendations on management.
July 5:	Seek Funding Councils' approval.
July:	Consult sector on progress to date.
July to September:	Advise on final deal.
September 30:	Deal with publisher(s) finalized.
September:	Make final recommendations on charging/management.
October:	Invite tenders for managing agent.
December 31:	Appoint managing agent.

As the project progressed, naturally some of these target dates slipped. Progress to date is described below. The library communities were kept in touch to some extent but were understandably uneasy about some of the implications for such a project (Chapman, 1995). Links between the Funding Councils tended to be direct with university vice chancellors and not directly with libraries, perhaps to avoid some of the early hostility expressed toward the project by librarians. The head of policy for HEFCE met with publishers, agents, and librarians to explain the pilot (Bekhradnia, 1995).

E. Choosing the Publishers

In May 1995 (scarcely a month behind timetable), an "invitation to express interest in the pilot project for a national site license for scholarly journals within the UK higher education sector" was sent to 65 publishers in Europe, which had at least 35 journals on their lists. It went out under the signature of the HEFCE head of policy. There had been considerable discussion over whether European Community procurement regulations would come into play and whether the exercise would have to be publicly advertised. However, because library material purchases are not an EC procurement priority, it was decided that the open nature of the invitation, combined with the commitment to include further publishers at a later date, would not necessitate such an advertisement. Given the tightness of the timetable, this was a helpful decision, as such advertisement involves lengthy waiting periods after the notice is posted.

The invitation to tender explained the background to the pilot project and its goals. Publishers were given a month to provide a five-page expression of interest, addressing the specific matters outlined below. They were told that some would be shortlisted and one or a small number would be chosen during July. Interviews would be held with a shortlist before final decisions were taken.

F. Objectives of the Pilot Project

The objectives for the pilot were laid out under five headings: the product, formats and delivery, the site license, intellectual property rights, and commercial models. (Quotations are from the letter of May 1995 from the HEFCE head of policy to publishers.)

1. The Product

"Objective: the funding bodies wish to test within the initiative the ability of the site license concept to deliver scholarly material more widely to the academic community." Under this heading, publishers were invited to propose a package of not less than 30 and not more than 300 international, refereed journals, with a preference for primary research titles, for an annual license. A subset of a publisher's output could be proposed if it provided at least 30 English language titles. A spread of subjects was preferred, with proposals for increasing coverage during the 3 years.

2. Formats and Delivery

"Objective: the funding bodies wish to test within the initiative the dissemination of scholarly material to the Higher Education sector through a variety of formats, including electronic versions." Publishers were advised that journals in a variety of formats would be required and their attention was drawn to possible vehicles for electronic versions in either image or coded character format. Recommendations on access and retrieval software were required. Publishers' attention was drawn to NISS (National Information Services and Systems) based at Bath University, which provides general computer services; and BIDS (Bath Information and Data Services), which is the world's first database geared specifically to higher education and MIDAS (Manchester Information and Database Service), which provides data such as the UK census online, as well as HENSA (Higher Education National Software Archive), which gives access to public domain and shareware software. Other methods of providing electronic journal access could be suggested by publishers.

3. The Site License

"Objective: the funding bodies wish to test the model(s) adopted in the pilot for the legal arrangements for a national site license programme." Publishers were invited either to confer a license on all potential sites with central funding councils payment to publishers or to individual sites on payment by each of a fee, after payment of a lump sum by the funding councils. These models are later referred to as A and B. Sites were defined as all staff and students of higher education institutions funded by the four councils.

4. Intellectual Property Rights

"Objective: the funding bodies wish to test within the initiative the ability of the site license concept to allow the academic community more flexibility in the use of scholarly material." Ownership of all intellectual property rights remains with the publishers and authors. However, publishers were expected to agree that any licensed institution could be allowed to make as many printed or electronic copies as required in the pursuit of *bona fide* research. They were invited to suggest how this could be policed, bearing in mind that the copyright remained with the publisher and authors. The funding bodies agreed on their part to draw on their own expertise in the software and datasets areas for the protection of material in copyright.

5. Commercial Models

"Objective: the funding bodies wish to explore within the initiative the possibilities for increased value for money from the site license concept." Publishers were asked under this heading to show how their pricing mechanisms would fit with the overall objective to better use existing funds for higher education libraries and also provide better value for money than existing journal purchases. It was not expected that any license fees payable would have an impact on funds used to purchase journals from publishers not playing a part in the pilot project. Any pricing model or formula for the pilot should be sustainable beyond the pilot phase in some form, and year-on-year variations in price for the pilot should be proposed.

Aside from the five major objectives, publishers were told that a managing agent would be appointed for the pilot and monitoring and evaluation would take place. The pilot was intended to last 3 years beginning in January 1996, and appropriate sunset clauses on reinstatement of original paid subscriptions were envisaged. The flow of business to a healthy publishing industry was intended to be maintained. Difficulties for serials librarians were minimized.

In the five pages of their expressions of interest, publishers were asked to cover

1. Background issues: company size and ownership, involvement in electronic products, and existing involvement in licensing
2. Program: journal titles to be provided
3. Technical issues: methods of delivery and support services
4. Contractual issues: restrictions on usage with information on copyright notices and warranties
5. Commercial issues: charging proposals with formula for annual extension and procedures for termination.

Further information was given to publishers on the funding councils and on JANET, as well as a short description of the Follett report.

G. Expressions of Interest

Seven publishers submitted substantial "expressions of interest," although 10 others showed some initial interest. The request to send only five pages of submission was liberally ignored by the provision of extensive appendices. Documentation was sent out to the HEFCE advisory group and scored under seven major headings:

1. Overall probity and experience of the publisher relevant to the pilot.
2. Ability of the publisher to deliver scholarly material more widely to the academic community.
   a. number and range of journals
   b. quality of material for higher education
   c. increasing availability of material
   d. scope of "site" (e.g., are all students/staff included or any restrictions)
3. To increase flexibility in use of material
   a. flexibility
   b. restrictions on copying/storage
   c. policing/monitoring/reporting requirements

4. Variety of formats proposed
    a. range of formats
    b. electronic versions (including backup)
5. To test the legal arrangements for a national site license
6. To increase value for money
    a. value for money in the pricing model
    b. robustness of annual uprating proposals
    c. value for money on growth proposals
    d. savings from electronic formats
7. Management arrangements

Assessors from the advisory group were able to add general comments and provide questions to be used at subsequent interviews. Assessment was carried out very speedily over 5 days, concentrating on the ability of individual publishers to test the concept and on the practicability of proposals.

The seven publishers who expressed interest in the pilot project were all well-established houses, ranging from a list of 20 journal titles to one of 180. There was a preponderance of science and technology titles offered, probably because these are more likely to be available in electronic form.

It would not be proper here to name the applicants, but an outline description of their applications may be instructive. It should be said that because expressions of interest had to be drawn up to a very short time scale, this certainly discouraged some publishers from applying.

1. Publisher A

A small university press offering some 30 research titles in medicine and social sciences. They already worked with OCLC, ISI, and ADONIS and, although not all technical features were yet worked up, they were enthusiatic to take part in the pilot. They showed a particular concern over the number of users who would have access to their material.

2. Publisher B

A specialist scientific publisher offering 22 titles well down the road of providing World Wide Web, CD-ROM, and other electronic versions of journals. They gave the impression of having more interest in providing services directly to researchers rather than to libraries. However, they were willing to provide a right for participants to purchase hard copy at "deep discounts."

3. Publisher C

A large prestigious academic publisher offering 150 STM journals. Their existing experience in ADONIS and other such services showed them to have the relevant knowledge and expertise in-house. The proposal concentrated on electronic access, but they usefully proposed the setting up of an expert group to carry on the experiment.

4. Publisher D

A large prestigious academic publisher offering 80 titles in life sciences and social sciences, to a limited number of sites. All journals offered would be available electronically. Little was offered in the way of print copies. Their existing experience in licensing showed their capabilities in the area.

5. Publisher E

A major print and database publisher in a specialized scientific area offering 45 titles. Their experience in providing electronic access and work with OCLC as well as an existing help desk were all demonstrated. Various kinds of access (print, electronic, remote, local, and via commercial hosts) were offered with unlimited simultaneous usage.

6. Publisher F

A large prestigious academic publisher with a spread of 52 titles in science and social science offered. Relevant experience in ADONIS and other delivery modes was offered, with existing technical support. They showed particular concern over pricing of the license and suggested a third party to audit compliance with any negotiated terms.

7. Publisher G

A large academic publisher offering 180 varied titles in science with some social science. Relevant experience in ADONIS and work on licenses elsewhere was demonstrated. The offer included print and electronic versions with a gradual increase in the latter over the pilot period. All potential sites could be licensed.

H. Final Choices

Following the receipt of expressions of interest and the ranking by six members of the advisory group, interviews were held with four of the publishers. The interviews were conducted by the HEFCE head of policy, the university computing service director, and a specialist consultant who had been advising the group. No librarian members of the group were involved in the interviews. The interviews focused on the opportunities provided by each publisher's proposal to test the objectives set out in the invitation to express interest and on the practicality of publishers' proposals. The interviewers were keen to explore both commercial charging models as previously defined.

After the interviews it was decided to refer one of the proposals to FIGIT because it relied heavily on electronic access. The other three publishers, Academic Press, Blackwell, and the Institute of Physics, were invited for further discussion to develop more detailed proposals. These proposals would have to be approved by the Council of the Funding Bodies in early July 1995.

Academic Press proposed access to all their journal titles (200 plus) initially through libraries but eventually directly to academic staff and students. Paper and electronic versions would be available using price model A, i.e., license purchased centrally by the funding bodies.

Blackwell Publishers offered a license to cover a range of 80 titles from their three companies (Blackwell, Blackwell Science, and Munksgaard), which work as a consortium. Electronic journals would be available via their Infobike system. During the pilot, the number of journals could increase. They offered to operate under price model B, i.e., a fee paid by the funding bodies and discounted subscriptions paid by each institution or licensed site. Munksgaard later withdrew from the pilot before it started.

Institute of Physics Publishing offered an integrated comprehensive site license covering their material in all formats and forms. Using pricing model A, they would provide access to their material which, by January 1996, would all be available in flexible electronic form.

I. Progress of the Pilot Project

Following the choice being made of the three publishers, approval was granted by the funding councils in early July. Intense negotiation then began. Further attention was given to the appointment of a managing agent for which three major serials agents had already thrown their hats in the ring. A job specification for the managing agent was drawn up.

University vice chancellors were sent a letter in the early summer asking whether their university would like to take part in the initiative. This was followed in late August with information on the three publishers chosen for the pilot, but with scant detail on the proposed operation of the scheme. Negotiations with publishers were still in train (Richards, 1995). Libraries were advised to make periodical renewals in the normal way. Refunds for discounted subscriptions from the chosen publishers would be organized later. Library staff was assured that they would be consulted during the extensive review of the project and that full terms of participation would be sent out in due course. Press releases were sent out from the funding councils on August 31st.

More details on how to participate in the project were sent to universities in early November.

J. Terms and Conditions of the Pilot Project

1. General Licensing Terms

The letter to universities in November 1995 set out the ground rules for licensing: Academic Press is licensing under model A, whereby the publisher licenses the four funding bodies who then sublicense individual sites direct; and Blackwell and the Institute of Physics are intending to operate under model B and will license sites direct themselves. The licenses, although contractually different, will be similar as far as libraries are concerned.

Separate licenses will be needed for paper and electronic subscriptions for each site, but not for each individual subscription. For the purposes of the license, a site is defined as the premises of a higher education institution funded by HEFCE, SHEFC, HEFCW, and DENI, together with other places where staff and students work, including residences, lodgings, and homes of staff and students. Each site can obtain a free license and subscribe to as many or as few printed journals as they choose. The licenses are handled by the Joint Information Systems Committee (JISC) of the funding councils and JISC appointed an individual as the managing agent. On provision of any fees, initially set at a nominal £10 for Academic Press (free from the other two publishers), sites will be sent requisite passwords and search tools for electronic access. Payments for paper versions of journals are to be made (at discount) through libraries' normal periodical agents. If a library decides to participate in the project, it must take both electronic and paper (if it wants both) inside the terms of the license. Administrative complexities preclude taking one inside the license and one outside. Of course it will not be compulsory for universities to join the scheme, but the discounts proposed are likely to make the prospect attractive.

2. Intellectual Property Rights

Unrestricted photocopying of paper journals in the pilot project will be allowed so long as it is for *bona fide* research and not "for profit." Use of copyright material in the United Kingdom is determined by the 1988 Copyright, Designs, and Patents Act. Electrocopying is also allowed, but is restricted to use within the United Kingdom with no systematic downloading allowed. Copying articles for the provision of interlibrary loans is also allowed, as it is for study packs. The funding councils will retain archive copies of the electronic files.

3. Financial Terms

The funding bodies have paid the three publishers an undisclosed lump sum related to current usage of their material in UK university libraries. This money gives the universities the right to buy the designated publications at discount and to enjoy the copying use just described. A separate payment has acquired access to the publishers' databases for electronic materials.

Individual sites will pay for paper periodicals through their usual agents at discounts announced by the publishers and described later. Some recouping of the lump sums paid up front by the funding bodies will be made from individual sites according to their usage. This will be effectively administered by a reduced discount rate with publishers. Connection to electronic versions of the journals may require a nominal fee for Academic Press, payable probably to CHEST on acceptance of the license.

Every year the funding bodies will renegotiate their lump sum payments with the publishers. Higher take up by individual sites may reduce the lump sum payments and therefore the unit cost of information. It should be kept in mind that if connection to the electronic versions proves very popular, the initial connection charge may have to increase. Librarians are naturally concerned that their individual universities may claw back from them some of the money top sliced by the funding councils to pay the publishers, which affects the discounts to libraries.

Many (if not all) university libraries will have made their overall subscription decisions before first year licenses become available. Publishers will inform them through their agents how to obtain refunds and how to take out new subscriptions at the discounted rate. In practice, libraries have been sent lists directly from the publishers and are left to sort out the discounts for themselves. Agents are also preparing lists for libraries.

K. Publisher Press Releases

In the event the cart came well before the horse and the three publishers contacted libraries before the funding bodies did so, and indeed before contracts were signed.

Academic Press gave their participation the acronym APPEAL (Academic Press Print and Electronic Access License) and explained how libraries could obtain refunds for any of the periodicals to which they had already subscribed at full price. Their discount rate for paper copies was announced at 60% of published price.

Institute of Physics Publishing announced a rate of 70% for all their publications. Blackwell announced their discount rate at 60% on a restricted list of their journals.

For the first year of the pilot in 1996, libraries would probably get discounts before actually being licensed. Provision has been made for libraries to return discounts if they decide not to participate once they have seen the licenses.

L. Monitoring and Evaluation

Decisions have not yet been taken on exactly how to conduct monitoring and evaluation for the pilot. Bearing in mind the objectives expressed in the invitations to publishers, the monitoring and evaluation will be separated, with the former considering the mechanics of the pilot and the latter taking a measure of quality. It is hoped to be able to appoint an independent body to carry out this work. Librarians will be keen to check that publishers do not use the pilot to substantially alter their product. Publishers and the funding bodies will want to know what the libraries spend their saving on. Serials agents will want to quantify the effect on their business.

Termination notice of participation in the pilot is set at 2 years in order to give both publishers and librarians time to make alternative arrangements if they do decide to end the experiment.

M. Prospects for the Pilot Project

At the time of this writing, the UK Pilot Site License Initiative is poised to begin. Nobody can yet say how big the take-up will be or how successful the whole project will prove. However, it does show certain characteristics that set it apart from other licensing experiments. This is a national project that combines both print and electronic journal products. It presents libraries with discounts on paper products with a small one–off connection charge for electronic access and no ongoing transaction charges.

It will be fascinating to see how this project progresses and how it fits into the developing world of licensing by publishers. There is no doubt that negotiating the licenses has been a difficult and complex task. This was envisaged by Hunter (1992) when she said that "negotiating a truly national site license is an awesome challenge."

IV. Implications of Licensing

A. General Effects

Because licensing of periodicals (and other material) is fairly new on the scene in libraries, it is worthwhile speculating on its possible effects on the major players: authors and publishers, serials agents, and finally libraries and their users.

As a general point, there is some disappointment that what is being licensed is either existing hard copy or an electronic version of the same. Breaking the mold of the journal structure has scarcely been attempted. Because most licensed products are electronic, with the exception of the UK

Pilot Project, the need for common user interfaces is enhanced. Users do not want to have to learn more and more sets of software. Electronic products are also rooted in the areas of science and technology, with some social science, notably at Tilburg University. Humanities seldom enter the frame.

Despite these caveats, testing licensing as a concept is a worthwhile exercise for all parties (except perhaps the agents). The pricing models will probably prove to be the greatest stumbling block in any future developments. The effects on all links in the information chain will be different but inextricably linked.

B. Effects of Licensing on Publishers

For publishers, licensing in the current climate of library cuts and cancellations is a logical extension of their work. To some extent licensing allows greater dissemination of their material in a more flexible way. Publishers will retain revenue, perhaps a more assured revenue, using a subscription format as before instead of transaction charges (Kutz, 1992). Indeed, publishers, who must be remembered do not enter licensing with philanthropic attitudes toward libraries, can breathe new life into the old body of journals, from which they have made so much income in the past. They may not even need to provide discounts to agents if they deal directly with subscribers for bundles of titles.

Naturally there are inherent dangers to publishers in going down the road of licensing. University libraries with separate licenses could work together to provide distributed electronic access between them, something along the lines of a national periodicals centre (Kutz, 1992). They are of course concerned about copyright and downloading of material for further copying. The policing of the UK license will depend heavily on the experience of CHEST in policing distributed database use (University of Bath, 1993).

Pushed to its ultimate extreme, publishers could face a monopsony where a powerful single university, or group of universities, becomes a controller of the market for a particular publisher. Even halfway along the line publishers will become separated from their familiar market. They could even have to change roles to become agents themselves with all the bureaucracy that entails (Hunter, 1992).

Licenses as they currently operate are at least transitory or experimental, but they are certainly not long term. If libraries move in and out of such experiments they cannot guarantee to continue subscribing to material they may have accessed during the period of a license. Equally they cannot, with present funding pressures, agree to continue licenses which become more expensive as pilot projects end. While publishers may face a diminishing market, freedom of choice for librarians may also be curtailed. Publishers may promise much for pilot project purposes when in fact they cannot deliver. The introduction of hitherto unavailable electronic products for the UK Pilot will undoubtedly take some time to deliver after the start date.

C. Effects of Licensing on Serials Agents

Serials agents, used to being caught in the middle between publishers and libraries, are potentially facing the greatest squeeze from licensing. As licenses are adopted they will face the messy business of myriad cancellations without compensatory new business. This loss of revenue comes on top of the squeeze on discounts that they are already facing from publishers.

Librarians, from bitter experience, are already worried by potential bankruptcy in the world of agents. Canceling and transferring subscriptions are time consuming and costly. Perhaps they will effectively be forced to lose the services of agents who handle their myriad invoices, processing, and claims needs with multiple publishers.

Agents could have a valid role by helping libraries negotiate licenses, set up passwords, or monitor use. It will be up to agents to involve themselves in order not to be ignored.

D. Effects of Licensing on Libraries and Their Users

1. Collection Considerations

One of the first concerns expressed by librarians over the site license project in the United Kingdom was the potential for central control over acquisitions and collection development in libraries. They were concerned not only about being coerced into taking products they would not otherwise purchase, but also that the status of certain poorly regarded journals might be raised when they appeared as part of a license. If users had access only to certain journals they might assume that these were the best and only journals in a particular field. Conflict and overlap between different bundles of journals, under different licenses, could accentuate the squeeze of periodicals on books. Libraries might be obliged to duplicate coverage and costs in order to get access to titles they require.

The reliance on science has already been mentioned as a particular influence on the licensing scene. Librarians might be forced to take unwanted material because the price is attractive to their budget holders or purchasing departments. At the furthest extreme they fear that licensing could be a publishers' scam to get them to buy material that publishers are not getting sales for and that libraries do not want.

2. Financial Considerations

On the financial side, licenses will provide libraries with the comfort of a known fixed price unless there are transaction charges to be met. The unit cost of information may actually reduce (at least for electronic access) not least because service charges to agents could disappear. On the latter point, some libraries do get discounts from agents for prompt payment. However, there is no guarantee for publishers that savings will be spent by libraries on more periodicals. A major concern of libraries may be that once they have signed and paid for licenses, publishers could take advantage of the situation to change formats, size, or publishing rates as well as the content of journals. At the higher level the fair price for a license is difficult for libraries to calculate and they may be uncertain of their ground. Pricing for institutions, versus pricing for individuals, may be complicated if publishers are not getting the revenue they consider essential.

3. Legal and Technical Considerations

For libraries the licensing world may present even more complexity than the database networking licenses they currently try to negotiate. Added to this is the difficulty of policing the licenses as a creative computer-literate community pits their wits against technology. Electronic access begs again the need for a common user interface, not the proliferation of software. Underlying the electronic licenses are the absolute costs of the necessary hardware and training for libraries.

Of course electronic access can free up expensive shelf space as well as staff costs in the circulation of print materials. To be set against this there are the problems of long-term archiving, one of the traditional roles of libraries. Who will store back files of the licensed material? In the United Kingdom the funding councils will fulfill this role in agreement with the publishers. This will in itself enable a reduction in interlibrary loan or other document delivery services. But can we be sure that long-term archiving of electronic material will be secure? ADONIS advertises itself as a secure archive on CD-ROM, but there may be storage problems allied to the sheer number of discs. At the end of the day would libraries have to return holdings after a license ends? On the whole it is not likely that publishers will be interested in an archival role.

4. Advantages and Disadvantages for Libraries

The points made so far in this section would seem to indicate a negative attitude toward licenses but there are advantages. As the UK Pilot Project shows, wider dissemination of scholarly material is possible. Access can become more flexible and, with due care over pricing, value for money can be improved. These advantages have obvious spin-offs for library users who will see cheaper print-off costs and, depending on the license, on-demand printing of multiple copies for classes. The copyright barrier may be lowered somewhat. More information could be free at the point of use. License initiatives may also please authors because, as a subset of library users, their work could get a wider readership.

What we may also see, however, is the bypassing of libraries themselves, as licenses purchased by university authorities (not libraries) go straight to library users' computers, missing out entirely the route via the library (Lindsay and Roberts, 1994). The onus will be on librarians to ensure that this does not happen.

V. Conclusion

Libraries are at an experimental stage in licensing the output of publishers. Pilot projects have really only gone live during the 1990s and are still feeling their way. Most license projects depend on the printed periodical, particularly the scientific periodical, as a base. However, there are moves to go beyond print versions with Web access and beyond science as publishers and libraries diversify. The UK National Site License Pilot Project is an ambitious and potentially rewarding initiative.

Librarians need to keep a watchful eye on developments in order to remain firmly fixed in the information chain. The part they play in information transfer cannot be guaranteed, and their worth needs to be proven to library users and nonusers alike. Serials agents need to carve out a new facilitating role for themselves. Publishers need to be aware of current publishing outside the mainstream. We may eventually see electronic licensing as one of the nails in the coffin of paper periodicals. What librarians must not lose sight of is their duty to their users, to provide the best available service in whatever form that appears.

References

Bekhradnia, B. (1995). Pilot site licence initiative for academic journals. *Serials* **8**, 247–250.
BioMedNet. (1995). *BioMedNet the worldwide club for biomedical scientists.* http://BioMedNet.com/ BioMedNet/biomed.htm.
Blackwell Science. (1995). *ADONIS home page.* http://adonis.blacksci.co.uk.
Butter, K. (1994). Red Sage: The next step in delivery of electronic journals. *Medical Reference Services Quarterly* **13**, 75–81.
Campbell, R. (1991). ADONIS: A prophecy fulfilled. *The Bookseller* **4480**, 1304.
Chapman, L. (1991). Book acquisitions in higher education libraries in England: Collection development or damage limitation. *Library Acquisitions: Practice and Theory* **15**, 287–294.
Chapman, L. (1995). The HEFCE Pilot Site Licence initiative. In *Endangered species? Evolving Strategies for Library Collection Management* (H. Woodward and M. Morley, eds.), pp. 49–56. UK Serials Group and National Acquisitions Group, Loughborough.
DeLoughry, T. (1993). Effort to provide scholarly journals by computer tries to retain the look and feel of printed publications. *Chronicle of Higher Education* **39**, A19–A20.

Designers and Artists Collecting Society (DACS). (1995). DACS slide library licence briefing: Report on meeting at the National Portrait Gallery. London, 19 June 1995. *Audiovisual Librarian* **21**, 270–275.

Dijkstra, J. (1994). A digital library in the mid-nineties, ahead or on schedule? *Information Services and Use* **14**, 267–277.

Elsevier Science. (1995). *TULIP: The University Licensing Program.* http://www.elsevier.nl/info/projects/tulip.htm.

Geleijnse, H. (1994). Journal articles on the desktop: Elsevier and Tilburg experiment. *Managing Information* **1**, 34–35.

Gelfand, J., and Needleman, M. (1995). TULIP: Participating in an experiment of electronic journal access: Administrative and systems challenges to ensure success. IATUL Proceedings **4**, 150–159.

Hunter, K (1992). The national site license model. *Serials Review* **18**, 71–72, 91.

Hunter, K., and Zijlstra, J. (1994). TULIP: The university licensing project. *Journal of Interlibrary Loan, Document Delivery and Information Supply* **4**, 19–22.

Kutz, M. (1992). Distributing the costs of scholarly journals: Should readers contribute? *Serials Review* **18**, 73–74, 96.

Law, D. (1994). The development of a national policy for dataset provision in the UK: A historical perspective. *Journal of Information Networking* **1**, 103–116.

Lindsay, J., and Roberts, B. (1994). Academics can do it for themselves (serial publishing). *Serials* **7**, 153–156.

Lucier, R. (1992). Towards a knowledge management environment: A strategic framework. *Educom Review* **27**, 24–31.

OCLC. (1995). *Elsevier Science/OCLC Electronic Publishing Pilot Program.* http://www.oclc.org/oclc/promo/els9254/9254.htm.

Pica. (1995). *Pica connects libraries.* http://www.pica./nl.

Richards H. (1995). HEFCE buys the right to copy freely. *Times Higher Education Supplement* **1182**, 1.

Stern, B., and Compier, H. (1990). ADONIS: Document delivery in the CD-ROM age. *Interlending and Document Supply* **18**, 79–87.

UK Educational and Research Networking Associations (UKERNA). (1995). *JANET home page.* http://www.jnt.ac.uk.

UK Higher Education Statistics Agency. (1995). *University Statistics.* Annual. UCAS, Cheltenham, Glos.

UK Joint Funding Councils' Libraries Review Group. (1993) *Report.* Higher Education Funding Council for England, Bristol.

University of Bath. (1993). *Combined Higher Education Software Team: Code of Conduct for the Use of Software or Datasets.* University of Bath, Bath.

University of Bath. (1995). *BIDS home page.* http://www.bids.ac.uk.

University of California, San Francisco. (1995). *The Red Sage Project.* http://www.library.ucsf.edu/lib/gen/redsage.html.

University of Michigan. (1995). *TULIP: The University Licensing Project.* http://circe.engin.umich.edu/tulip/tulip.html.

Willis, K., et al. (1994). TULIP—the university licensing program: Experiences at the University of Michigan. *Serials Review* **20**, 39–47.

Domain of Adult Fiction Librarianship

Liangzhi Yu*
Department of Information Management
Nankai University
Tianjin, People's Republic of China

Ann O'Brien
Department of Information and Library Studies
Loughborough University
Loughborough, Leicestershire LE11 3TU, England

I. Introduction

This review focuses on adult fiction provision in libraries. The area of children's and young adults' fiction is, of course, very important but needs special consideration beyond the scope of this chapter. The review is primarily concerned with the general collection management of fiction: understanding fiction as a type of library material, understanding fiction readers, collection management issues such as acquisition, current methods of making fiction available both on the shelves and through conventional and novel retrieval systems, the promotion of fiction to library readers, and reference services.

In the library and information profession, the term "fiction librarianship" is still a relatively fresh one. It appeared in 1981 in Atkinson's monograph *Fiction Librarianship*. But the academic area to which it refers can be traced back much further to the various controversies on fiction provision of more than a century ago. The implication of this debate on the formation and the development of fiction librarianship has been twofold. First, it signaled a professional concern with fiction provision in the library. As Atkinson (1981) noted "the debate as to whether fiction provision is justifiable at all, and if so, to what extent and with what restrictions and provisos it should be supplied, has been the brooding Mount Etna of librarianship for generations" (p. 7). Second, it revealed a set of prejudices against fiction provision and the related emerging academic domain.

* Present address: Department of Information and Library Studies, Loughborough University, Loughborough, Leicestershire LE11 3TU, England.

151

This early professional concern with fiction and its provision in the library was nurtured by the rapid increase in fiction lending in public libraries from the end of the past century. The continuing popularity of fiction among library readers and its establishment as one of the major resources in libraries proved that fiction deserved more serious attention than simply being treated as a nuisance. This was well exemplified by the increasing research interest in fiction classification on which Burgess (1936) commented: "If classification is a really good thing, why should not the fiction reader share its benefits?" (p. 179).

In recent years the growing interest in fiction services has gradually built up to a quite distinguished area in librarianship, which is characterized by its aim to improve professional performance in serving the public whose interest in fiction is basically recreational rather than academic. The heritage of the early social prejudice against fiction provision, however, has suppressed, to some extent, the development of the domain. Its growth has consequently been agonizingly slow.

It is clear that any domain can be strengthened internally by critical review. This is of special significance in a developing area such as fiction librarianship where a research paradigm has not yet been established and problems due to this lack might hinder the further development of the domain.

This chapter therefore aims to: (1) look at recent progress on the major aspects of fiction librarianship, based mainly on the literature published since 1981; and (2) highlight the general problems in current research. For these purposes, "fiction librarianship" refers here to the research area that aims to improve library services for fiction reading as a leisure activity.

II. An Operational Delimitation of the Domain

Research in this area has been predominantly driven by different practical problems and rarely guided by any conceptual framework throughout the 1900s. Consequently, the domain has remained rather amorphous. At the stage when Atkinson proposed "fiction librarianship" as its heading, there did not even exist any certainty as to which aspect of the subject on which to concentrate (Dixon, 1986, p. viii).

This section attempts to propose an operational structure of the domain in order to form a context in which each piece of research can be examined in relation to others. It is called an operational structure because the authors are well aware that an examination of the conceptual framework underpinning the practice of fiction services is beyond the scope of a review such as this.

Such an operational structure has been laid down by a number of general works in the domain. Atkinson (1981) traced the origin of fiction librarianship back to the debate over various historical problems with the subject, which were concerned mainly with a theoretical view of a library's true function. His outlook on fiction librarianship, however, is rather pragmatic. He defined the area as being composed of the principles and practice of several major professional activities: acquisition, processing, promotion, and preservation. Dixon (1986) incorporated studies on different types of fiction, as well as surveys on users. Kinnell (1991), by contrast, provided a much broader view of the domain, which was initially proposed for the purpose of staff training. The domain knowledge required of professional librarians as she outlined, includes:

1. The nature of fiction
2. Genres of fiction
3. The fiction industry
4. Readership
5. Selection and acquisition
6. Organization
7. Promotion
8. Information sources

This broader view encompasses the major elements involved in the communication between the author and the reader, in which fiction functions as media, libraries being the major channel. It is hardly surprising that this broader view provides a more comprehensive and realistic picture of the domain knowledge because linking the author and the reader in the process of their communication is really what fiction service is about.

The broader view is, therefore, also applied in this chapter. Viewed from this perspective, four research focuses emerged from previous studies, dealing with different elements of the communication process:

1. Fiction itself—research focusing on this aspect deals with the characteristics and functions of fiction, from the library's point of view.
2. Professional activities—related research focuses on libraries' performance in fiction provision; e.g., fiction acquisition, fiction processing and representation, fiction promotion, collection management, and so on.
3. Fiction readership—fiction readers' needs and behavior.
4. Fiction policy—which reflects general attitudes toward fiction on the one hand, and to fiction readers on the other hand, and the perceived professional function in linking the reader to the book.

The professional activities, which outline the domain of a specific aspect, play a paramount role in the development of the whole domain. Such fiction services, on the one hand, raise problems and engender demand for practical

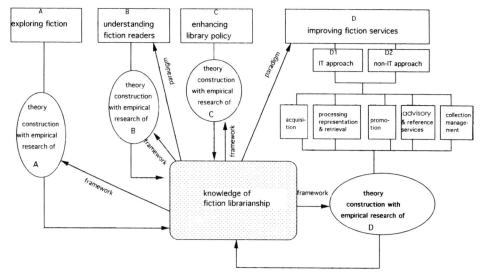

Fig. 1 The structure of the domain of fiction librarianship.

research, and on the other hand, put forward questions and evidence for theory construction.

With new technology prevailing in many professional activities, it is possible to distinguish two modes of services and related research: (1) IT based professional activities and (2) conventional professional activities.

Whatever areas are studied, it is expected that this will contribute to the domain in either or both of two ways: to improve the practice of fiction services or to build up the body of the domain knowledge, which in turn, provides a theoretical base or principles to both practice and further research.

The domain structure with all contingent areas discussed above is illustrated in Fig. 1.

III. Exploring Fiction as a Type of Library Material

Research in this context, unlike literary criticism, sees fiction as a special type of library material, waiting to be integrated into an individual library's stock to be processed and disseminated to the reader.

From this perspective, the following issues have been of special interest to previous researchers:

Fiction attributes/features
Possible dichotomy in fiction
Value/function of fiction

A. Fiction Attributes/Features

Fiction is different from nonfiction, especially in terms of its content attributes. At its most superficial level, fiction is commonly regarded as consisting of works of imagination, while nonfiction consists of fact. Pejtersen (1978, 1979a; Pejtersen and Austin, 1983) and Beghtol (1991, 1994) went much deeper in examining the special attributes of fiction contents, for the purpose of fiction processing and retrieval. Pejtersen did this from the users' point of view. In order to understand how the "aboutness" of fiction is perceived by the reader, she observed actual conversations between fiction readers and librarians. The verbal expression of readers' needs were analyzed. The study suggested that fiction content is usually perceived from different perspectives: subject, author's intention, and setting. She further argued that the author's intention is the most problematic. It is open to varying interpretations and thus brings about great subjectivity in fiction analysis (Pejtersen and Austin, 1984).

Beghtol (1991, 1994) studied the attributes of fiction content from the point of view of literary warrant. Her analysis of fiction works (fiction warrant) and literary critical works (critical warrant) revealed that fiction usually consists of multiple elements (corresponding broadly to Pejtersen's dimensions): characters, events, space, time, and other elements. The most remarkable difference between Beghtol's and Pejtersen's perception of fiction content is that Beghtol disproved the position of more abstract information such as author's intention in fiction analysis. She argued that "the 'atmospheric aspects' and 'ideological patterns' suggest a different level of interaction with narrative, that is they seem less like sources of 'data' about a fictional world and more like 'information' constructed from a summation of data elements and possibly further cumulated into 'knowledge' " (Beghtol, 1994, p. 128).

B. Possible Dichotomy in Fiction

Ideologically, the distinction between so-called "high-brow" fiction and its opposite has existed throughout the debates over fiction provision from the last century. Mann (Mann and Burgoyne, 1969; Mann, 1982a, 1982b) first conceptualized the dichotomy of serious fiction and light fiction in his sociological study of books and reading. He warned that they are actually two contrasting points along the continuum of types of fiction and that to dichotomize them in practice might be dangerously misleading.

Serious fiction, according to this study consists of works of "imagination which aspire to being genuine contributions to thought and culture. Dealing as they do, imaginatively with the personal problems of characters in special social situations, the novels are a commentary on contemporary or historical society" (Mann, 1982a, p. 17). Light fiction, however, "is written for entertainment and escapism. . . . It is much more time filling in its function and is rarely considered as having any creative or intellectual element" (Mann, 1982a, p. 17).

Spiller (1980), in his study of fiction readers' behavior, applied Mann's concept and model to examine readers' general preference. He broke down fiction into recreational fiction and serious fiction. (This study is reviewed in more detail in Section IV,D.) Evidence exists that in other surveys such dichotomy was also often applied (Dixon, 1986).

C. Value/Function of Fiction

Mann (Mann and Burgoyne, 1969; Mann, 1982a) related the function of fiction to its "seriousness" and "lightness." He argued that the function of serious fiction is to challenge the reader's beliefs and attitudes and reading it confers status on the reader. The function of light fiction is purely to entertain and reading it is intrinsically satisfying for the reader.

The social and cultural attitudes related to such a distinction—the cultural discrimination against light fiction—has also engendered a number of defenders. It is first of all defended for its entertainment function. Rosenberg (1986) argued that the glamour of genre fiction is that it is for entertainment and the reading of it is carefree. Gerhard (1991) stated that among all value constituents of mystery fiction—recreational or entertainment value, value of mental stimulation, knowledge value, literary value—the recreational or entertainment value is the most important. Abbey (1981) in her defense of science fiction, remarked that "Science fiction has its own values. First, it provides entertainment and escape. . . . It also isolates aspects of our world so that we can examine them clearly and see them in a new way " (p. 587).

Light fiction has also been defended for its value of conveying meanings. Treuherz (1984), for example, sees romance as a genre that not only reflects social and moral values, but also reflects and communicates changes in these values to many who read little else. Hugo (1985), through a critical analysis of a number of well-known fictional books, argued that good stories convey meaning in a similar way as myth does. "Myth endures because it speaks to elements in us that are at the core of our being. The drive to endure. To love and procreate. To survive" (p. 172). Furthermore, a good story often bears in it value judgment by showing the defeat of wickedness by virtue. Bodart (1994) defended horror also on these grounds: "Maybe, learning that evil exists in all kinds of forms, and in many of them it can be vanquished, will remind us that we can fight back just as hard as the characters in the books we read" (p. 25). Abbey quoted Bodem to make explicit this value of fantasy:

> Since the morning of mankind, fantasy has delighted young and old, has given wings to the mind, revealed deeper meanings of being, brought symbolic satisfactions to the needs of self and with a sense of wonder has refreshed men for the tasks of reality. (Bodem in Abbey, 1981, p. 584)

The studies reviewed above have seen fiction as a special type of library material. Their general aim is to contribute to the body of knowledge of fiction librarianship by establishing a set of fiction attributes and values and hence provide guiding principles for its processing and collection evaluation. Although the domain has seen remarkable achievements toward this objective, fiction still remains a problematic library material. It must also be noted that a large proportion of works reviewed here consisted mainly of personal opinions. Many arguments were without solid empirical evidence. Even when evidence was produced, secondary information sources played an overriding role compared with empirical investigation.

IV. Understanding Fiction Readers

Although fiction dominates what people read for pleasure, the fiction reader, however, had remained a humble and fairly marginal topic in general reading studies up to the early 1980s. Examples of such general studies include Rubakin's (Rubakin and Bethmann, 1937) study of reading psychology, Bryan's work (1939, 1940) about the therapeutic function of reading, and Mann's sociological study about books and reading (Mann and Burgoyne, 1969; Mann, 1982a, 1982b).

The lack of understanding of fiction readers has hampered the development of fiction services in libraries, as Spiller (1980) argued in the case of British libraries and Pejtersen and Austin (1983) in the sphere of fiction retrieval.

Prompted by these researchers, the 1980s and the first part of 1990s have seen a number of studies of fiction readers. Among them are Spiller's (1980) study on general fiction readers, in which 500 people from five U.K. public libraries were investigated with a structured interview, asking what types of fiction were issued and how novels were chosen; Pejtersen's (1979b) study on readers' construction of their searching strategies, in which 134 librarian–reader conversations were observed and analyzed; Jennings and Sear's (1986) study on how readers actually choose their books, in which 135 readers from a public library were interviewed; Spenceley's (1980) and Mann's (1980) studies on literary fiction readers, in which 100 literary fiction readers were interviewed; and Goodall's (1989) review of several studies on readers' browsing behavior in public libraries.

A. The Fiction Reader

The profile of the fiction reader, revealed in these studies, is more likely to consist of women than men. Women constituted 63% in Spiller's (1980) sample, 68% in Jennings and Sear's (1986) sample, and 65% in Spenceley's (1980). Mann (1991) confirmed that such figures are in accordance with Euromonitor's survey on national readership (Mann, 1991).

Findings regarding the reader's profile in terms of age group show less agreement. The general reader in Spiller's and Jennings and Sear's studies tend to be much older than the literary reader in Spencely's. Whether such findings suggest some sort of correlation between readers' age and types of books is not clear.

B. Reading Needs and Motivation

The concept of "needs" or "motives," according to McClellan (1981) and Hatt (1976), refers to the drives that operate below the surface of the consciousness. "Often, we have little control over our needs. . . . What we have at a more conscious level are goals. We set up our goals in order to satisfy our wants" (Hatt, 1976, p. 41).

This concept was applied by Brewis, Gericke, and Kruger (1994) to identify a number of motives that give rise to the action of fiction reading. These motives include: reading for pleasure (this is an inner satisfaction that gives rise to profound psychological relaxation, amusement, and entertainment); reading to relieve tension (this is to alleviate the tension imposed by individual's social roles with the experience of fictional tension); reading for communication purposes; reading for societal consciousness; reading for the reinforcement of personal and social values; reading for education; reading for escape; and reading for assistance in resolving personal problems.

These motives, however, according to McClellan (1981), are still surface motivations. Deeper motivations in the light of theories of psychology, are:

1. The testing of plans, i.e., to see how other people's plans and experience have worked out
2. The search for meaning—orientation in relation to life and other people
3. The need to allow the conscious mind to maintain an undisturbed rhythm so permitting the conscious part of the mind to deal with problems and frustrations
4. Confirmation—the realization that others think and feel as we do

5. The sense of belonging
6. Discharge of feelings
7. Extending our range of conceptions
8. Empathy—putting oneself into another's situation

The relationship with other people seems to be the fundamental element underlying these deeper motivations. This is explained by psychologists such as Harding with the concept of "readers as onlookers," watching and studying humans "in motion" while reading (Harding in McClellan, 1981) because "stories bring the abstractions [of the psychological analysis of the individual] to life by presenting specific examples of the individual acting in a social setting" (McClellan, 1981, p. 79).

These studies, from a theoretical perspective, examined different levels of motivation for fiction reading. At the deepest level seems to lie people's unrelenting interest in examining other people for meaning, for testing plans, for confirmation, for a sense of belonging, and for emotional exchange. At the more superficial level lie various motives for pleasure, for escape, for communication, for education, and so on. These needs and motives eventually lead people to set up a goal of reading fiction, among other goals in their daily life. Therefore, the reading context for each person, as well as his or her response to a particular text, possesses a uniqueness. "The prediction of responses by a number of unknown potential readers is virtually impossible" (McClellan, 1981, p. 78).

From this proposition, McClellan went further to warn those who tend to assess fiction with certain standards that "we cannot, therefore, with any certainty, assess the kinds of values which actually emerge from the reading of a particular text" (McClellan, 1981, p. 78).

C. Readers' Formulation of Their Needs

Perhaps the next stage in the chain that runs from needs and motivation through goals to the act of reading is to form certain criteria about the books that the reader expects to meet his needs. Pejtersen (1978, 1979a) is among the pioneers who saw the importance of such criteria—the formulation of readers' needs—in system design and other fiction services. Her research has been almost the sole contribution to the theory of such formulations.

The empirical research from which her theory about readers' enquiries was developed, consisted of observation and analysis of actual conversations between fiction readers and librarians. It was found that fiction readers tend to express their needs in a multidimensional way. Four dimensions were identified from this study:

1. Subject: the subject content of a novel, what the story is about, including action and course of events, psychological development and description and social relations.

2. Frame: the setting in time and place chosen by the author as the scenario of a work.
3. Author's intention: the theme of a novel; i.e., the author's attitude toward the subject or the set of ideas and emotions that the author wants to communicate to his readers, including emotional experience and cognition and information.
4. Accessibility: the level of communication, described in terms of those properties that can facilitate or inhibit communication; e.g., difficulty of language.

This theory has been implemented in many of her subsequent studies on fiction retrieval and representation, which are discussed later (see Sections VI,B and VI,C).

D. Book Searching and Selection Methods

Pejtersen's research was concerned mainly with the conceptual perception of readers' enquiries. This perception, unfortunately, has hardly ever been implemented either in development of searching tools or in the arrangement of library stock. The question of how readers actually select books in the absence of retrieval or searching tools are treated in a number of other studies.

The practical methods readers apply in their book searching and selection can be roughly broken down into two types: (1) browsing, and (2) searching for specific author/title.

Browsing, as a method of book selection, involves "looking around," with the reader hoping to encounter desired books or serendipity. It is used as the major method by more than half of the readers when they choose books (Goodall, 1989).

It has also been found that browsing involves scrutinizing a large amount of information from the book itself. The sources of such information, e.g., title, blurb, and so on, formed the actual decision-making factors in book selection (Goodall, 1989; Jennings and Sear, 1986; Spiller 1980). Although the names of the sources and their exact role-ranking vary from survey to survey, it is agreed that blurb, text, cover, and title play the most important part in browsers' decision for book selection. Goodall suggested that blurb and text (particularly the blurb) are the deciding factors. Speak (1990) also emphasized type size as an important factor in elderly people's browsing.

Searching for specific books relies heavily on author's names. Spiller (1980) found that searching with author names is as important as browsing in the fiction section. Most of his respondents had a small list of favorite authors. Some even carried with them notebooks full of author names. People usually like to borrow books by authors they have read (Goodall, 1989), but they may also try new authors if these are recommended by reliable resources such as friends, book reviews, television, and so on (Spiller, 1980).

These studies have also revealed a large amount of transformation between browsing mode and specific searching mode (Goodall, 1989; Spiller, 1980). In Spiller's study, the combination of these two modes reached the high percentage of 77.6%. Such transformation most frequently happens when readers fail in their specific searching and resort to random browsing and this can result in a large number of substitution books. Goodall (1989) therefore suggested that there is a high substitutability among fictional books.

It is difficult to evaluate these practical searching techniques with conventional measurements of retrieval performance, because readers appear to be able to find some books whatever searching modes they have applied. Goodall (1989) found that 94% of readers succeeded in finding some books to borrow. But many studies did attempt to reach a sort of evaluation by checking readers' satisfaction with these techniques. Most studies obtained readers' reactions directly by interview. For example, Goodall found that when interviewed, about half of the library users said they had experienced search failure. Some research attempted to established correlation between search method and reading satisfaction. For example, a number of studies (Spenceley, 1980; Turner in Goodall, 1989) indicated that there is a correlation between a reader's knowledge of a book before borrowing it and the resulting satisfaction level with that book. The more a reader knows about a book in advance, the more he or she will enjoy reading it. Therefore, specific searching results in a high satisfaction level in reading while random browsing results in a low satisfaction level.

Although it is not clear to what extent the above correlation can be generalized and accepted (because of the sample size, sampling methods, and above all, the lack of statistical inference), the studies and other evaluations seem to suggest that at least two cautions should be kept in mind in the interpretation of findings regarding searching techniques. First, although most readers' book selection involved random browsing, there is a danger of jumping to the conclusion that they are in favor of such a search mode because, in reality, they have few alternatives. Second, it might be misleading to emphasize solely the need to improve fiction browsing simply on the ground that the majority are using it, especially when the potential of complex searching facilities has not been fully explored.

E. Book Preference

Readers' preference for categories of books and formats of books (paperback vs hardback) has also been investigated either by survey or circulation studies.

There seems to exist a preference for light fiction or recreational fiction. Jennings and Sear (1986) checked preferred author names in their interview with 135 readers and found most of them were light fiction authors. Spiller (1980) examined the categories of returned books, of which 76% were found to be recreational books. Dixon (1986) summarized the result of a number of surveys including many in-house surveys and concluded that in no survey did the proportion of light fiction ever fall below 50% of the issues. Sumsion (1991, 1992), making use of data from the U.K. Public Lending Right, also showed an apparent bias toward light fiction.

In terms of book format, research findings tend to suggest that most library users do not have a particular preference between hardback and paperback books (Christensen, 1984; Goodall, 1989), although evidence in favor of paperback has also been noted in some cases (Hayden, 1987). Research also showed that fiction readers do not favor short stories (Sumsion, 1992), but they do not care much about copyright date (Christensen, 1984; Moore, 1982).

V. Enhancing Library Policies

The rationale of whether to stock fiction has been one of the major concerns of early professional controversies. The objective of the debate was to work toward an acceptable and working policy on fiction and fiction readers in a society with disdain for both of them. In the United Kingdom, the debate did gradually come to a resolution of sorts in the early twentieth century, which was stated in a policy form without dissent:

1. The function of a public lending library is to provide good literature for circulation amongst its readers, and that the same test must be applied to its works of fiction as to the books in its other departments: they must have literary or educational value.
2. Every public library should be amply supplied with fiction that has attained the position of classical literature.
3. The provision of mere ephemeral fiction of no literary, moral, or educational value, even if without offense, is not within the proper province of a public lending library (Sturges and Barr, 1992, p. 25).

Today the issue of whether to stock fiction is more or less resolved, but controversy over the library's attitudes toward the dichotomy of light fiction and literary fiction has never diminished, as indicated by the discussion over Baltimore County Public Library's "give 'em what they want" policy (Sweetland, 1994). Arguments on this issue actually signaled the modern professional dissent between two different library policies: a library function-oriented policy and a market-oriented policy. Although the former emphasizes the library's postulated professional role, the latter places the user at the center of any activity.

Although less fashionable today, the library function oriented policy is not without advocates. Hermenze (1981), for example, questioned the policy adopted by some public libraries that "stock the library with multiple copies of currently advertised titles so that people won't have to wait for the books they seek" (p. 2191). He argued that a professional librarian, whose service the public has paid for with their taxes, should be able to meet much higher expectations than just provide what the reader wants. A librarian should know what the standard, important books are and make them available to the public.

> One of the functions of the public library is to serve as a place where a citizen can educate himself or herself. Trash novels and books on the latest fad diet do not provide much of an education. The librarian who is content with buying only what is currently popular, beside abdicating the professional role as book expert, is doing a serious disservice to the community by eliminating the educational mission of the public library. (Hermenze, 1981, p. 2192)

A similar argument was put forward recently by Riel (1993) more recently to emphasize libraries' educational function in fiction service. "People want many things but it does not follow that the state should freely provide them. The most popular fiction is easily available elsewhere and is not expensive to buy. . . . We need to be able to demonstrate that libraries are pro-active and educative in their approach to fiction" (p. 84).

However, there seems to be an increasing move toward market-oriented policy. In the United Kingdom, the strengthening of market-oriented policy is attributed to much social and political shifting over the past decade (Kinnell and MacDougall, 1994), resulting in the decline of book funds and the growth of fiction titles (Goodall, 1991). The policy is promoted (by its advocates) as the likely means for libraries to survive in future society. "Library purists may be horrified at what they see as a 'supermarket' approach to librarianship. Without orientation towards its users, the library is in danger of dying" (Reader, 1982, p. 41). These "cautious anti-marketing attitudes toward fiction must be replaced by the 'go for it' proactive attitude of the commercial world if libraries are to survive" (Goodall, 1991, p. 138). Libraries should learn from the policy of industry: to listen to the customers, for readers do know what they want (Williams, 1990).

VI. Improving Fiction Services

Fiction services—activities in libraries to manage fiction resources and make them available for readers' use—roughly fall into the following categories:

Fiction acquisition
Fiction processing

Fiction representation and retrieval
Fiction promotion
Fiction readers reference/advisory services
Fiction collection management

A great deal of research has been devoted to the improvement of these activities.

A. Fiction Acquisition

Fiction acquisition in U.K. and U.S. libraries more or less follows certain standard procedures, which are well described in such textbooks as Atkinson's (1981) and articles such as Sweetland's (1991, 1994).

Despite the long history of these procedures, they are still found to be lacking in scientific elements. "As a specialism, the art of selecting novels for adults is virtually dead in public libraries. . . . The selection of adult fiction as it has been practised recently, has relied more on the judgement of the supplier than the local librarian" (Labdon, 1991, p. 36).

The reason for such a situation may not only lie in the lack of research interest in acquisition practice but also in the lack of application (or awareness) of existing research findings to the practice. This subsection presents the major findings of research concerning fiction acquisition.

1. Factors Affecting Fiction Acquisition

A number of studies have attempted to explore the various factors involved in librarians' decisions in fiction selection. Major factors to emerge from these studies include: book reviews; reader's demands (Mann, 1980; Palmer, 1987, 1988, 1991; Shaw, 1991; Sweetland, 1994); bestseller lists (Sweetland, 1994); features of books, e.g., its author and text (Oosthuizen, 1994; Wiener, 1983); and availability of other selection aids (Palmer, 1991).

a. Book Reviews.   This factor is identified as the most important factor for hardback purchase and the second most important factor for paperback purchase in Sweetland's (1994) questionnaire survey on medium-size U.S. public libraries, which consisted of 200 randomly chosen libraries. It appeared as the second most important factor in Mann's (1980) questionnaire survey of literary fiction acquisition in British library authorities. It is also listed as one of the most important factors in Curry's (1994) case study on the acquisition of controversial books. The strength of this factor has also been statistically examined by Palmer (1988) and Shaw (1991) with correlation between the number of reviews a title received and the number of holding libraries. Shaw surveyed 200 reviewed American titles against their availability in

78,011 OCLC libraries. Palmer surveyed 182 novels that had been reviewed in *Canadian Book Review Annual* and their availability in the OCLC database and in *Book Review Index*. In both cases, there was a very positive correlation between the number of reviews a book received and the number of holding libraries (r = 0.90 in Palmer's; r = 0.67 p < 0.01 in Shaw's). Shaw's study also found that a power curve ($y = ax^b$, r = 0.84) represents a better fit.

However, a questionnaire survey by Palmer (1991) in 120 Ontario public libraries showed a much more complex picture regarding the book review factor in book acquisition. The survey showed that while reviews were regarded as a major source of acquisition aid in 67% of libraries they were only moderately important in other libraries and in some libraries they were used very little.

The result makes one cautious in coming to definite conclusions about the effect of reviews, especially in the interpretation of the correlations. What these studies may suggest is that book reviews do play an important role in book selection decision, but the effect is perhaps much less significant than the correlations have suggested. This is because the review factor may be highly correlated with other factors, e.g., author's reputation. So until more rigorous control is exerted over these correlating factors, a simple correlation coefficient does not make much sense.

b. Author's Reputation. Wiener (1983) shed some light on this factor by examining the acquisition of first novels in academic libraries. This study investigated the availability of 30 first novels in 100 randomly chosen academic libraries. It was found that few first novels are held in these libraries. Those that were acquired by these libraries seem to have had advance publicity or honors. This finding indicates that author's reputation plays an important role in librarians' book selection.

c. Readers' Requests. This factor was found to be the most important in Mann's survey (1980) and in Sweetland's (1994) for paperback purchase. It was ranked second in Sweetland for hardback purchase. It was also found to be one of the most important factors in Curry's (1994) survey.

2. Evaluating Books for Acquisition

Broadus (1981) suggested three criteria for general book evaluation: interesting, verisimilitude, and literary quality. However, as Wagers (1981) argued, it is almost impossible to apply standard criteria to all fictional works. Many librarians actually apply two completely different standards. As far as more serious or literary fiction is concerned, there are certain conventional criteria, such as vivid characterization, complex imaginative plotting, and so on. Light fiction, however, poses many problems, especially because they are rarely reviewed. He suggested that librarians draw implications from popular culture studies to set up standards for light fiction evaluation. Futas (1994) suggested that the standards for light fiction evaluation consist of principles at a more general level and criteria at a more specific level. The principal standard is set up by those worthwhile and lasting materials, usually but not always limited to the classics of the field, as *Wuthering Heights* sets the standard for Gothic. At the more specific level, he suggested criteria such as plausible plot, effective characterization, imaginative writing, accurate era descriptions, and ability to sustain readers' interest.

The evaluation process steps into the intriguing area of censorship as soon as the social implication of a text is taken into consideration. This is where opinions especially conflict. For example, Asheim (1983) argued that it is the right of the people in a democracy to have access to the widest possible variety of choices and freely to choose for themselves on the basis of their own judgment. "The social responsibility of the library is to preserve freedom of choice, and the selection policies of the librarians are designed to foster it" (Asheim, 1983, p. 81).

Vincent (1986), however, argued that these comments confused the right to intellectual freedom with the damage that some materials do to some minorities in society. "It is within this framework that librarians must select stock, and selection cannot be made in isolation" (Vincent, 1986, p. 132).

3. Models of Decision Making in Fiction Acquisition

a. Model 1. Oosthuizen (1994) presented a visual model of the decision-making process in fiction selection. The model stated that the decision to purchase a book or not is actually a function of the book value itself and its conformity with the library's objective and the library's purchasing ability. The book value is again a function of the quality of text (different types of text apply different quality criteria), the library's policy over readers' demand and needs, and the coherence of the text in the context of existing collections.

b. Model 2. Baker (1994) pointed out a pitfall in fiction acquisition that confuses the concept of demand and quality. She proposed a visual model based on her reappraisal of these concepts; that is, demand and quality are two independent concepts with their own continuum. So the decision on book selection should be based on where the book is located along these two continuum.

4. Automation of Fiction Acquisition

Decision making in book selection, as shown by Oosthuizen's model is a highly complex process that remains, at least presently, human work, but

Labdon's (1991) case study provided an example of an attempt to automate part of the process. Although not statistically generalizable, the results of the study do have a certain pertinence to other library authorities. It stated: "The supply environment within which [the acquisition process] must work is too diverse and unregulated to enable a routine acquisitions system to be developed. . . . But the administration of the acquisition process can be reduced to a routine and it is here that electronic intervention is required" (Labdon, 1991, p. 44).

B. Fiction Processing

Fiction processing—subject analysis, indexing and classification, and so on—has been ignored almost by all general classification and indexing schemes such as Dewey Decimal Classification (DDC), Universal Decimal Classification, and Library of Congress Subject Headings (LCSH). The lack of direct subject access to imaginative literature in general and fiction in particular has made "the work of the public librarians more difficult and the experience of using the library frustrating for many patrons" (Ranta, 1991, p. 7).

For this reason, processing fiction for enhanced subject access has consistently attracted many researchers. Proposed fiction processing schemes have experienced dramatic change and development from Haigh's (1933) crude fiction adaptation of DDC through Burgess's (1936) detailed enumerative system to Walker's (1958) PMEST-based facet system.

Walker's facet system, which is theoretically and technically supported by Ranganathan's concepts and devices, represents a change from a monodimensional processing approach to a multidimensional approach. This new approach has been developed and expanded by Pejtersen (1978, 1979a, 1980, 1994; Pejtersen and Austin, 1983, 1984) based on her own theory about fiction readers' enquiries and Beghtol (1989, 1990, 1991, 1994) based on an extensive analysis of literature warrant, as well as the American Library Association's (ALA) (1989) *Guidelines*. Therefore the 1980s and 1900s in fact have seen the multidimensional approach getting mature, although not necessarily always implemented. It is not surprising that Hayes (1992) called this period "an era of enhanced catalog access to imaginative literature" (p. 445).

The following section therefore looks at the major multidimensional fiction processing schemes that have appeared in the recent past.

1. Analysis Mediation of Publications (Pejtersen, 1978, 1979a, 1980, 1994; Pejtersen and Austin, 1983, 1984)

Analysis Mediation of Publications (AMP) aimed to improve fiction retrieval in public libraries. It consisted of four dimensions and their subdivisions based on a conceptual perception of readers' expressed enquiries, developed from Pejtersen's own empirical reader studies that were discussed earlier (Section IV). These four dimensions and their subdivisions are shown below:

1. Subject matter
   a. Action and course of events
   b. Psychological development and descriptions
   c. Social relations
2. Frame
   a. Time: past, present, future
   b. Place: geographical, social environment, professional work
3. Author's intention
   a. Emotional experience
   b. Cognition and information
4. Accessibility
   a. Readability
   b. Physical characteristics, literary form

Further subclasses are allowed to be developed to suit individual libraries' particular needs. These dimensions and subclasses are not mutually exclusive but supplement each other: when a novel is classified, it is simultaneously placed in every dimension and category in which it would be reasonably expected to be found.

Sapp (1986) found this system very impressive. Indeed, the system has a number of notable features. First, it developed and extended Walker's multidimensional method from the readers' point of view and therefore consolidated the position of multidimensional approach in fiction processing. Second, the scheme legitimatized the inclusion of subjective concepts such as emotional states in fiction-processing schemes. Third, it has undergone tests both in a laboratory setting and with real public library readers. It demonstrated the possibility of in-depth fiction processing and the benefits such processing can offer to the readers.

This system has been criticized by some researchers mainly for two reasons. First, it is a combination of classification and indexing, which Pejtersen called "hybrid." But in maintaining such a "hybrid" nature, she also discarded major underpinning principles of both classification and indexing. She argued that "there is no reason to insist on these principles in a scheme which does not function as an arrangement system" (Pejtersen, 1978, p. 7). It consequently lost many advantages of both classification (e.g., rigorous control of class relations) and indexing (straightforwardness). This, plus inadequate definition of the scope of classes has greatly affected the usability of the system. It is mainly for this reason that Beghtol (1990) regarded it as principally a "tool for writing annotations" (p. 23).

The system has also been criticized for its theoretical framework. The theory on which it based—the conceptual perception of readers' enquiries—is not a very solid one. Since Pejtersen drew this theory solely from analysis of readers' expressed request, the validity of the theory relies very much on the assumption that the observed readers are representative of general fiction readers and readers' expressed demands reflect their real needs. However, this is not an assumption most user studies would support. It its not surprising to read one librarian's comment on the system: "her criteria do not match the kinds of user questions and problems with which my library is presented. Therefore, I do not find her method meets the needs of my patrons" (Guard, 1991, p. 12).

2. Guidelines on Subject Access to Individual Works of Fiction, Drama, etc. (American Library Association (ALA), Subject Analysis Committee, 1989)

The genesis of the *Guidelines* was in January 1986, with the creation of the Subcommittee on Subject Access to Individual Works of Fiction, Drama, etc. of the ALA. The *Guidelines* recommend provision of subject access to four aspects of fiction: form/genre, characters, setting, and topics. Form/genre headings indicate what the work is. Librarians are instructed to assign as many topical subject headings as necessary to bring out the topics covered, as determined after a superficial review of the publication in hand. Character access provides names whenever these names appear prominently in three or more different works. Setting access includes headings for location and time period.

This scheme enjoys two exceptional advantages: the authority of ALA and its compatibility with LCSH. It also assimilates some merits of previous research, for instance, the multidimensional approach, the special attention to characters and settings.

Ranta (1991) noted that its problems seem to lie in the inadequacy of its speculation about assignment of subject headings. "Methods for providing topical access are barely hinted at" (p. 15). For example, librarians are told not to attempt to discern topics that have not been made explicit by the author or publisher, but no criteria of explicitness are given.

As Ranta commented, while the *Guidelines* constitute an important step toward improving subject cataloging for imaginative literature, the recommendations need development, especially with regard to topical access.

3. Experimental Fiction Analysis System (EFAS) (Beghtol, 1991, 1994)

The system aims to provide an operable preliminary prototype system for fiction analysis. It is based on fictional and critical warrant. Beghtol carried out an extensive analysis of fictional works and critical works looking for characteristics of fiction's content and form. Four main content elements (characters, events, spaces, and times) plus an "other" element were developed.

These five potential data elements of a given book are joined with an expressive notation, which consisted of EFAS's own coined notations, interpolation notations from other classification systems, verbal expressions from LCSH, and verbal expressions made by classifiers themselves. Therefore, a book that consists of one time element, one space element, three event elements, three character elements, e.g., David Adams Richards' *Nights Below Station Street* will have the following descriptions as the result of its analysis with EFAS (Beghtol, 1994, p. 287):

T1 cu(+1972/1973)[S1,E1,2,3,C1,2,3]
S1 ev(715)ej(New Brunswick) [T1,E1,2,3,C1,2,3]
E1 gq(392.5)gm(weddings) [E2ghj,E3ghi] [T1,S1,C1,2,3]
E2 gq(551.555)gm(Blizzards) [E1ghj,E3ghj] [T1,S1,C1,2,3]
E3 gq(307.767)gm(Community life)[E1ghi,E2ghj][T1,S1,C1,2,3]
C1 jst(572)jrsjqv(056)jqt(041)jqq(0814)jpv(112)jpt(0623:0694)
   jpr(282)jo (Walsh,Joe) [C2jmm(0655),C3jmn(0431:0411]
     [T1,S1,E1,2,3]
C2 jst(572)jrsjqv(056)jqt(042)jpv(112)jpt(0623:0694)
   jpr(282)jo(Walsh, Rita)[C1jmm(0655),C3jmn(0431:0441]
     [T1,S1,E1,2,3]
C3 jst(572)jrsjqv(055)jqt(042)jpv(112)jpt(0623:06947)jpr(282)jpp(374)
   jo(Walsh,Adele) [C1jm(0431:0441),C2jmn(0431:0441)
     [T1,S1,E1,2,3]

As this example illustrates, it is possible to analyze fiction in great detail with EFAS. However, this is unfortunately a double-edged sword. The device EFAS uses to express all these details is its notation, which was designed to identify not only the major data elements but also other related information such as the relationship between these elements, their literary meaning, their position in other major classification systems, e.g., DDC, the uncertainty or transformation in each element (e.g., the uncertain existence of the governess' ghost in Henry James's *The Turn of the Screw*), and the transformation between a human body and an animal in some science fiction. Such a notation results in extremely complicated and unwieldy descriptions. Even in a computerized environment, it is doubtful that such descriptions would be as easily identifiable as a description using natural language. It is also doubtful that a reader would carry out his search by an uncertain access point, considering that people usually express their needs based on what they know. For example, it is unlikely that a reader would search for a character who moves from

England to Constantinople and back to England before he or she has read Woolf's *Orlando*, or search for an ent-like creature before he or she reads Tolkein's *The Lord of the Rings*.

In addition, the practicability of the system is also restricted by its reliance on too many assumptions. Among these are that: (1) the system will be used only in a computerized retrieval environment; (2) before the construction of its EFAS descriptions, a work of fiction would have already received descriptive cataloging, subject analysis, and a call number, according to the policies of the library that required it, and (3) a cataloger would know a great deal about the content of the cataloged book. These assumptions restrict the system to a very limited applicable scope and therefore make it rather impractical.

Having presented the major individual multidimensional schemes, it is perhaps a good time to go back to the general trend of multidimensional subject approach toward fiction processing. As has been noted, the approach, on the whole, has progressed a great deal since Walker's (1958) initial proposal. However, the individual schemes are not easy to apply to library practices. Many problems remain to be tackled. For example:

Exactly what dimensions should the system represent?
Should fiction processing systems, especially classification systems, take book shelving into account?
Should the scheme have notation? What roles does the notation play?
Should the scheme also be multilayered on some or all of the dimensions (i.e., provide both denotative and connotative information?)

C. Fiction Representation and Retrieval

Pejtersen's research has made the most important contribution in bringing fiction into the territory of modern information retrieval. From the beginning of the past decade, her work has formed the cornerstone in nearly all of the following aspects related to fiction retrieval.

1. Theoretical Considerations

One of the most notable features of Pejtersen's research on fiction retrieval is that it is theoretically based. Apart from applying a general theory of information retrieval, she also proposed several other theories particularly applicable to fiction retrieval.

a. Attributes of Readers' Demands. Fiction readers tend to perceive book contents from a number of different angles. Readers therefore often construct their information needs with multidimensional concepts. Four major dimensions have been identified from the empirical study of librarian–

reader communications: subject, author's intention, frame, and accessibility (Pejtersen, 1979a, 1980; Pejtersen and Austin, 1983, 1984) (Section VI,B,1).

b. Searching Strategies. From the same empirical research as above, Pejtersen (1984, 1988, 1989, 1992b) also developed four major searching strategies in the context of fiction retrieval:

1. Analytical search strategy—utilizes the dimensions of a user's needs as the basis for suggesting books.
2. Bibliographical search strategy—is a search for a known item.
3. Empirical strategy—is based on the librarians' classification of users into typical categories (stereotypes) which are associated with a known set of books.
4. Search by analogy—is a search for new books based on a model book.

c. Readers' Value Structures. This theory is the result of an examination of how humans value information. It states that the human value function in fiction retrieval is related to fiction attributes (four dimensions and their subdivisions) and the relative importance of these attributes. It conforms to an additive linear model. This function was incorporated into a computer-based fiction retrieval system and further tested in an experiment in which nine subjects searched fiction from the computer system. The experiment showed that a relatively small number of attributes account for the major part of a book's perceived value (in this experiment, five best categories account for 89.5% total value). Among the four dimensions, subject matter and author's intentions were approximately twice as important as frame and accessibility. The most important to least important categories are: (1) emotional experience, (2) cognition/information: criticism, (3) psychological description, (4) social relations, (5) readability, (6) action/course of events, (7) time, (8) setting, (9) cognition/information: agitation, (10) place, and (11) typography (Morehead, Pejtersen, and Rouse, 1984).

The implication of all these theories in fiction representation and retrieval is explained by Pejtersen (1984) when she suggests that an understanding of how people store, retrieve, and manipulate information; the strategies they employ in searching; and how they actually process that information should be the basis for the design of better retrieval systems.

2. Fiction Representation and Retrieval Systems

Fiction representation is defined here as description of the physical and content features of a work of fiction (in language and/or pictures or any other signs) presented in a particular medium, e.g., a computer system. This definition exhibits two essential elements: the information being represented and the means of representation. The combination of these two elements in a computer system determines the nature and the function of the system.

With reference to these two elements, four types of fiction representation systems have been identified in the literature surveyed by this chapter.

a. Systems That Represent Bibliographical Information Using a Traditional Linear System. An online catalog is an example of a linear system. As a survey by Marriott (1993) indicated, information represented in such systems is usually elementary, typically comprising title, author, keyword, and ISBN, occasionally with subject and fiction category.

Recent enhancement of fiction retrieval with such systems follow mainly two approaches: The first approach is to expand subject access points in existing online catalogs. For example, in the United States an OCLC-sponsored project was designed and conducted cooperatively by a group of libraries to enrich fiction records by listing additional subject/category headings as set forth in ALA's *Guidelines.* Previously, Library of Congress cataloged fiction according to author, title, publisher, place and date of publication, page length, and call number (Quinn and Rogers, 1992).

Yee and Soto (1991) addressed the problem with searching for fiction characters in current online catalogs. Most require users to specify a term from title, subject, or author with which to search. However, fiction characters are a type of heading that do not fall neatly into one of these broad groups. Yee and Soto's questionnaire survey with reference librarians indicated that fiction readers who were looking for fiction characters had difficulty in deciding which type of access point to pick. Two solutions were suggested to enhance existing catalogs' ability to cope with such problems: for smaller libraries, it is possible to create a general index which does not require the user to specify a particular access point. Large libraries might consider the solution of double indexing. For example, fiction characters could be indexed in both the name/author and the subject index.

The second approach is to design special catalogs for fiction materials. McKenna (1987) reported the design of a fiction catalog for school libraries named Fiction Finder. This catalog classified fiction for children and young adults from different angles: subject, readability of the text, interest level of the reader (readers' age group), gender of characters, and length of the book. Readers can specify any of these criteria or their combinations in their fiction retrieval. Each book record contains a very brief annotation (usually one sentence) in addition to basic bibliographic data such as author and title.

b. Systems That Represent Multidimensional and Multiple Types of Information with Traditional Linear Systems. Software called Novelist Readers' Advisory introduced by CARL Corporation in September 1994 may be taken as an example of this type of system. It has four functions. "Match a novel" uses a reader's favorite author or title to retrieve a list of titles with similar content. "Describe a plot" uses keywords provided by the user to allow subject browsing or uses those keywords to find titles that may be of interest. "Explore fiction types" uses genre headings in an icon-based environment to retrieve titles of interest for the user. "Best fiction" is totally customizable and can feature awards, such as the Pulitzer and Nebula prizes, bestsellers, or local favorites. The editing feature allows for timely updates for these locally created databases. This software is now available in a windows-based format with a graphical user-interface, as well as in Dos operating systems (Novelist, 1995).

c. Systems That Represent Bibliographical Information with Hypertext Systems.
"Science Library Catalog," although consisting of more than fictional books, can be taken as an example of such systems, because books in this catalog, fiction and nonfiction, are all basically for pleasure reading. It is a HyperCard catalog for elementary school students. The essential feature of its design is that it allows users to navigate a database in a hierarchical manner by selecting subjects on the screen. Each selection reveals 10 subordinate subjects, depicted as 10 shelves with signs. Clicking on the topic at the bottom level will lead the user to book lists on this topic. From the booklists, the user can click on a title of interest and visit screens containing all the available bibliographic information for that item. From the book record the user also can click a button to visit the library map, which actively draws the path to the current book's physical location relative to the user's position in the room (Borgman, Gallagher, Krieger, and Bower, 1990; Borgman, Walter, Rosenberg, and Gallagher, 1991).

d. Systems That Represent Multidimensional Information and Multiple Types of Information with Hypertext Systems.
A catalog for children in Colfax, Washington can be cited as an example. It is a catalog written for use in a bookmobile that was not staffed by a professional librarian. This catalog not only contains bibliographic information, but also book illustrations, plot summaries, and so on. Children can also read comments by other children who have read the books (Bertland, 1992).

Another important and influential work of this type is Pejtersen's (1989, 1992a,b) Bookhouse. This is a hypertext computer system that represented fiction books with multidimensional information.

The system applies AMP (Section VI,B,1) as the processing scheme and therefore provides multidimensional information—subject, author intention, frame, and accessibility—for each book in its database.

Bookhouse employs a graphical user interface. Information both in and about the database (as well as the various means of communicating with it) is represented as pictures/icons in different locations in a virtual space. For example, the category "time" is represented as a clock on the wall. Access to this category can be activated by clicking on the clock with a mouse.

The whole system features four types of searching: (1) intuitive browsing for browsing along all book records within a icon-represented category, (2) associative retrieval based on analogies between known books and unread books, (3) analytical retrieval using dimensions and their subdivisions, and (4) bibliographical retrieval for a known item.

The retrieved book records contain all information of the four dimensions in the format of subject keywords and annotation, as well as bibliographical data.

Icon/pictorial representation is one of the most remarkable features of Bookhouse. Pejtersen's empirical research on users' cognitive association between meaning and the icons showed that the icon/pictorial analogy can be used efficiently to represent fiction. The advantages of such representation are that: first, it enables a direct mapping onto effective cues/signs for action at the manipulative level and at the same time onto the semantic organization/content of the database for use in planning and decision-making. This makes it possible for the user to develop efficient skills in communicating through the interface quickly without the need for complex mental juggling to convert one representation to another. Second, icons are faster to read than text, since one icon can communicate complex messages (Pejtersen, 1992b).

A number of trends might be noted from all of the above systems: (1) the incorporation of various nonbibliographical information with the aid of hypertext/hypermedia technology, (2) the enhancement of the browsing function and incorporation of other functions, e.g., readers' advisory function, and (3) the provision of access points that are neither bibliographical nor subject, e.g., "analogy-of-book" access point.

3. System Evaluation

The problem of evaluating retrieval systems has not yet been fully explored. Pejtersen and Austin (1983, p. 23) have applied the traditional "precision," "recall," and "relevance" measurements to evaluate their system but they were well aware of the limitations in such an evaluation, as, in the case of fiction, "relevance" may have an unorthodox meaning.

D. Fiction Promotion

Fiction promotion is one of the most frequently used concepts in fiction librarianship, yet it is also one of the least defined. Basically, it is seen as a library activity that employs various publicity methods—personal contact, publicity materials and "atmospherics" or "image," and such—to create awareness and visibility of particular fiction services and books (Goodall, 1991; Marriott, 1993). Goodall (1991) sees it as one of the major tools for marketing. Its importance also lies in the fact that over half of fiction readers in public libraries are random browsers (Goodall, 1989) and are readily open to the influence of promotion schemes.

Promotion, as Goodall suggested, is "expensive both in terms of time and money. It must be professional with methods agreed and defined, targets identified and practical and the message to be conveyed appropriate and effective" (Goodall, 1991, p. 142). Promotion usually occurs as a special event rather than daily routine in the library and usually focuses on a certain part of the library stock rather than the whole.

It is also very prevalent, especially in public libraries. In the United Kingdom, many library authorities have regular regional fiction promotional schemes (Goodall, 1991). Individual libraries also quite commonly design small-scale promotion activities (Corns, 1995). Most previous literature consist of descriptive studies related to one or more of these schemes. The rest are more theoretical study on the effect of different promotion techniques.

1. Promotion Schemes and Affecting Factors

Goodall (1991) offered an extensive study of major regional promotion schemes in United Kingdom. Nottinghamshire fiction promotion featured a clearly defined promotion goal; that is, to lead people away from obvious authors but without being too highbrow. Leicestershire "Fiction Addiction" was thought to be very successful in combining striking publicity material and plenty of relevant stock. "Well worth Reading" (McKearney and Baverstock, 1990) aimed to encourage the reading of quality contemporary fiction and involved cooperation with other library authorities, publishers, and bookshops. In the "Dare you . . ." scheme in the United Kingdom (Bidston, 1995), staff involvement was noted as the most important factor in its success. In the United States, the "Classics and Readable" scheme (Hermenze, 1981) was initiated and participated in by the target readers and was made attractive by the brand new condition of the promoted books.

A number of factors affecting the success of the schemes emerged:

Goals
Environment: this includes the associated community, local governmental environment, etc.
Stock: the physical condition and the availability of promoted stocks
Promotion techniques
Cooperation

Sponsorship
Staff involvement
Target readers

2. Promotion Techniques

Most promotion schemes used one or more of the following promotion techniques:

Book display
Booklist/bookmarks
Author activity
Mass media publicity
Book discussion
Readers' review and amateur writing

Among these techniques, the effect of book display and booklist have also been studied at a more theoretical level.

a. Book Display. The effect of book display as a promotion technique has been examined by a number of experimental studies. Jennings and Sear's (1989) experiment was designed to test the effect of the display method on circulation and readers' satisfaction level with the books. In this experiment, a categorized area called "Novel Ideas" was set up and separated from the main A–Z shelves. Circulation of these books and readers' reaction to it (collected by questionnaire and interview) was monitored for 6 months. It was found that the majority of readers did enjoy using this area. It also improved the chance of a reader finding a book he or she enjoyed.

The relationship between book display and fiction circulation was tested with more rigorous experimental design and statistical analysis in Goldhor's (1972, 1981) and Baker's (1986a, 1988) experiments. Goldhor's first study (1972) was carried out to test the hypothesis that "Public library circulation of these titles will be significantly greater when they are collected and placed in a prime location than when they are scattered on the shelves of even an open-stack collection" (Goldhor, 1972, p. 371). It was tested with a pretest and posttest experimental design and accepted after a statistical analysis applying X^2. In his second experiment (1981), he applied another pretest and posttest experiment with three groups of books carefully selected with the same criteria, acting respectively as the control group, experimental group one, and experimental group two. During the 3-month pretest period, none of the groups received any experimental treatment. Their circulation was found to be approximately the same. During the 6-month experimental period, no special handling or treatment were given to the control group, a treatment of special display location named "Good Books You May Have Missed" was given to experimental group one, a booklist was compiled and distributed for experimental group two. The posttest showed that both experimental variables resulted in increase in circulation of seven and four times respectively, while the number of loans in the control group stayed essentially the same. The author suggested that there exist causal relationship between devices or techniques with the guidance function and the circulation of library's fiction collection.

In Baker's (1986a, 1988) study, physically separating classified fiction in a display area formed one of her experimental treatments. The circulation of these books was compared with circulation of books that did not receive any treatment. It was found that the experimental books were circulated significantly more frequently than the control books.

b. Booklists. The distribution of booklists was found to result in significantly more circulation in Goldhor's (1981) experiment presented earlier. The effect was confirmed by Wood in a similar experiment with the fiction collection of an academic library (Wood, 1985).

E. Fiction Readers' Advisory and Reference Services

Most research works on fiction reference services are practical, aimed to provide various kinds of reference aids. Mann (1985) and his successor's work (Huse, 1993), which provide relationships between fiction authors, are examples of such practical research. There is now also an electronic version of Mann's *A Readers' Guide* developed by Robert Clayton (1993) with Hyper-Card. In addition to cross-reference between similar authors, there are genre access points so that a reader can access a list of novelists of a certain genre from the genre title. On getting a list, the reader can click on any of the authors whom he or she has known or read, he or she will then be led to a list of authors who write in a similar way as the chosen one. This system was tested in three public libraries in Leicestershire, UK, and has received a very positive response from the readers.

Another example is Rosenberg's (1986) *Genreflecting.* This guide classifies popular fiction into genres and subgenres. Within each subgenre, authors that are popular and prolific as well as important are introduced with their important titles.

Greenhalgh (1991) offered an extensive survey of a wide range of such reference sources, including indexes, bibliographies, and current and retrospective book reviews. He also proposed the idea of greater reader involvement in fiction reference services.

The philosophy of fiction reference services is not strongly represented in the literature. Views are merely traceable from general speeches or essays.

For example, Mann (1982b) argued that fiction reading is a very personal matter. Individual taste should be highly respected and taken as the base of the reference service. Therefore, a reader who likes Kingsley Amis should be guided to authors such as William Boyd or Malcolm Bradbury. Catherine Cookson fans should be led to Victoria Holt or Doris Eden. By and large, he is against reference services that involve the librarian's own judgment. "It really is difficult trying to judge for others in fiction and it is made all the more difficult when people try to press their own judgement (prejudice?) on others" (p. 15).

Fiction readers' advisory services have only recently attracted some serious research interest, though it can be argued that it was mentioned as a marginal area in some early research, such as Rubakin's (1937). Ross (1991) attributes this new interest to two major factors. First, social attitudes toward fiction reading is not so negative as it was before. "New thinking about popular culture and pleasure reading has set the stage for the resurgence of a new kind of readers' advisory service in libraries" (p. 504). Second, "fiction overload"—a concept initially proposed by Baker (1986b)—is forcing readers to narrow their choices and they therefore may miss a large number of books with the potential to satisfy their needs.

This new interest is first demonstrated by the emergence of discussions featuring fiction advisory services, such as Ted Balcom's (1988) *Rediscovering Readers' Advisory—And Its Rewards* and Ross's (1991) *Readers' Advisory Service: New Directions.* Balcom reported a discussion on practical advisory skills, e.g., writing annotated bibliographies and leading adult book discussions. Ross, however, points to the new direction of advisory services today, based on her own interview survey with more than 100 fiction readers. The new direction, as she suggested, is to respect the idiosyncrasy in pleasure-reading and help to satisfy each individual's need.

New interest in the resurgence of fiction readers' advisory service is also revealed from the incorporation of an advisory function into fiction retrieval systems, such as Bookhouse and Novelist, as discussed earlier (Section VI,C).

F. Collection Management

Studies on collection management deal with the library collection as one unity and seek the efficient use of this resource by means of collection arrangement, stock assessment/control, and library cooperation in provision and preservation.

1. Collection Arrangement

Not treated in traditional classification systems such as DDC, the arrangement of the fiction collection has remained a perplexing issue for decades. Librarians have resorted to two strategies as solutions:

1. Distinguishing types of fiction with spine labels or separate shelves, which is usually referred to as categorization.
2. Applying A–Z order according to authors' names. It used to be seen as almost the only method (Dixon, 1986) and it is still applied in most libraries to the so-called general fiction, which is not applicable to the first strategy.

a. Categorization. Categorization, compared with A–Z arrangement, seems to be well supported by two underpinning propositions.

First, developed after the 1960s in the overall reappraisal of collection arrangement based on the concept of "user oriented service" (Ainley and Totterdell, 1982), it was seen as the strand of the emerging "reader interest arrangement" and believed to be more congenial to readers' needs and there-fore resulted in greater reader satisfaction. Related empirical research seems to support these convictions by showing that while a minority of readers are looking for specific materials, the majority are just seeking something interest to read (Ainley and Totterdell, 1982; Goodall, 1989; Spiller, 1980). This can be helped by gathering together books of the same genre. Further investiga-tions tend to suggest that categorization increases ease of use of libraries (Goodall, 1989; Jennings and Sear, 1989; Sapp, 1986) and decreases readers' information overload and dependence on their own knowledge about authors (Baker, 1988).

Second, it is believed that there is a positive relationship between categori-zation and an increase in books circulated. There has been an attempt to verify this by some experimental studies (Jennings and Sear, 1986; Baker, 1988).

Both of these propositions have encountered little questioning. However, for the categorization–circulation relationship to be more solid as a theory, it needs much more rigorous testing. The internal validity of the existing experimental studies may have been contaminated by a number of defects in their experimental design, especially the sampling method and the experimen-tal treatment. For example, in Baker's sample, only two categories were involved. In both Jennings and Sears and Baker's studies, the categorization treatment was mixed with other factors, such as separating the experimented books into a better-equipped area.

Techniques of categorization vary from library to library. Harell (1985) and Corns (1995) have noted three major techniques:

1. Spine labeling—this involves denoting the books' category through letter notations, graphic picture or color codes, while maintaining the A–Z run.
2. Separation—this involves physically separating genre novels and plac-ing them within a separate area.

3. Amalgamating 1 and 2—certain genres are separated and others remain interfiled.

Researchers' attitudes toward these techniques also vary. For example, Sear and Jennings (1991) criticize spine labeling as a compromise that only exposes the disadvantages of both A–Z arrangement and separation. But Dixon (1986) praises it because it keeps the alphabetical sequence, makes the reader go around the shelves, and it highlights the books rather than the author.

There are considerable variations under each technique. For example, with the method of separation, the categorization schemes applied by different libraries vary greatly. Harrell's (1985) survey showed that in 49 large U.S. libraries that apply categorization, a great diversity of categories was encountered, without standardization.

Categorization has demonstrated the role of collection arrangement in improving the congeniality of public libraries but is not accepted as a definitive solution. The major disadvantages are (1) the dispersion of authors (Dixon, 1986), and (2) nonexclusiveness of categorization schemes (Dixon, 1986; Hayes, 1992; Pejtersen and Austin, 1983).

2. Stock Assessment and Control

Stock assessment occurs when librarians look back at the collection and attempt to determine how good it is in terms of its strengths and weaknesses. This assessment may be unconnected with any selection decisions (Futas, 1994) but it usually leads to fiction weeding. Futas classified the methods for stock assessment into two groups: quantitative and qualitative.

a. Quantitative Assessment. This group of methods is basically related to circulation records. Senkevitch and Sweetland's (1994) survey indicated that methods of this type applied by small American libraries includes: circulation date (98% of evaluating libraries), publication date (78%), collection growth rates (28%), turnover rates (13%), and internal reserves (37%).

Research on the scientific use of circulation data for the purpose of fiction weeding has not progressed much since Slote's (1971) model in which he found that the period needed to account for 95% of fiction circulation varied among the libraries from 2 to 23 months (i.e., by the end of this period, 95% of all fiction being circulated had already been checked out at least once before). For 99%, the time varied from 5 to 70 months. Once the time needed to account for 95 or 99% current circulation was established for each library, then the library could safely weed materials remaining on the shelf that had not circulated.

b. Qualitative Assessment. Methods of this type are usually related to use of criteria book lists. Senkevitch and Sweetland (1994) reported that the criteria list used by libraries in his questionnaire survey included: best-seller lists (66% of the evaluating libraries), recommended lists (63%), and prize and award lists (45%). In addition, methods such as staff input and comparison with other libraries are also commonly used.

3. Cooperative Provision and Preservation

Regarding cooperative fiction provision, one project reported, SEALS (Selection, Acquisition and Loan Systems), in the U.K. West Midlands Regional Library System, is worth special note. This project aimed to provide improved access to European adult fiction by establishing collections of novels and short stories in French, German, Italian, and Spanish. Lending of its collections is based in each of 11 participating library authorities. This project was found to be of great interest and significance both practically and theoretically. Practically, cooperation among regional library authorities and links with European libraries were established, new methods of collection management were tested, and special needs of each library authorities with foreign language fiction were considered. Readers also benefit from it by having much wider access to European language fictions. Theoretically, it brought about a series of related research, e.g., research on the European book market (Goodall, 1993).

The importance of cooperation in fiction preservation has been well exemplified in the United Kingdom by various projects such as the London Joint Fiction Reservation Scheme and the Provincial Fiction Joint Reservation.

These schemes offer many lessons that other libraries can learn from in coping with fiction preservation; for example, speculations concerning what books can be lent and the charges for the lent books, coordination on national level to reduce duplications; cataloging of reserved fictional books, and policy toward ephemeral fiction (Samways, 1980).

VII. General Remarks on the Problems in Current Research in the Domain

Despite the large amount of research in fiction librarianship as shown above, the domain has never developed into one of the more important areas in librarianship. Major problems with the research revealed from this review are listed here.

A. The Lack of General Concern from the Wider Profession

That fiction librarianship has attracted little serious research interest from librarianship is almost unanimously acknowledged by those who do see its importance and care about its development:

> That this [librarians' reluctance to do research on fiction reading] should have been the case is not particularly surprising when one considers that neglect of fiction as a serious topic in the library literature to the present day. This twentieth century unwillingness to treat fiction provision as a really important issue is partly a legacy of the nineteenth century prejudice. (Sturges and Barr, 1992, p. 23)

and

> From about the mid-60s, the subject of fiction provision has been almost completely ignored as a topic of professional concern at conference and in librarianship journals. (Dixon, 1986, p. 87)

Bryon (1985) also noted the disproportion between the small volume of research on fiction services and the large amount of money, staff time, and shelf space allotted to it. Riel attributed this situation to the remaining social prejudice to light fiction reading:

> It's much more culturally ok to say you watch *Neighbours* [an Australian television soap opera] than to say you read Mills & Boon. . . . The complicated taboos and snobberies which surround attitudes to reading fiction have reinforced the reluctance of public library staff to enter the danger zone of developing policies in this area. Provision has been largely passive and user demand the main criterion. (Riel, 1993, p. 81)

B. The Overriding Body of Exploratory Research Compared with Explanatory Research

The majority of studies are descriptive and exploratory rather than explanatory in nature, i.e., the purpose is to describe phenomena, answer questions, or develop propositions for further research rather than to test hypotheses.

C. The Lack of Quality Research

The lack of quality research is first of all indicated by the large proportion of nonresearch works in the domain literature. Nonresearch works, in Creswell's definition, refer to publications of essay type or opinions, typologies, and syntheses of past research (Creswell, 1994, p. 27). These type of works normally do not involve research design and data collection and therefore lack solid evidence. In the domain of fiction librarianship, they are well exemplified by the majority of works that have appeared during the long debate over fiction provision.

> The debate as to whether fiction provision is justifiable at all and if so, to what extent and with what restrictions and provisos it should be supplied . . . has over the years irregularly but inevitably erupted with great heat and subsided into quiescence, when the dust settled, it is always seen that nothing has really changed. (Atkinson, 1981, p. 7)

Research works—studies that attempt to pose a question or hypothesis, collect data, and try to answer the question or support the hypothesis—were often carried out without rigorous research design in this domain. This is reflected in the following aspects of their research design:

1. The mixture of research paradigms, e.g., quantitative data collection, was applied to untestable hypotheses, or hypotheses were dealt with without statistical data analysis.

2. The lack of a theoretical framework in quantitative research. Few studies have applied solid theories to provide clearly defined concepts and variables and to establish statistically testable hypothesis.

3. Nonrigorous data collection and data analysis. Both procedures were seldom found to be guided by clearly stated research questions or statistically testable hypotheses. Data collection instruments, such as the most frequently used interview and questionnaires, have hardly ever been tested with validity and reliability of variables. Only in occasional situations was statistical data analysis applied. Such defects in data collection and analysis made the generalization of research findings very difficult.

D. Lack of Theoretical Research

In addition to the unsatisfactory research design, the domain of fiction librarianship is also marked with a common lack of intention for theory construction. The lack of interest in theoretical study is, at least to a certain extent, responsible for the very slow growth of the body of domain knowledge.

Underdeveloped as it is, the domain has seen a more fruitful 1980s and a promising 1990s, with the appearance of such major books as Kinnell's (1991) and Beghtol's (1994) and a large number of major papers. There is also evidence to suggest that the major research in this domain has shifted from Europe to America with the advent of 1990s. At the beginning of 1990s, Sweetland remarked:

> There is considerable amount of work from the British and European point of view regarding adult fiction. . . . In the USA, on the other hand, most of the research involves children's material, with much of the remainder concerned with censorship. (Sweetland, 1991, p. 81)

However, much and constant research interest has been seen both from the United States and Canada thereafter, including a series of studies on the collection management of fiction, a number of studies of fiction analysis and processing, as well as the increasing institutional concerns of ALA and LC.

VIII. Conclusion

The original debates about fiction continue, nowadays in the context of decreasing budgets and shrinking services. The new weapons of the manager such as performance indicators will certainly give us new data to measure and analyze. This also may act as a double edged sword. On the one hand, increasing use of IT should give more and better data that can be measured and this should result in more justifiable studies. The qualitative argument, however, may still not be so easy to resolve, for, as this review has shown, reliance on quantitative data is only one part of the research paradigm in the still developing world of fiction librarianship. The 1990s sees a promising future of research in this area, but its further development may rely very much on two factors: the upgrading of the social and cultural status of fiction and fiction reading in society and the improvement of research efforts from the profession.

References

Abbey, K. (1981). Science fiction and fantasy: A collection proposal. *Wilson Library Bulletin* **55,** 584–588.

Ainley, P., and Totterdell, B. (1982). *Alternative Arrangement: New Approaches to Public Library Stock.* Association of Assistant Librarians, London.

American Library Association (ALA) Subject Analysis Committee. (1989). *Guidelines on Subject Access to Individual Works of Fiction, Drama, etc.* ALA, Chicago.

Asheim, L. (1983). Selection and censorship: A reappraisal. *Wilson Library Bulletin* **58,** 180–184.

Atkinson, F. (1981). *Fiction Librarianship.* Bingley, London.

Baker, S. L. (1986a). The display phenomenon: An exploration into factors causing the increased circulation of displayed books. *Library Quarterly* **56,** 237–257.

Baker, S. L. (1986b). Overload, browsers and selection. *Library and Information Research* **8,** 315–329.

Baker, S. L. (1988). Will fiction classification schemes increase use? *RQ* **27,** 366–376.

Baker, S. L. (1994). Quality and demand: The basis for fiction collection assessment. *Collection Building* **13**(2/3), 65–68.

Balcom, T. (1988). Rediscovering readers' advisory—And its rewards. *Illinois Libraries* **70,** 583- 586.

Beghtol, C. (1989). Access to fiction: A problem in classification theory and practice: Part 1. *International Classification* **16,** 134–141.

Beghtol, C. (1990). Access to fiction: A problem in classification theory and practice: Part 2. *International Classification* **17,** 21–27.

Beghtol, C. (1991). *The Classification of Fiction: the Development of a System Based on Theoretical Principles.* PhD thesis, Faculty of Information Studies, University of Toronto, Canada.

Beghtol, C. (1994). *The Classification of Fiction: The Development of a System Based on Theoretical Principles.* Scarecrow, Metuchen, NJ.

Bertland, L. (1992). Hypermedia in young adult services. *Journal of Youth Services in Libraries* **5,** 301–304.

Bidston, P. (1995). Dare you . . . create your own book promotion? *Public Library Journal* **10**(1), 10–11.

Bodart, J. R. (1994). In defense of horror fiction. *Book Report* **12**(March/April), 25–26.

Borgman, C. L., Gallagher, A. L., Krieger, D., and Bower, J. (1990). Children's use of an interactive catalog of science materials. In *ASIS '90: Proceedings of the 53rd Annual Meeting of the American Society for Information Science, serial no. 27.* (D. Henderson, ed.), pp. 55–68. Learned Information Inc., Toronto, Canada.

Borgman, C. L., Walter, V. A., Rosenberg, J. B., and Gallagher, A. L. (1991). The science library catalog project—Comparison of children's searching behavior in hypertext and a keyword search system. In *ASIS '91: Proceedings of the 54th Annual Meeting of the American Society for Information Science, serial no. 28.* (J. M. Griffiths, ed.), pp. 162–169. Learned Information, Medford, NJ.

Brewis, W. L. E., Gericke, E. M., and Kruger, J. A. (1994). Reading needs and motives of adult users of fiction. *Mousaion* **12**(2), 3–18.

Broadus, R. N. (1981). Prose fiction. In *Selecting Materials for libraries* (R. N. Broadus, ed.), pp. 382–389. H. W. Wilson, New York.

Bryan, A. I. (1939). The psychology of the reader. *Library Journal* **64,** 7–12.

Bryan, A. I. (1940). The reader as a person. *Library Journal* **65,** 138–140.

Bryon, J. F. W. (1985). Home reading: Fiction. *New Library World* **86,** 186–187.

Burgess, L. A. (1936). A system for the classification and evaluation of fiction. *Library World* **38,** 179–182.

Carrier, E. J. (1965). *Fiction in Public Libraries 1876–1900.* Scarecrow Press, New York.

Carrier, E. J. (1985). *Fiction in Public Libraries 1900–1950.* Libraries Unlimited, Littleton, CO.

Christensen, J. O. (1984). Management of popular reading collections. *Collection Management* **6**(3/4), 75–82.

Clayton, R. (1993). *A Hypertext Reader's Guide to Fiction Authors: The Potential and Reality.* Unpublished master's dissertation, Department of Information and Library Studies, Loughborough University, UK.

Corns, I. (1995). *A Study into Fiction Categorization.* Unpublished master's dissertation, Department of Information and Library Studies, Loughborough University, UK.

Creswell, J. W. (1994). *Research Design: Qualitative and Quantitative Approaches.* Sage Publications, London.

Curry, A. (1994). American psycho: A collection management survey in Canadian public libraries. *Library and Information Science Research* **16,** 201–217.

Dixon, J., ed. (1986). *Fiction in Libraries.* Library Association Publishing, London.

Futas, E. (1994). Collection development of genre literature. *Collection Building* **12**(3/4), 39–44.

Gerhard, K. H. (1991). Mystery and detective fiction: A qualitative approach. *Public Library Quarterly* **10**(4), 49–59.

Gertz, M. B. (1989). Fiction in the public library. *Cape Librarian* **33**(1), 6–9.

Goldhor, H. (1972). The effect of prime display location on public library circulation of selected adult titles. *The Library Quarterly* **42,** 371–389.

Goldhor, H. (1981). Experimental effects on the choice of books borrowed by public library adult patrons. *The Library Quarterly* **51,** 253–268.

Goodall, D. (1989). *Browsing in Public Libraries.* Library and Information Statistics Unit, Loughborough University, UK.

Goodall, D. (1991). Marketing fiction services. In *Managing Fiction in Libraries* (M. Kinnell, ed.), pp. 138–158. Library Association Publishing, London.

Goodall, D. (1993). Improving access to European fiction. *Library and Information Research News* **16**(56), 18–20.

Greenhalgh, M. (1991). Fiction information: Sources and services. In *Managing Fiction in Libraries* (M. Kinnell, ed.), pp. 120–137. Library Association Publishing, London.

Guard, A. (1991). An antidote for browsing: Subject headings for fiction. *Technicalities* **11**(12), 10–14.

Haigh, F. (1933). The subject classification of fiction: An actual experiment. *Library World* **36**, 78–82.

Harrell, G. (1985). The classification and organization of adult fiction in large American public libraries. *Public Libraries* **24**(Spring), 13–14.

Hatt, F. (1976). *The Reading Process: A Framework for Analysis and Description.* Bingley, London.

Hayden, R. (1987). If it circulates, keep it. *Library Journal* **112**(10), 80–82.

Hayes, S. (1992). Enhanced catalog access to fiction: A preliminary study. *Library Resources & Technical Services* **36**, 441–458.

Hermenze, J. (1981). The classics will circulate. *Library Journal* **106**, 2191–2195.

Hugo, L. H. (1985). A defense of popular fiction. *South African Journal of Library and Information Science* **53**, 170–177.

Huse, R., ed. (1993). *Who Else Writes Like?: A Readers' Guide to Fiction Authors.* Library and Information Statistics Unit, Loughborough University, UK.

Jennings, B., and Sear L. (1986). How readers select fiction: A survey in Kent. *Public Library Journal* **1**(4), 43–47.

Jennings, B., and Sear, L. (1989). Novel ideas: A browsing area for fiction. *Public Library Journal* **4**(3), 41–44.

Kinnell M., ed. (1991). *Managing Fiction in Libraries.* Library Association Publishing, London.

Kinnell, M., and MacDougall, J. (1994). *Meeting the Marketing Challenge: Strategies for Public Libraries and Leisure Services.* Taylor Graham, London.

Labdon, P. (1991). Acquiring adult fiction. In *Managing Fiction in Libraries* (M. Kinnell, ed.), pp. 34–47. Library Association Publishing, London.

Mann, P. H. (1980). *The Literary Novel and Its Public: A Report to the Arts Council Literature Panel.* Sheffield University, Sheffield.

Mann, P. H. (1982a). *From Author to Reader.* Routledge and Kegan Paul, London.

Mann, P. H. (1982b). *Libraries and the Reading Habit: A Paper Presented to the Library Association Public Libraries Group Weekend School in Sheffield.* Public Libraries Group, Library Association, Penzance, UK.

Mann, P. H. (1991). Fiction readers: What people want to read. In *Managing Fiction in Libraries* (M. Kinnell, ed.), pp. 1–16. Library Association Publishing, London.

Mann, P. H., and Burgoyne, J. (1969). *Books and Reading.* Andre Deutch, London.

Marriott, R. (1993). How well do libraries inform their public? *Library Association Record* **75**, 161–163.

McClellan, A. W. (1981). The reading dimension in effectiveness and service. *Library Review* **30**, 77–86.

McKearney, M., and Baverstock, A. (1990). *Well Worth Reading: An Experiment in Fiction Promotion.* Well Worth Reading, Winchester, UK.

McKenna, M. C. (1987). Using micros to find fiction: Issues and answers. *School Library Media Quarterly* **15**(2), 92–95.

Moore, C. (1982). Core collection development in a medium sized public library. *Library Resources & Technical Services* **26**, 37–46.

Morehead, D. R., Pejtersen, A. M., and Rouse, W. B. (1984). The value of information and computer-aided information seeking: Problem formulation and application to fiction retrieval. *Information Processing and Management* **20**, 583–601.

Oosthuizen, B. L. (1994). Selection of fiction in the public library: A model of the decision-making process. *South African Journal of Library and Information Science* **62**(3), 85–95.

Palmer, J. W. (1987). An inquiry into the availability of Canadian fiction in US libraries with special attention to the influence of reviews. *Library Acquisitions: Practice and Theory* **11**, 283–295.

Palmer, J. W. (1988). Factors responsible for the acquisition of Canadian fiction by US public and academic libraries. *Library Acquisitions: Practice and Theory* **12**, 341–356.

Palmer, J. W. (1991). Fiction selection in Ontario public libraries, how important are reviews? *Public Library Quarterly* **10**(4), 39–48.

Pejtersen, A. M. (1978). Fiction and library classification. *Scandinavian Public Library Quarterly* **11**(1), 5–12.

Pejtersen, A. M. (1979a). The meaning of 'about' in fiction indexing and retrieval. *Aslib Proceedings* **31**, 251–257.

Pejtersen, A. M. (1979b). Investigation of search strategies based on an analysis of 134 user–librarian conversations. In *The 3rd International Research Forum in Information Science* (T. Henriksen, ed.), pp. 107–131. Statens Biblioteksskole, Oslo.

Pejtersen, A. M. (1980). Design of a classification scheme for fiction based on an analysis of actual user-librarian communication, and use of the scheme for control of librarians' search strategies. In *Theory and Application of Information Research* (O. Harbo and L. Kaijberg, eds.), pp. 167–183. Mansell, London.

Pejtersen, A. M. (1984). Design of a computer-aided user-system dialogue based on an analysis of users' search behaviour. *Social Science Information Studies* **4**, 167–183.

Pejtersen, A. M. (1988). Search strategies and database design. In *Tasks, Errors and Mental Models* (L. P. Goodstein, H. B. Andersen, and S. E. Olsen, eds.), pp. 171–190. Taylor and Francis, London.

Pejtersen, A. M. (1989). *The Bookhouse: System Functionality and Evaluation.* Riso National Laboratory, Roskilde, Denmark.

Pejtersen, A. M. (1992a). The Bookhouse: An icon based database system for fiction retrieval in public libraries. In *The Marketing of Library and Information Services* (B. Cronin, ed.), Serial no. 2, pp. 572–591. Aslib, London.

Pejtersen, A. M. (1992b). New model for multimedia interfaces to online public access catalogues. *The Electronic Library* **10**, 359–366.

Pejtersen, A. M. (1994). A framework for indexing and representation of information based on work's domain analysis: A fiction classification example. In *Proceedings of the 3rd International Society for Knowledge Organization Conference* (H. Albrechtsen and S. Oernager, eds.), pp. 251–263. INDEKS verlag, Frankfurt/Main.

Pejtersen, A. M., and Austin, J. (1983). Fiction retrieval: Experimental design and evaluation of a search system based on users' value criteria: Part 1. *Journal of Documentation* **39**, 230–246.

Pejtersen, A. M., and Austin, J. (1984). Fiction retrieval: Experimental design and evaluation of a search system based on users' value criteria: Part 2. *Journal of Documentation* **40**, 25–35.

Novelist now available in window-based graphical user-interface. (1995, Feb.). [2 paragraphs]. Public-access Computer System News. [online serial] 6(2). Available E-mail: @earn-relay. ac.uk:PACS-P@UHUPVM1.UH.EDU.

Quinn, J., and Rogers, M. (1992). OCLC/LC Fiction headings project: Too little, too late? *Library Journal* **117**(1, Feb.), 14–15.

Ranta, A. J. (1991). The new literary scholarship and a basis for increased subject catalogue access to imaginative literature. *Cataloguing and Classification Quarterly* **14**, 3–26.

Reader, D. (1982). User orientation in a Hertfordshire branch. In *Alternative Arrangement: New Approaches to Public Library Stock* (P. Ainley and B. Totterdell, eds.), pp. 3–26. Association of Assistant Librarians, London.

Riel, R. V. (1993). The case for fiction. *Public Library Journal* **8**(3), 81–84.

Rosenberg, B. (1986). *Genreflecting: A Guide to Reading Interests in Genre Fiction.* Libraries Unlimited, Littleton, CO.

Ross, C. S. (1991). Readers' advisory service: New directions. *RQ* **30**, 503–518.

Rubakin, N., and Bethmann, M. (1937). The psychology of the public library. In *Nicholas Rubakin and Bibliopsychology* (S. Simsova, ed.), pp. 9–25. Clive Bingley, London.

Samways, A. J. (1980). The Joint Fiction Reserve: An appraisal. *Journal of Librarianship* **12**, 267–279.

Sapp, G. (1986). The levels of access: Subject approaches. *RQ* **25**, 489–497.

Sear, L., and Jennings, B. (1991). Organizing fiction for use. In *Managing Fiction in Libraries* (M. Kinnell, ed.), pp. 101–119. Library Association Publishing, London.

Senkevitch, J., and Sweetland, J. (1994). Evaluating adult fiction in the smaller public library. *RQ* **34**, 78–89.

Shaw, D. (1991). An analysis of the relationship between book reviews and fiction holdings in OCLC. *Library and Information Science Research* **134**, 147–154.

Slote, S. J. (1971). Identifying useful core collections: A study of weeding fiction in public libraries. *Library Quarterly* **41**, 25–34.

Speak, M. (1990). A survey of reading patterns of elderly people using the Age Concern Centre Library, Leicestershire. *Health Libraries Review* **7**(1), 8–13.

Spenceley, N. (1980). *The Readership of Literary Fiction: A Survey of Library Users in the Sheffield Area.* Unpublished master's thesis, Department of Information Studies, Sheffield University, UK.

Spiller, D. (1980). The provision of fiction for public libraries. *Journal of Librarianship* **12**, 239- 266.

Sturges, P., and Barr, A. (1992). The fiction nuisance in nineteenth century British public libraries. *Journal of Librarianship and Information Science* **24**, 23–32.

Sumsion, J. (1991). *PLR in Practice: A Report to the Advisory Committee, 2nd ed.* Registrar of Public Lending Right, Stockton-on-Tees, Cleveland, UK.

Sumsion, J. (1992). Who reads what in libraries? In *Reading the Future: A Place for Literature in Public Libraries* (R. V. Riel, ed.), pp. 47–50. Library Association Publishing, London.

Sweetland, J. H. (1991). Managing adult fiction collections in public libraries. In *Managing Fiction in Libraries* (M. Kinnell, ed.), pp. 81–100. Library Association Publishing, London.

Sweetland, J. H. (1994). Adult fiction in medium-sized U.S. public libraries: A survey. *Library Resources & Technical Services* **38**, 149–160.

Treuherz, T. (1984). Lending romance. *Assistant Librarian* **77**(1), 53–55.

Vincent, J. (1986). Censorship and selection in public libraries. In *Fiction in Libraries* (J. Dixon, ed.), pp. 127–134. Library Association Publishing, London.

Wagers, R. (1981). Popular fiction selection in public libraries: Implications of popular culture studies. *Journal of Library History* **16**, 342–352.

Walker, R. S. (1958). Problem child. *The Librarian and Book World* **16**, 21–28.

Williams, T. (1990). Fiction: What should we buy? *Public Library Journal* **5**(5), 121–124.

Wiener, P. B. (1983). Acquisition of first novels in academic libraries. *Collection Management* **5**(Fall/Winter), 25–36.

Wood, R. (1985). The experimental effects of fiction book lists on circulation in an academic library. *RQ* **24**, 427–432.

Yee, M., and Soto, R. (1991). User problems with access to fictional characters and personal names in online public access catalogs. *Information Technology and Libraries* **10**, 3–13.

Librarian–Faculty Partnerships in Instruction

Evelyn B. Haynes
Social Sciences and Humanities Reference Librarian
Colorado State University Libraries
Fort Collins, Colorado 80523

I. Introduction

Academic librarians are inclined to think of themselves as full-fledged members of the scholarly community and to regard the libraries that they manage as central and essential to the mission of their institutions. Their unique position within the academic community, however, may set them apart in ways that interfere with their full integration and participation in the educational life of their campuses. Although they are educators within the broad definition of that term, they seek to understand the breadth of knowledge in all fields rather than the in-depth, compartmentalized knowledge of a subject discipline. They function in partnership with, and in support of, the teaching goals of all campus units, not in typical academic isolation from their colleagues in other departments.

The concept that librarians are integral to academic life is most likely to be recognized outside the library world by those who think broadly and deeply about the purpose and benefits of education as a whole. The most prominent example is the often-quoted Ernest Boyer (Breivik, 1987, p. 46), president of the Carnegie Foundation for the Advancement of Teaching, who identified this basic function of librarians in his address at the Symposium on Libraries and the Search for Academic Excellence in March, 1987: "Those in charge of information services on a campus are the renaissance people who are able to guide students through the typology of knowledge and help them discover the relationships that no single department and no single professor can provide." Librarians refer to Boyer frequently in articles related to bibliographic instruction, possibly because he stands virtually alone among educators who speak with clarity and authority in articulating this holistic vision of education.

ADVANCES IN LIBRARIANSHIP, VOL. 20

II. The Academic Library and Its Parent Institution

Words like Boyer's are heartening to librarians, but his assumptions are certainly less widely accepted within the larger academic community, despite the cliché that the library is the "heart of the university." One hears at conferences and reads in the literature the questions that librarians ask themselves about how relevant they are to the real work of their institutions, to the learning that takes place within them. When they observe materials that remain on the shelves unopened and unused, faculty disregard for their expertise and potential contribution as educators, or students making superficial or inexpert use of the library's resources, along with declining financial and administrative support, they understandably may conclude that their perceptions don't match those of the rest of the campus. Boyer (Brandehoff, 1987, p. 444) concurred with this pessimistic assessment in his address to the Symposium on Libraries and the Search for Academic Excellence: "Libraries are shockingly neglected as the centerpiece of undergraduate education," Boyer said. He placed the responsibility for this neglect "squarely in the classroom at the feet of the professor." "We [the Carnegie Foundation] found a passivity on campus," he said, "a feeling that learning takes place only in the classroom and resources outside the classroom are no business of the faculty."

Consequently, librarians spend a large percentage of their resources and energies justifying the contribution of libraries and librarians to the educational mission of their institutions. In preparing a rationale for their existence and function, librarians should be aware that faculty perceptions may differ significantly from their own. For example, librarians tend to identify themselves with their libraries, whereas faculty may perceive the relationship differently. The distinction that Evan Farber (1978) described a number of years ago between being "library minded" and "librarian minded" may find its more recent expression in ways that are discomforting to librarians. Kellogg's (1987) observation that most administrators and faculty are thinking about libraries, not librarians, when they refer to the "heart of the university" is corroborated by a survey taken at the University of Manitoba (Divay, Ducas, and Michaud-Oystryk, 1987, p. 33). "It was remarkable that many [faculty] participants [in the study] seem to consider the library simply as an institution, with little regard for the people who are instrumental in its functioning." More than one academic library's faculty has probably found itself in the uncomfortable position of hearing the institution's faculty express a willingness to sacrifice library personnel in order to shelter the book acquisitions budget and retain journal subscriptions.

Hardesty's (1995, p. 343) perceptive article on faculty culture provides some useful insights into the sources of these attitudes: "Why then do many faculty members expect, even demand, the development of relatively large library collections but often resist efforts by librarians to teach students how to use these collections?" He finds answers in the emphasis of most academic disciplines on research, content, and specialization and a deemphasis on teaching, process, and undergraduates. The interdisciplinary nature of the role of librarians in itself sets them apart from their academic colleagues whose reputations rest on their subject expertise rather than their ability to transmit knowledge to their students. But it is through the less-valued teaching function that librarians can make their most valuable contribution to student learning.

In the landmark Carnegie report on undergraduate education, Boyer (1987) describes the library's role:

> The quality of a college is measured by the resources for learning on the campus and the extent to which students become independent, self-directed learners. . . . The college library must be viewed as a vital part of the undergraduate experience. . . . All undergraduates should be introduced carefully to the full range of resources for learning on a campus. They should be given bibliographic instruction and be encouraged to spend at least as much time in the library—using its wide range of resources as they spend in classes. (p. 21)

The report goes on to say, "This means encouraging students, through creative teaching, to become intellectually engaged."

For librarians, the link between the goals of the kind of information literacy described and bibliographic instruction is automatic; the former cannot be accomplished without the latter. Again, this assumption is not necessarily shared by their colleagues in the institution. However, it is explicitly stated by Simmons (1992) as spokesman for the Middle States Association Commission on Higher Education (CHE):

> The centrality of a library/learning resources center in the educational mission of an institution deserves more than rhetoric and must be supported by more than lip service. An active and continuous program of bibliographic instruction is essential to realize this goal. . . . Nothing else matters much if the resources are not used. (p. 17)

III. Faculty Perceptions of the Library

Although librarians share an important part of the responsibility of guiding student research, they do not often have the opportunity of determining its direction. It is primarily the function of the teaching faculty to decide whether and to what extent their students use the library for information research. The educational philosophy and teaching style of the faculty, who manage the course of their students' education and determine its rewards, are much more powerful influences on students' research behavior than librarians' efforts to motivate.

Numerous studies, most of them conducted by librarians, bear out this assumption. Despite the desire and efforts of librarians to exert a stronger influence on students, the results remain constant. One early survey of academic libraries (Allen, 1970) reported its finding that the most notable factor influencing undergraduate student utilization of the library has been found to be the attitude of individual instructors. McInnis (1978, p. 3) agrees: "More than any other factor, the value the classroom instructor attaches to library research determines the students' interest in use of library materials. Instructors give direction and motivation to students as to how library materials are to be used in meeting course requirements." The expected result is summarized by Baker (1989, p. 320): "Most students will use library materials in their courses only if professors require them to. . . . Not surprisingly. . . many students do not use the library as a primary information source."

In view of the overwhelming effect of faculty influence on library use, it is essential for librarians to understand faculty attitudes toward, and knowledge about, the library. Studies revealing faculty attitudes have been cited previously; a closer look at how these attitudes translate into events may be enlightening. Fewer studies exist yet to provide information about faculty *knowledge* of library resources and usage. One suspects that much good material on these subjects continues to reside in numerous filing cabinets or computer files of academic libraries throughout the country. One common thread running through the sources that are available points to a prevailing dichotomy between what librarians and teaching faculty know and believe about librarians and their institutions.

For example, a survey of faculty attitudes toward the library (Colorado State University, 1986) found that 75% of respondents agreed with the statement: "Adequate instruction is available in library use." When asked to explain what they meant by "the best way to teach my students about library use," 54% checked "written library guides," 36% checked "lectures and tours of the library tailored to my course," 21% checked "elective library courses given by librarians," and 16% checked "lectures by librarians in my classroom." A later study (Colorado State University Libraries, 1993) concluded that "We had no reason to think that attitudes would have changed significantly in the past six years." What was evident to the librarians was a disparity between the opinions of teaching faculty and those of librarians on the issue of library instruction; library staff had been planning for development based on their perceived inadequacy of existing instruction programs. The questions concerning space planning in the same study found that ". . . both faculty and students considered ample space, equipment, and assistance for electronic information resources among the top five priorities; but 'space for instruction in computerized information for class groups' was one of the lowest" (Colorado State University, 1993).

A survey of user instruction needs (Colorado State University Libraries, 1993) conducted in focus group sessions with faculty and student groups who had already expressed, or were known to have, some strong interest in the library, revealed some unsettling opinions about the educational mission of the library. Although not a scientific sampling, the survey results from the 50 faculty who attended the sessions are important as possible indicators of thinking across campus. Among the faculty attitudes expressed, the following are indicative of items that should concern the library staff:

First of all, as to knowledge about library instruction services:

1. Many did not know about such services as CD-ROM training workshops, or that librarians were available to give instruction. Few knew about the library's credit course. There was agreement that services would be used more if people knew about them.

2. About a dozen people had experience with library instruction involving a librarian, either through a formal class or an assignment. Most were satisfied with the service. Some people who emphasize library use in their teaching did not know that the library offered instruction services.

Second, as to the need for library instruction programs:

3. Nearly everyone thought that, at the level they were teaching, students (including graduate students) should have the basic library skills, and nearly everyone found that they do not.

4. However, several people said that, at the graduate level, the instructor should be able to assume that students know how to use the library; therefore they do not think it is appropriate to include formal training in the curriculum.

5. Most agreed that these skills are critical because of the rate of change of knowledge and the fact that it is not possible to cover everything in courses.

Third, as to what faculty were doing to provide library instruction:

6. All but one or two agreed that they require their students to use library resources: books, scholarly journal articles, and specialized reference tools. Not everyone believed that this pattern was typical of faculty in their departments, however.

7. Many agreed that as teachers it is their responsibility to show students the literature of their discipline and to teach them to evaluate it. Several said it was a responsibility they had been shirking, i.e., by assuming that students would have acquired these skills somewhere else.

8. Most had not significantly changed their teaching, even when aware of the rapid increases in knowledge, although several commented that a change in teaching was inevitable.

9. Some people are developing their own materials, with and without help from librarians.

Fourth, as to recommended means of library instruction:

10. One person thought that everyone should take the library's credit course in research methods; many agreed that appropriate library instruction should be part of most research methods courses and some of the survey courses for beginning majors. The concept of library assignments integrated into courses was well received.

Readers will probably note that not all of the faculty interviewed consider librarians a necessary participant in user instruction. If one can base certain assumptions on discussions heard at library conferences and readings in the professional library literature, these opinions may be typical of those on many campuses. An assessment of faculty views from surveys conducted over a period of years supports these assumptions:

> Only a few surveys have been conducted in the past that were specifically designed to assess faculty attitudes toward library research instruction. Common findings among several of them were that faculty were not happy with the level of their students' library research skills; that they recognized the need for library research instruction, but did not generally care to provide this themselves; and that faculty did not make heavy use of librarians to provide this instruction for their classes. (Cannon, 1994, p. 525)

A more recent survey of faculty attitudes at York University in Ontario, Canada (Cannon, 1994, p. 537), found that, at their institution, attitudes were essentially no different today. However, they did discover an openness to collaboration with librarians, which signaled an unmet need of large proportions:

> Despite the high percentage of faculty who provided some form of library research instruction to their classes without the obvious intervention of librarians, 85 percent thought librarians alone or librarians and classroom faculty together should provide this. . . . Fifty-five percent of those who haven't had a librarian teach a subject-specific session in one of their classes would like to have this. Forty percent of faculty did not know it was available. (Cannon, 1994)

A series of surveys reported in another article (Ivey, 1994) reveal some common faculty attitudes about librarians that may influence the extent to which they collaborate with librarians in research instruction. (1) They emphasized the *service* (may be understood as *subordinate*) role of librarians, rather than the educational role; (2) they viewed librarians as professionals but not as academic equals; (3) they were often unaware of the amount of instruction given by librarians; (4) most of them frequently or sometimes referred their students to a librarian; and (5) although almost two-thirds believed that librarians had some involvement in their students' education, less than one-fourth saw that involvement as substantial.

One Earlham faculty member (Thompson, 1993, pp. 103–104), who probably expresses an unusually positive orientation to library instruction, deplores the attitudes of some of his colleagues toward librarians. "They [faculty] regard librarians as they regard secretaries and grounds keepers, as their errand boys and girls, not as their colleagues." His candor is refreshing but disturbing. "How can you treat colleagues in the library like that? What does it do to the ethos of an entire community when a cohort of people are treated like flunkies? The intellectual life is supposed to be cooperative."

A more scientific study (Oberg, Schleiter, and Van Houten, 1989, p. 223) provides a rational basis for much of what faculty think. "The current study demonstrates that more than two-thirds of our respondents do not consider librarians to be their peers. These faculty members cite as their reasons insufficient teaching and research and inadequate educational credentials."

The culminating effect of these attitude studies and observations could negatively influence those inclined to accept the status quo. Librarians, however, are a hopeful lot, and their culture and experience have traditionally predisposed them to accept such negatives as challenges rather than obstacles. These arguments are essential for librarians to understand, however, if they wish to overcome the resistance of many faculty to their bibliographic instruction efforts. It is important that they be less concerned with how faculty regard them, as equals or subordinates, than with ways that they can build constructive relationships and affect classroom learning. Although their role may remain supportive in the overall framework of the courses they teach, it is an essential and distinctive contribution that only they can make.

A study by Nitecki (1993) suggests the need to develop "a shared frame of the library" as a means of bridging the perception gap and developing a common understanding of what libraries and librarians are and do:

> The identification of metaphors about libraries, cited by academics in their communications, offers library administrators insights into academic library users' conceptualisation of libraries. . . . As we learn more about the metaphoric stories our users tell about libraries, the better we may understand their criteria for judging our success in resolving the problems perceived with our libraries. Furthermore, as we better understand the basis for their perceptions of libraries, the easier it should be to direct our efforts to influence these perceptions by manipulating metaphors we use in communications about libraries with them. (p. 273)

In view of the influence that faculty exercise over their students' learning, knowledge of attitudes such as these should provide librarians with effective tools for building instruction programs. They understand that their task is broader than simply teaching research methods to students. It includes agreement with faculty on the pedagogical principle of the value of exploratory learning, demonstration that knowledge is cumulative and dependent on what has been learned before, valuing discipline-oriented learning that depends on the organization of knowledge, and integrating present learning with previous knowledge. Whether faculty or librarians, or both in cooperation, provide the instruction, the significance of the task argues convincingly for instructors to be knowledgeable information researchers themselves. Although their need to use the library for their own research and information gathering is conditioned by the other information networks available to them, their students do not usually have access to these alternative sources. For students, the library remains their most important information source, next to the faculty themselves. Faculty who neglect insuring that their students develop adequate information research skills may be depriving them of an important part of their education. They may also handicap their students' ability to pursue the lifelong learning required in an occupationally mobile, information-dominated society.

One source (Moran, 1990, p. 513) postulates that individualized library-centered learning provides a more effective way of preparing students for the real world than traditional methods do: "After graduation, students will not learn from lectures and reserve books. They need to be prepared for this future now by being taught how to gather, evaluate, and utilize sources on their own." She even suggests that professors model their own learning methods for their students.

> Faculty members expect to transmit knowledge by lecture, but how much of their learning do they get by that means . . . ? They gain new knowledge by reading journals, exchanging references, talking to colleagues and keeping up with the literature that appears in their fields. In short, their learning takes place outside the classroom. (Moran, 1990, p. 513)

IV. Faculty Knowledge and Use of the Library

Since faculty exercise the strongest influence on student use of the library, it is useful to learn something about how and how well they instruct their students when they do undertake the task of teaching research skills themselves. One study (Clark and Silverman, 1989) discerned a tendency of faculty to recommend to their students the use of computer sources over print, even when the choice was inappropriate for the subject matter. It is clear to any reference librarian that even misinformation from faculty members is more authoritative than knowledgeable and accurate information from a librarian. Students' *perception* is a stronger motivator than reality.

In order to teach information research skills effectively, faculty must have first-hand knowledge of, and experience with, the information system. They will be required to know the power and potential of research in order to enable their students to explore the invaluable world of peripheral and relational data, or students will not be directed toward appropriate resources.

No clear picture exists to tell librarians how much their faculty members know about using the library. What library has had the temerity to administer a test of library knowledge to its faculty? Most evidence relies on experience and anecdotal data. Both suggest that a large number of faculty remain ignorant of how to use the library and hence undervalue its potential as an information laboratory for student learning. This reality is asserted by both faculty and librarians. One source (Burlingame, 1980) estimated that perhaps only one third of the faculty on a given campus has an adequate knowledge of their library resources.

A history professor's experience (Swieringa, 1984, p. 391) led to this pessimistic observation: "It would not shock professional librarians if I assert that the university library is *terra incognita* for many, if not most, students. Unfortunately, this is also true of graduate students and even professors." Another faculty member (Lacey, 1980, p. 21) speaks candidly about his own experience: ". . . I did not know how to help my students figure out how to do research, how to distinguish good from bad material to use for research. . . . I have a sense that my colleagues do not know much more about research than any of us did when we first got out of graduate school. . . . If I am right in this, it would follow that many of us who are now teaching in colleges and universities are only slightly at home in libraries."

Another concurs (Stephenson, 1980, pp. 81–82): "Most of us faculty, however, lack the training in library skills, accessing, and developing search strategies. Overall, we lack the training for effectively incorporating library training into our academic courses and into our departmental programs. I know this from my own experience." The same faculty member (Stephenson, 1993) writes a number of years later, after a period of intense and effective bibliographic instruction, of changed perceptions and practices:

> . . . our new, young faculty members participate in bibliographic instruction with much greater avidity and ease than did we older teachers when we were first exposed to it. They recognize its power and its importance in the scientific disciplines of today. . . . In the biology department at Earlham College, library training has become an integral and significant part of our curricular program. My colleagues and I cannot imagine effective teaching without it. (p. 27)

Librarians have reason to hope that a decade or more of bibliographic instruction efforts, some of it directed toward or at least involving faculty, have changed negative perceptions. A survey of faculty attitudes (Thomas, 1994) conducted at California State University, Long Beach, in 1990 that updated a 1982 survey, showed some hopeful signs of change. In the 1990 survey, faculty showed a greater tendency to value library instruction and less dependence on students' ability to learn research methods on their own than revealed in the 1982 survey. However, the literature suggests that inade-

quacies persist. An English professor (Thompson, 1993) describes the research
methods of his colleagues:

> Most people who have PhD's do not really know how to do research and never did. There
> are all kinds of ways you can get your research done to get a doctorate, and most of these
> ways are very inefficient. Dissertation topics are so narrow that they do not call for the
> kind of research skills required of broader undergraduate projects. When you can focus
> narrowly, you really do not have to be a particularly good seeker of information. (p. 103)

The fact is that few faculty were taught how to use libraries when they
were students; it was apparently assumed (as confirmed by the California
State study for that institution at least) that they would "pick up" library
usage skills somehow on their own. However, there is no reason to expect
that they know as faculty what they never learned as students. Even for those
who did receive instruction in library research methods, the shift to machine-
based information systems requires mastery of new concepts and different
skills. "But one does not learn to use today's large research libraries intelli-
gently without months of practice, in addition to considerable help from the
people who work there. This the faculty, for the most part, do not realize
or do not want to acknowledge. The fact is that few university professors
know very much about bibliographic research, even in their own disciplines"
(McCarthy, 1985, p. 142).

An ESL teacher at Cornell (Feldman, 1989) confirms the value of librarians who enable faculty to keep their research skills up to date.

> I found that I was depending more and more on the librarians' talks and information, both
> for my own knowledge and for my students. Though I well understood the concepts and
> motivation for bibliographic skills, my details were as out of date as the textbooks. . . .
> The ESL teachers certainly feel that our own skills are sharpened by our direct contact
> with library professionals. . . . (p. 162)

However, the fact that many faculty lack information research skills
should not be interpreted to mean that they do not possess sophisticated
research abilities appropriate to their area of specialization. What some may
need to learn is how to integrate information research into their overall
research and teaching. "Unlike instruction in online searching for students,
which focuses on how to construct a research strategy of which online searching is a part, instruction for faculty emphasizes how online searching fits in
with and enhances the research methods they already use" (Steffen, 1988,
p. 18). Faculty who are educated in this manner will be more likely to integrate
information research into their class requirements than those who have no
such orientation. They will also be able to assign more appropriate and
workable research problems.

Troublesome as it is to librarians to think about the many students
who seldom or never choose, or are not motivated to use, the library as an

information resource, their real problems arise from ill-prepared or inade-
quately motivated students who do use the library. The sometimes divergent
and even conflicting roles of faculty and librarians often intersect at the time
students enter the library to do their "library assignment." It is difficult from
the library perspective to deal with the proliferation of what seem to be
poorly designed and executed library exercises that appear to have no better
purpose than to "get students into the library." Librarians tend to view these
faculty-generated assignments as naive, inaccurate, and unworkable (as they
sometimes are). Despite their qualms, however, their professionalism requires
them to help students (the ones who have the courage to ask) with any
research problem. Their morale and self-esteem may suffer from the failure
of faculty to treat them as colleagues, or even as subordinate lab assistants, in
that they were not consulted or informed about the assignments beforehand.
However, they do not have the choice of refusing to help. Many librarians
no doubt try to contact the faculty authors of these difficult assignments, but
they may be misunderstood as complaining about the extra work load rather
than trying to improve the quality of library research.

It is possible in some instances, however, that these opinions may be
based on a lack of awareness of the rationale behind the assignments, of what
the teacher had in mind or hoped to accomplish. They may be the result of
the faculty's tendency to bypass the librarians in writing these assignments.
Librarians may resent being overlooked in the process, but their energies
could be better directed toward seeking ways to collaborate in constructing
assignments that combine the intention of the faculty with workable, reasonable methods directed toward achieving the desired goals. Constructive solutions will lead librarians to confer with faculty, to learn their attitudes toward
the library, what they expect of the library, what they tell their students about
the library, and what uses they require their students to make of the library.

Because they are usually asked to intervene only when there is a problem,
it is possible that librarians acquire through experience a pessimistic view of
the faculty–library connection. They may not be aware of the many students
who carry out intelligent library research assignments in a reasonable manner
without any help from a librarian. They may function without a clear sense
of the whole range of assignments and research tasks that require students
to use the library. Consistent and ongoing communication between librarians
and faculty is essential in order to acquire a complete and accurate picture
of the extent to which the library supports student and faculty research.

V. The Library's Unique Contribution

Knowledgeable librarians can make a strong case for their ability and willingness to support the teaching programs of the institution and are likely at the

same time to further the objective of insuring research-oriented faculty. It should not be difficult to demonstrate that the library has needed resources that will further the important goals of instruction. If librarians will only marshall these resources, they should be well prepared to articulate and justify how the library can contribute to learning in ways that are positive and assertive. Numerous examples may be found in the literature to support these arguments.

A. Integrated Instruction for Students

A number of libraries have discovered an open door for library instruction through collaboration with the many writing-across-the-curriculum (WAC) or writing-intensive-curriculum (WIC) programs (Sheridan, 1995) that have been introduced at more than 400 colleges and universities. Educators have found in them a way to improve what many faculty see as the deplorable quality of student writing, but their greatest selling point has been proof of the theory that writing can be a mode of learning. Many instructors have recognized that for writing as learning to happen, students must have something to write *about*, and the library becomes the natural and essential resource as the principle repository of knowledge. Students are expected to integrate new knowledge as the essential matter of their learning through writing.

A noteworthy example of the interrelationship between research and writing is the Writing in American Studies course at Arizona State University West (Isbell and Broaddus, 1995). An unusual class, in that an English professor and a librarian share equally in responsibility and contribution, this course integrates the elements of writing and research to an unusual extent. "The organization of the course stresses the organic nature of research and writing, and how the two are intertwined and part of a continuous process." The assumptions underlying this theory have important implications for integrating classroom learning with bibliographic instruction:

1. Research and writing in a scholarly setting are a seamless whole; each feeds on the other and cannot be separated.
2. Scholarly writing is a dialogue between the writer, his or her sources, and colleagues.
3. Scholarly writing is a creative activity—the writer adds to the dialogue by contributing new syntheses, new conclusions, or new insights (Isbell and Broaddus, 1995, p. 53).

Other programs have demonstrated that the principles of collaboration can operate on a smaller scale than one requiring equal partnerships between librarians and faculty. Successful efforts have been recorded of varying levels of contribution by librarians at such disparate institutions as state university systems, small liberal-arts colleges, and community colleges (Sheridan, 1995). Courses in subject matter as varied as graphic design and aquaculture at Oregon State University lent themselves equally well to teaching with WIC principles, demonstrating that students could learn the subject matter, discover how to do effective information research, and improve their reasoning and communication skills. The campuswide writing program at the University of Massachusetts–Amherst operates on the premise that writing is an essential component of education ". . . for self-reflection, for learning and presentation of their ideas, for civic participation, and for professional life . . ." and that library research is a necessary means by which students conduct inquiries for their writing projects (Sheridan, 1995, pp. 168–169).

Nontraditional courses at the University of Rhode Island in women's studies and human services, which by their nature could not depend on the traditional textbook/lecture approach, found the library indispensible as their students' primary source of information. Teachers in the writing-intensive program at the University of Vermont discovered soon after the inception of the program that "As writing-intensive courses are developed at first-year or advanced levels, it becomes apparent that students will require outside resources to complete their projects satisfactorily. Faculty have worked with librarians to develop quite an array of research or library assignments that go beyond the traditional research paper" (Sheridan, 1995, p. 190). Among the benefits of faculty/librarian collaboration in Whatcom Community College's WAC program were the following:

1. Increased interest in topic and in research process, due to ease of use
2. Increased energy on creative use of materials rather than on burdensome searching
3. Increased preparation to undertake future research projects and to pursue deeper research questions and more sophisticated research projects
4. Enhanced learning of both library/research skills and course content (Sheridan, 1995, p. 201)

The success of alliances between the writing program and library research with academically at-risk students has been demonstrated at Richard Stockton College, a small state-supported undergraduate institution in New Jersey. Oral interviews with individuals who had experienced a historical event or movement sparked student interest in learning more about its history. Individual advising by a librarian enabled students to complete the intimidating task of library research, fulfill their class assignment, and satisfy their own curiosity (Sheridan, 1995, pp. 161–163).

Another source (Marino, 1992) emphasizes but also cautions that a shared view of the nature of the research process by librarians and faculty is essential for these programs to succeed. The projects described above provide evidence that such a shared view is possible.

Once these principles are espoused by both librarians and faculty, they have promise of even wider application to other types of course-related instruction. "Both team instructors [at ASU West] have taken ideas from Writing in American Studies and applied them to other classes, such as active learning techniques that foster collaboration and discovery" (Isbell and Broaddus, 1995, p. 61). Another writer (Fister, 1995, p. 34) sees similar affinities. "Of course, this is a description of course-related bibliographic instruction programs. Or is it a description of the writing-across-the-curriculum movement? These programs share so many characteristics that it is hard, in the abstract, to tell them apart."

Examples of other course-related library instruction have appeared over time in the literature of librarianship, and to a certain extent, in that of the larger field of education. Increasingly of late these articles have exemplified the principles of course-*integrated* teaching.

Geology professors at Kent State University (Schloman and Feldmann, 1993) discovered in the library an indispensible resource for teaching students the use of secondary sources as a means of discovering primary records and for developing an understanding of the overall structure of the literature of geology itself, both important goals of the undergraduate program. Graduate students were then taught to build on these skills to understand the different kinds of information needs of a practicing geologist and the means of meeting these needs quickly and efficiently.

Psychology students at St. Olaf College (Huber and Sherman, 1992) are taught the principles of scholarly networking, defined as "a body of materials produced by a community of individuals, working in concert to advance knowledge of the discipline." They follow the development of a contemporary researcher's ideas during recent years, learning how this person's thinking fits into a particular psychological topic, and determining the current status of the field by what questions are being asked about it today. In addition to teaching traditional library research tools to these classes, librarians have emphasized the importance of citation indexing in understanding the principles of scholarly networking.

An instruction librarian (Bodi, 1992, pp. 75–76) urges her colleagues to incorporate critical thinking skills into their teaching, rather than relying solely on emphasizing information-finding techniques, by encouraging students to examine their assumptions and biases about a subject: "Librarians can help students find the many differing points of view on an issue; they can help them to evaluate conflicting opinions and to arrive at their own well-reasoned, carefully documented, and effectively argued views."

A psychology professor and librarian team (Mark and Lee, 1992) have demonstrated an effective way to incorporate the teaching of critical thinking into a process-research approach. By this method, students are guided through their assignments, and they receive feedback and approval from the teacher and librarian before proceeding to the next step.

An education professor (O'Brien and Warmkessel, 1994) came up with a novel idea of how to animate an ordinarily dull class in the philosophy of education and collaborated with a librarian in developing library-related assignment objectives. Students were asked to assume the persona of a well-known educational philosopher, become thoroughly familiar with that person's ideas and present them at a mock conference in keynote addresses, workshops, and informal discussions. The course proved to be an effective way of weaving together course content, classroom teaching, and library instruction.

Another faculty–librarian team at Rensselaer Polytechnic Institute's School of Engineering (Holmes, Irish, and Haley, 1994) have developed an interactive model for library instruction in a large-enrollment undergraduate course required of all majors, Introduction to Engineering. The program uses the Karplus learning cycle, which includes exploration, inventing concepts and applying concepts, using library research to complete each phase. Librarians involved in teaching these classes have gained invaluable experience in integrated classroom instruction but also in understanding faculty and student perceptions of the information process.

The demonstrated success of experiential learning methods such as those described gives librarians a convincing argument for the educational relevance of library research and provides faculty a powerful tool for enhancing classroom learning. Faculty are certainly aware of the limitations of the typical class period as a medium for instruction, and they must routinely make the difficult choices required for determining what can be reasonably taught and assimilated. Given this pattern of teaching, it is probable that students cannot be provided all the information they will need to function effectively in their chosen profession through classroom instruction alone. The rate at which knowledge becomes obsolete, especially in scientific and technical fields, necessitates continual relearning, as does the rate at which information is lost through the memory. These limitations mean that students must augment their learning by exploring, testing, and evaluating facts and theories for themselves, especially in the information-rich environment of the library. Developing learning habits that will enable students to continue this process throughout their professional lifetimes will prepare them far better for living and working in the modern information society than will mastering a finite amount of information. The purpose of a college education, then, is to learn how to learn. Astute educators will place a deemphasis on information transfer and an increased emphasis on teaching students how to learn (Stanford, 1992).

Librarians have not been slow to recognize the enormous advantages of new technological information retrieval capabilities, not only for opening up the world of knowledge to their users but also in providing a highly effective, interactive bibliographic instruction tool. Electronic access through online bibliographic searches and computer-based reference services to many of the available databases provides powerful discovery and intelligent, purposeful selection capabilities not available through traditional searching means.

The ability to construct search inquiries for precise retrieval of information, once minimally possible with print indexes, is now greatly enhanced with electronic retrieval methods. These provide numerous access points to information that were not previously available as well as the ability to define specifically what the searcher wants. They enable precision in the inclusion of desired items as well as the exclusion of undesired. The process of selecting search specifications also requires researchers to refine their queries and to define the purpose and scope of the research project, necessities often dealt with only vaguely in traditional search methods.

As an example, professors in a dissertation proposal class at Colorado State University were pleased to discover that Boolean logic used in electronic searches for information admirably illustrates and accommodates the development of dissertation research questions or statements. These will typically include an antecedent/predictor independent variable, possibly a second independent variable, an outcome/criterion dependent variable, and participants or subjects. The process of planning a computer search requires students to think about and determine the ideas and vocabulary that they wish to include in each of these categories.

In view of the claims of most database vendors that their search programs that have created these capabilities are self-instructional, it may be necessary for librarians to demonstrate the value that their intervention can add to database researchers' learning. An early study of OPAC use (Matthews and Lawrence, 1984, p. 369) concluded that "those who receive at least some initial training and assistance [in system use] are more satisified and successful than those who do not." Although trained users experience greater success in searching, according to the same study, users seem reluctant to seek training on their own, or even to read available documentation. Updated studies could provide librarians with some vital information as to whether attitudes have changed and skills have developed over more than a decade of users' experience with electronic searching systems. Experience suggests that instruction still provides a means of introducing database options, shortening the learning curve, allaying anxieties of the computer phobic, and improving the quality of searching methods and results.

The immediacy of the means used and results obtained enable librarians to demonstrate, to a degree not possible before the introduction of technology, the learning power inherent in the research process. Several of Butler's (1985) principles of the teaching/learning model are applicable to, and illustrated by, electronic database searching:

1. . . . the principal basis for motivation and purpose is the perceived value and meaning of the new knowledge or skill for the learner.
2. . . . the more distinctive features we can differentiate, the more and the stronger the connections we can make among the elements of a situation, the new learning, and related prior learning (Butler, 1985, p. 17).
3. The mere act of organizing information involves a certain degree of comprehension. . . . (Butler, 1985, p. 7).
4. . . . learning complex knowledge and skills is nearly impossible without the help of visual and verbal representations that model the underlying structure and meaning (Butler, 1985, p. 9).
5. Regardless of the instructional media or method, some means must be used to insure that students directly interact with the new information conveyed, as it is conveyed.
6. We must also teach students when, where, and how to transfer and translate generalizable knowledge and skills to new contexts and to new tasks (Butler, 1985, p. 12).

Librarians who teach electronic information research quickly realize that their success has created its own dilemmas. Students are faced with an overwhelming amount and variety of information, and they may not be able to deal with the unprecedented abundance of resources without some organizing principles, or concepts, that enable them to understand the significance and interrelatedness of knowledge. These concepts can be imbedded in, or explicitly taught, through carefully designed instruction, but they are also objectified and reinforced in the way that libraries and information sources are organized to provide systematic and convenient access. The vocabulary that students learn in the research process teaches a great deal about the structure of the subject, often dealing with its hierarchies through expression of broader and narrower subject ranges but also providing an introductory approach to the discipline.

An important task of student education is acquiring the ability to reflect on the content and manner of learning and to evaluate the quality and validity of the ideas they encounter. This process may be practiced in the library where adequate information exists for relating, comparing, and synthesizing ideas. A library instruction workshop (Lin, 1994, p. 169) for culturally diverse populations used the library as an object lesson for teaching unifying principles

to both Oriental students who ". . . tend to emphasize the holistic, organis-
mic, and macroscopic aspects of the world . . ." and Westerners who ". . .
tend to focus on specific, mechanistic, and microscopic aspects."

In an age of narrowing subject specialization, there is at the same time
a countertrend toward cross-disciplinary programs such as women's, ethnic,
and area studies, and toward ideas that seek to integrate knowledge. Involvement in these programs will require faculty and students to learn in new
disciplines and to pay renewed attention to interdisciplinary questions. The
integrative function of contemporary education is perceptively described by
Cleveland (1985):

> The Scientific Revolution, and its younger sibling the Industrial Revolution, were made
> possible by our capacity to divide into separable disciplines the proven methods of inquiry,
> and to retrieve from bins of manageable size and complication the knowledge we accumu-
> lated by observing, experimenting, and theorizing. But in the latter part of the twentieth
> century, we came to realize that most of our troubles stem from neglecting the interconnect-
> edness of knowledge and the interdisciplinary character of all real-world problems. (p. 10)

One faculty member (Talbot, 1989) has discovered that the library offers
a readily available means of discovering how knowledge is interrelated:

> The point is not that one should try reading or hearing everything in its entirety but rather
> that one should develop an awareness of the connections between selected passages and
> their surroundings. This is one reason that it is so important for students to be encouraged
> to use the whole library on a regular basis, not just the reserve room. One of the beauties
> of open stacks is their browsability; the physical relationship of books on the shelves reveals
> so much about patterns and history of thought. (p. 53)

Of course, these riches of information can be intimidating without a "road
map" for guidance. Researchers, both faculty and students, need generalizable
skills that are transferable to information needs in any subject area, skills
which librarians, by preparation and experience, are distinctively qualified
to teach.

These approaches to instruction demonstrate that the library has the
resources to become a useful ally to the faculty in motivating students to
learn. No amount of testing, grading, and in other ways "pushing" students
into learning will achieve as much success as will efforts to develop self-
motivated, self-directed learners. What the library can provide is an environment in which learning can happen and a laboratory where information exists
in sufficient quantity and variety to support exploration.

Programs such as these demonstrate the truism that one of the most
effective ways to ensure motivated learning is to engage students actively in
the learning process. The full use of the library's resources will require
students to become active participants in exploring significant questions that
justify the amount of time required to pursue them, attempting to find solutions to the pressing problems of the day, and engaging their minds and wills

in the discovery of knowledge. This quality of learning gives students a stake in the outcome of their education that goes beyond grades and degrees.

A library-sponsored faculty project developed at Northern Kentucky University (Werrell and Wesley, 1990, p. 172) produced a list of characteristics of effective, motivating library assignments that are given in brief here. Readers are urged to consult the original article for a full discussion:

> (1) Library assignments should originate from and be directly related to the course subject matter; (2) the students must understand the purpose of the project and how it will benefit them; (3) analysis should be emphasized over answers; (4) students should be encouraged to plan their research before and as they retrieve information; (5) the assignment should be a progressive project, with time and opportunities for concrete feedback from a variety of sources; (6) library research and information use should be presented at increasing levels of complexity, moving from basic retrieval of information to evaluating information sources; (7) students should be helped to generalize the skills they learn in one research project so that they may be applied to others. (Werrell and Wesley, 1990, p. 172)

Integrated programs of this type make it clear to students that information research provides direct and tangible benefits to their immediate course objectives. With emphasis placed on the development of these skills, library use is more likely to be viewed as providing faculty with an additional teaching tool, not as an "extra," which takes valuable time from the class schedule. It becomes integral to the course rather than peripheral. Syllabi could then be structured to include the type of information research that directly furthers the course objectives. Ideally such courses would be developed in consultation between librarians who understand the use of information resources and teaching faculty who know the subject matter and who determine the learning objectives of the course.

B. Library Instruction for Faculty

Although traditional user education programs have been directed toward students, a number of libraries have recognized and attempted to meet the need of instruction explicitly for faculty. At a national library conference several years ago, one speaker proposed, perhaps facetiously, the controversial thesis that all attempts to educate students in library research should be abandoned as too labor-intensive and ineffective, in favor of faculty library instruction. The apparent intention was that faculty would then teach their own students. That idea has apparently not caught on, but those libraries that have initiated effective faculty programs provide them in addition to those offered to students.

Among the most extensively documented (Lipow, 1979) are the faculty seminars offered at the University of California, Berkeley. Conducted annually since 1976, these sessions have emphasized advanced research in the social sciences and humanities and library updates on changing research tools and techniques. Of necessity, however, they have also covered basic research methods, with which many faculty are unfamiliar.

The experience gained by librarians at Berkeley through this program provides some insights for any libraries considering efforts to provide faculty library instruction:

> Finally, some generalities about what we have learned from this experience. I hope that the myth that faculty won't admit to their lack of library know-how is exploded. We now know that (1) many, if not most, faculty need an update course; (2) many faculty need guidance in elementary concepts and tools in addition to the more advanced ones; (3) if given the opportunity, faculty want to be educated about the library; (4) although it is true that most faculty may neither understand nor appreciate the crucial role of librarians in the information-retrieval process, faculty can be educated about this role, and no one but librarians can do the job. (Lipow, 1979)

Seminars offered in recent years have added an emphasis on access to electronic information sources (Lipow, 1992, p. 7), acting on the assumption that ". . . there are new bibliographic concepts to be learned, and faculty must learn them if they are to be successful library users and information seekers." Although the few hundred attendees at each series of workshops represent only a fraction of the total faculty at the university, they have the potential over time of creating what Thompson (1993) calls a "critical mass" of faculty opinion that can become allied with librarians seeking to change traditional campus culture relating to teaching methods.

A more recently introduced faculty instruction program at Northwestern University (Baker, Birchfield, and Weston, 1992, p. 75) has adopted the Berkeley model as part of its campuswide emphasis on faculty–librarian partnerships: "The Faculty Update Program at the University of California, Berkeley, remains the best model for informing faculty about new developments in information retrieval and bibliographic research." The rationale for the Northwestern design incorporates much of what has been learned in recent decades about essential changes in methods and means of information research:

> Faculty members unexposed to recent developments such as integrated bibliographic systems, CD-ROM publishing, computer networking, full-text databases, and electronic text manipulation are obviously often at a loss in taking advantage of them, and thus cannot easily incorporate them into their own teaching practices. The need to give faculty opportunities to learn about new technologies in a supportive environment, and in ways that are immediately applicable in their areas of teaching and research, is increasingly being recognized as an important educational issue. (Baker *et al.*, 1992, p. 71)

A similar emphasis on learning to search electronic sources has guided the development of faculty seminars at the University of Iowa (Forys, 1992) and Messiah College (Mark and Lee, 1992). At the latter institution, librarians were able to observe tangible outcomes in cooperative development of a sequence of library skills that were incorporated into a target course, and in the inclusion of knowledge gleaned from the workshops into library assignments for classes.

A program developed at the Library/Learning Center of the University of Wisconsin–Parkside (Piele, Pryor, and Tuckett, 1986, p. 377) consisted of a series of seminars to teach faculty the use of microcomputers in library-related research and teaching tasks. These included sessions on end-user searching, bibliography management and presentation graphics that were conceptual in approach, stressing the principles of information access and management. "Faculty . . . have been prepared to introduce their students to discipline-specific applications of microcomputers, which otherwise might have been ignored."

Similar workshops designed to teach the appropriate uses of, and searching methods for, online database indexes were developed by the University of North Carolina at Greensboro (Schumacher, 1989). Librarians were particularly concerned about the number of inappropriate recommendations from faculty that students use computer searching to meet any research need. They planned the workshops with two goals in mind: (1) to explain how computer searching could improve the quality of faculty research and/or classroom instruction; (2) to provide more complete and accurate information about computer searching to pass on to their students. The positive responses from the 15–18% of the university faculty who attended the workshops (voluntarily) indicated a significant sense of need as well as receptivity to instruction by librarians.

Librarians at Syracuse University (Stark and Waltz, 1988) conducted successful faculty workshops in online catalog searching to deal with some key problems often encountered by users of automated systems: word order, trying to key in too much information, initials, and finding too many hits. For solutions, they presented several distinctive features that characterize online searching in general, or that have special applications to computer searching: truncation, call number searching, combining subject searches, and choice of terminology. Although their instruction was based on their own online system, the principles have wide application to computer catalogs and indexes in general.

Efforts to provide user education for faculty appear to have better chances of success when approached from the perspective of learning electronic resources than using other means. It seems easier for faculty to admit the need to learn new research tools than to acknowledge that they don't fully understand the traditional ones. However, skillful presentations by librarians can use newer electronic methods to illustrate the principles that have always been required in order to perform intelligent information research. Other approaches that can prove the benefits of faculty–librarian cooperation, may not necessarily depend on electronic intervention.

A series of exercise-planning workshops at Northern Kentucky University (Werrell and Wesley, 1990, p. 172) concentrated on the design and writing of effective research assignments, using criteria that were developed jointly by faculty and librarians. A highly useful feature of the sessions was the opportunity to critique several anonymous exercises designed and used by faculty prior to the workshop. This activity allowed for peer review of both poor and well-designed assignments and helped to attain the desired result of defining the characteristics of good exercises. "The faculty–librarian collaboration resulted in assignments which promoted information literacy, while fulfilling the instructors' course goals."

As a means of coping with the growing complexities of knowledge, professors may be tempted to continue relying on their familiar information networks, such as consultation with trusted colleagues in their disciplines, use of their own subscriptions and personal libraries, and contacts at conferences or on research projects as their primary information sources. However, essential as these sources are, those who limit themselves to these means may miss information vital to their research and teaching as well as the opportunity of profiting by the comprehensive, systematic, organized and selective approach to information that is available through libraries. Whatever the faculty's need for the library may be, it should not be denied that their students must explore and use library resources, not only for their immediate information requirements, but also for educating their minds, enhancing the quality of their intellect, and promoting lifelong learning.

C. Administrative Support for Bibliographic Instruction

It must be clear to instruction librarians who wish to develop an effective campuswide user education program that the means of reaching this goal are dependent on more than the efforts of librarians. In some instances, methods of changing the entire institutional climate must be addressed; in others, existing readiness to participate on the part of faculty and administrators requires that libraries use their resources to take advantage of these receptive attitudes. For example, a recent survey of faculty attitudes at Dalhousie University (Nowakowski, 1993, p. 124) revealed an astonishing degree of support for information literacy: ". . . 84% agree that students should know how to do library research and 95% agree that it will be essential to students in later life that they are able to find information efficiently." Perhaps more surprising, in view of some negative results of other surveys, is that ". . . 88% agree that librarians and faculty are partners in the educational process . . ." and ". . . 89% of those surveyed agreed that it should be a requirement of

the Baccalaureate degree that students know how to do library research."
Librarians at institutions such as Dalhousie may experience more demand
than their resources can supply.

The experience of the University of Alaska, Fairbanks (Ruess, 1994),
provides a model for library response to an overwhelming demand. When
the university adopted a core curriculum in 1990 that ". . . emphasized the
integration of information, skills, and disciplinary perspectives," an existing,
well-established course in library and information research gained approval
as the library and information skills component of the core curriculum. The
all too-familiar scenario of mandating new programs without providing additional resources was repeated in the UAF experience, necessitating considerable reassessment of course objectives, reassignment of existing personnel,
and revision of methods. However, the process provides an example of a
functioning program mandated by the campus decision-making bodies outside
the library.

Another source of administrative support for library user education may
be found in the criteria of regional accrediting associations, especially those
of the Middle States and Southern Association.

The Director of the Middle States CHE (Simmons, 1992, p. 18) agrees
with Boyer's contention that information research is a necessary component of
undergraduate instruction. The association has made the goal of information
literacy a part of its accreditation standards and procedures:

> Because the Middle States CHE is concerned about the continuous improvement of
> quality, particularly at the undergraduate level, it believes that programs to improve
> the teaching and learning process in colleges and universities should include an appropriate
> emphasis on information literacy and other resource-based learning strategies. (Simmons,
> 1992, p. 18)

The association has developed a built-in mechanism for ensuring that
these objectives become an effective part of the accreditation process:

> CHE understands that it has a corresponding responsibility to ensure that this emphasis
> on information literacy through the medium of the library—as broadly defined—is realized
> in self-study and evaluation team reports, institutional assessment programs, program re-
> views, and in accreditation decision making. (Simmons, 1992, p. 18)

Unlike the prescriptions of educator–thinkers such as Boyer, which may
serve as clarion calls to action but have no means of effecting reform, the
Middle States CHE has a built-in change mechanism in its standards for
accreditation. Among the most detailed, and probably most effective, are
those that examine course syllabi for appropriate and creative library research
content that promotes critical thinking and learning (Simmons, 1992, p. 17).
Typical of questions asked to determine the extent of information research
required by individual courses may be some of the following:

How many syllabi include library-based assignments?

What is the nature of those assignments?

Are they appropriate for the program and its students?

Do they show evidence of thought and creativity?

Do they promote active learning?

Do they take advantage of primary sources when appropriate?

Do they display a knowledge of the range of resources available to students
at the institution?

Is there a sense that, as students progress from the beginning of the degree
program to its conclusion, they are required to use increasingly complex
library research skills?

It seems clear that the in-depth analysis required to answer these questions
precludes any superficial evaluation and necessitates a background of truly
course-integrated library instruction.

The criteria of the Southern Association (1994) are less prescriptive as
to the responsibilities of classroom instructors, but are more explicit about
the library's role: "Basic library services *must* include an orientation program
designed to teach new users how to access bibliographic information and
other learning resources" (p. 54). They make it clear that collaborative efforts
are expected: "Libraries and learning resource centers *must* provide students
with opportunities to learn how to access information in different formats
so that they can continue·life-learning. Librarians *must* work cooperatively
with faculty members and other information providers in assisting students
to use resource materials effectively" (p. 55).

The perspective of emphasizing the responsibility and initiative of the
library for user instruction seems to be a less effective method for bringing
about change than that of requiring a faculty role in teaching information
research. Librarians already understand and accept the challenge. However,
the support of professional associations when seeking an institution-wide
commitment should not be overlooked.

VI. The Library's Challenge

On many campuses the library remains uninvolved in the mainstream of
academic life, and students graduate from college without having learned the
basics of information research. The *Carnegie Report* observed that "The gap
between the classroom and the library, reported on almost a half-century
ago, still exists today" (Scully, 1986, p. 1).

The library can fulfill its role in the improvement of teaching only when
it is regarded by faculty as one of the vital campus resources for instruction.

The distinctive expertise of librarians in the field of information resources is fundamental to learning, even though this fact may not always be recognized by faculty. The crucial responsibility for librarians is to develop, maintain, and enhance that expertise, but more important, to take the initiative in demonstrating it to their faculty colleagues.

Partnerships formed between librarians and teaching faculty and collegial relationships forged in the classroom and on other projects are certain to improve and advance both areas of academic life. Without such collegiality, the library will probably remain underutilized in spite of the high financial and personal investment required to develop and maintain it and in spite of the abundance of resources that it contains.

Cooperative endeavors provide opportunities for classroom faculty to observe that librarians possess an area of expertise in the information world that they themselves may lack. When librarians share that special knowledge, it "allows faculty to observe a librarian as a teacher and an information consultant, two roles of a librarian that are unfamiliar to most faculty." This role establishes librarians as valuable colleagues who possess essential knowledge that they are willing to share (Steffen, 1988, p. 20).

It would be easy and convenient to blame the problems of noncooperation between the library and the classroom on bad attitudes of faculty toward librarians, lack of understanding by faculty of the value of the library's support for instruction, or any of the other misconceptions and errors dealt with previously. However, a more productive approach would be to ask how well librarians understand faculty perceptions and problems, how much they know about the goals of classroom instruction, and how extensively they participate in the active life of campus. The answers in most instances would probably reveal a serious lack of communication between librarians and faculty about learning objectives and methods:

> The teacher . . . believes that the student, *like himself* or *herself*, understands the library, and that for the most part he or she uses it in an orderly way, and, if not, has enough common sense to ask questions of librarians. In some ways our differing perspectives may be the result of our point of contact with the student. As a colleague insightfully remarked, faculty see the *outcome* and librarians see the *process*. (Lubans, 1983, p. 20)

These comments show some understanding of the communications gap that exists. The consequences for students are too important to allow the different perceptions to divide the process when collaboration between faculty and librarians can create an integrated and effective outcome: improved course work and increased learning. Hardesty (1986) places responsibility for this dialogue on librarians:

> Academic librarians interested in promoting educationally productive use of the academic library should develop a good understanding of the educational attitudes of the classroom

faculty and how these attitudes relate to the academic library. Librarians then need to develop coherent strategies to relate the academic library to the educational goals and purposes of the classroom faculty. This may involve some change of attitudes on the part of members of both groups. (p. 155)

Librarians who fail to make these essential connections with the faculty and the institution will find themselves left out of the mainstream of academic endeavors and irrelevant to the learning that takes place on campus. They may have invested a great deal of time and effort in programs that do not work and that are not used (Dennis and Harrington, 1990). In order to maintain a proper perspective on all that has been written about the unique contribution of libraries and librarians, the concept of the support role of the library must remain constant despite changing methods and technologies.

. . . librarians need to emphasize how they can help solve the problems of others. They need to make it clear that the agendas of . . . libraries are the same as those of their institutions, that libraries do have much to offer in the addressing of identified educational priorities, and that library personnel and resources can be strong tools of empowerment for achieving those priorities. (Breivik, 1989, p. 9)

The means available to librarians who wish to educate faculty and administrators about the value and necessity of bibliographic instruction are as varied as the institutions and personalities involved. However, one assumption remains constant; it is up to librarians to take the initiative and become active agents of change. This assignment may be exceptionally difficult in view of entrenched attitudes, lack of knowledge, and shrinking library faculties with diminished influence—difficult but not impossible. The Earlham faculty member previously quoted (Thompson, 1993) describes the challenge:

Though the librarian is more likely to be the victim than the victimizer in cases of poor bibliographic instruction, I do not see how collaboration can begin if the first steps are not taken by a librarian. I know they will not be taken by most faculty members. What I have described is a kind of seduction of the recalcitrant faculty member. It is the best (and perhaps the only) technique available to librarians with little institutional power. (p. 105)

A librarian (Sheridan, 1995) details the principles of change necesssary for librarians to understand and use:

In order to effect change, one should (1) build strong relationships in strategic areas; (2) assess the situation which needs change; (3) acquire sufficient information about it; (4) test possible solutions and then select one; (5) convince others to accept this solution; and (6) institutionalize the solution and gain wide acceptance for it. (p. 122)

Sheridan (1995) recognizes that librarians do not operate from a position of strength and will find it necessary to use finely honed persuasive skills. "Since much of this activity is dependent on personality and skill, librarians need to apply group dynamics principles to their efforts, learn how to work in teams, and recognize each other's strengths and gifts" (p. 122).

These principles provide some workable methods for changing attitudes and organizational structures, whether one is dealing with reluctant faculty and administrators, librarians who are already overloaded and overworked, or library administrators who must decide on how much emphasis and resources to allocate to instruction. In view of the obstacles, it would be natural, but also defeatist, to conclude that there are too many problems and not enough librarians and that the task is impossible. A more positive and productive approach would be to determine what is essential to be done, how much can be done with existing means, and what additional resources are needed to accomplish the goals.

Since the status and reputation of librarians within their institutions grant them very little influence, their task becomes that of informing, publicizing, promoting, and persuading the campus community of their strategic role. "Serious commitment cannot be mandated from above, or at the college, division, or department levels; it must untimately be a grass-roots phenomenon, worked out by faculty in collaboration with librarians. It requires constant monitoring, careful nurturing, and time" (Tierney, 1992, p. 68).

Another librarian (Sheridan, 1995) concurs: "The BI program and its effectiveness seems to pivot on an effective marketing program. This means it is necessary to take an aggressive approach with new faculty members and reaffirm personal contacts with tenured faculty. These relationships need to be built up over the years and constantly nurtured." Methods may be both formal and informal, but they can be applied on most campuses. ". . . We intentionally strive for more visibility for the librarians, through campus committees, union participation, and personal contacts. Many classes are scheduled over lunch" (p. 158).

It is probably true that libraries have experienced an unprecedented demand for instruction in the decade since Boyer issued his report. Much of the change can be attributed to the proliferation of important curriculum changes such as the many writing-across-the-curriculum and writing-intensive-curriculum programs and other active learning courses described previously but also to the benefits derived from the contributions of librarians to electronic search instruction. However, despite the natural affinity of these types of programs for library research, librarians cannot assume that faculty will always approach them when they need their help. The basic stance in many libraries continues to be reactive, but the work load increases. It is the responsibility of librarians to create the administrative structures within their unit that make such collaboration possible. Librarians must be granted the authority, responsibility, and time to develop the programs that will accommodate institution-wide curriculum needs, rather than merely responding to individual requests from those faculty who already recognize the importance of information research to their teaching.

Advocating assertiveness by librarians does not mean recommending arbitrary prescriptions about how faculty and students should use the library. Librarians, however, *are* expected to take the initiative in establishing dialog with faculty, learn how they perceive their own and their students' information needs, and articulate how the library can meet those needs.

Opportunities, probably exceeding the abilities of librarians to respond, exist on every campus. Committee memberships, especially on key groups such as those making ongoing curriculum decisions or core curriculum review task forces, provide an invaluable opportunity to participate in ground-floor curriculum building and to assess and represent the library's potential contribution to course instruction. The introduction of new programs, which generally involves broad campus participation, gives librarians another open door. When the WIC program was first introduced at Oregon State University, for example, a librarian attended the first workshops offered for faculty teaching the writing courses (Sheridan, 1995). Her intention was to understand the purpose and content of WIC classes and to identify ways that the library could support them. She continued to attend subsequent workshops to learn from faculty what they and their students needed from the library.

Library liaison assignments to academic departments may be purposefully expanded beyond those that are characteristically limited to collection development issues into discussion of instruction matters. Membership of librarians on accreditation teams provides opportunities to influence the adoption of bibliographic instruction criteria like those of the middle states and southern associations.

Library administrators play a pivotal role in the development of effective, campuswide library user education programs. Their decisions and policies will largely determine whether or not instruction is essential and central to the mission of the library, the relative priority of instruction in the organizational structure and resource allocations of their unit, the ratio of instruction librarians to the entire library faculty, and hiring decisions that work toward building a corps of librarian–teachers.

VII. Conclusion

The library is the principal unit of the college that supports all academic programs; the one location on campus where all disciplines are represented, organized, and integrated; and a fertile environment within which to explore the interdisciplinary aspects of knowledge. The librarians who staff the library are educators, perhaps the few remaining generalists in higher education. Librarians can capitalize on their unique position within the academic community and at the same time fulfill their mission by making themselves indispensable to faculty and students as the principal information provider.

The appearance of informal satellite libraries in various departments throughout campus, the tendency of faculty and students to seek other information sources as their first choice, the proliferation of scattered electronic database searching services, and declining support for libraries characterize many academic communities. These could all be symptoms of the possibility that libraries have abdicated some of their responsibility as information educators and providers or have failed to inform their public of the multiplicity of resources and services available in libraries.

Active cooperative instruction programs can serve to bring libraries into the mainstream of academic life. These will create effective opportunities, not only for librarians to listen to their faculty and learn what their information needs actually are, but also to inform them of how the library supports their study, teaching, and research.

In the final analysis, libraries will be judged less by the quality of their collections, the proliferation of their technological systems, or even the excellence of their staff, than by the expertise with which they interpret their mission and educate their constituencies.

References

Allen, K. (1970). Student and faculty attitudes. *Library College Journal* 3(4), 28–36.

Baker, B. K. (1989). Bibliographic instruction: Building the librarian/faculty partnership. In *The Reference Librarian, Vol. 24: Integrating Library Use Skills into the General Education Curriculum* (M. Pastine and B. Katz, eds.), pp. 311–328. Haworth, New York.

Baker, B. K., Birchfield, M., and Weston, N. (1992). Information technology and curriculum design: New approaches for library and faculty partnerships. In *Working with Faculty in the New Electronic Library: Papers and Session Materials Presented at the 19th National LOEX Library Instruction Conference* (L. Shirato, ed.), pp. 71–80. Pierian, Ann Arbor, MI.

Bodi, S. (1992). Collaborating with faculty in teaching critical thinking: The role of librarians. *Research Strategies* 10, 69–76.

Boyer, E. L. (1987). *College, The Undergraduate Experience in America: The Carnegie Foundation for the Advancement of Teaching.* Harper & Row, New York.

Brandehoff, S. E. (1987). A meeting of minds. *American Libraries* 18, 443–445.

Breivik, P. S. (1987). Making the most of libraries in the search for academic excellence. *Change* 19(4), 44–52.

Breivik, P. S. (1989). Politics for closing the gap. In *The Reference Librarian, Vol. 24: Integrating Library Use Skills into the General Education Curriculum* (M. Pastine and B. Katz, eds.), Vol. 24, pp. 5–16. Haworth, New York.

Burlingame, D. F. (1980). Faculty development from a librarian's point of view. In *Library Instruction and Faculty Development: Growth Opportunities in the Academic Community* (N. Z. Williams and J. T. Tsukamoto, eds.), pp. 11-15. Pierian, Ann Arbor, MI.

Butler, F. C. (1985). The teaching/learning process: A unified, interactive model. *Educational Technology* 25(9), 9–17, (10), 7–17, (11), 7–17.

Cannon, A. (1994). Faculty survey on library research instruction. *RQ* 33, 524–541.

Clark, J. M., and Silverman, S. (1989). What are students hearing about online searching? A survey of faculty. *RQ* **29**, 230–238.

Cleveland, H. (1985). *The Knowledge Executive.* Truman Talley Books, New York.

Colorado State University Libraries. (1986). *CSU Library Users Questionnaire, Rating Key.* Author, Fort Collins, CO.

Colorado State University Libraries: User Education Task Force. (1993). *The Empowering Library, A Plan for User Education at CSU Libraries: Report of the User Education Task Force.* Author, Fort Collins, CO.

Dennis, N., and Harrington, N. D. (1990). Librarian and faculty member differences in using information technologies. *Reference Services Review* **18**, 47–52.

Divay, G., Ducas, A. M., and Michaud-Oystryk, N. (1987). Faculty perceptions of librarians at the University of Manitoba. *College & Research Libraries* **48**, 27–35.

Farber, E. I. (1978). Librarian–faculty communication techniques. In *Proceedings from Southeastern Conference on Approaches to Bibliographic Instruction* (C. Oberman-Soroka, ed.), pp. 71–87. College of Charleston, Charleston, S.C.

Feldman, D. (1989). The international student and course-integrated instruction: The ESL instructor's perspective. *Research Strategies* **7**, 159–166.

Fister, B. (1995). Connected communities: Encouraging dialogue between composition and bibliographic instruction. In *Writing-Across-the-Curriculum and the Academic Library* (J. Sheridan, ed.), pp. 33–51. Greenwood, Westport, CT.

Forys, M. (1992). The electronic library: A faculty seminar. In *Working with Faculty in the New Electronic Library: Papers and Session Materials Presented at the 19th National LOEX Library Instruction Conference* (L. Shirato, ed.), pp. 143–148. Pierian, Ann Arbor, MI.

Hardesty, L. L. (1986). The role of the classroom faculty in bibliographic instruction. In *Teaching Librarians to Teach: On-the-Job Training for Bibliographic Instruction Librarians* (A. S. Clark and K. F. Jones, eds.), pp. 155–187. Scarecrow, Metuchen, N.J.

Hardesty, L. (1995). Faculty culture and bibliographic instruction: An exploratory analysis. *Library Trends* **44**, 339–367.

Holmes, C. O., Irish, D. E., and Haley, T. C. (1994). BI for an undergraduate engineering course: An interactive model for a large-enrollment course. *Research Strategies* **12**, 115–121.

Huber, K., and Sherman, B. (1992). Scholarly networking in action. *Research Strategies* **10**, 40–43.

Isbell, D., and Broaddus, D. (1995). Teaching writing and research as inseparable: A faculty-librarian teaching team. *Reference Services Review* **23**(4), 51–62.

Ivey, R. T. (1994). Research notes: Teaching faculty perceptions of academic librarians at Memphis State University. *College & Research Libraries* **55**, 69–82.

Kellogg, R. (1987). Faculty members and academic librarians: Distinctive differences. *College & Research Libraries News* **48**, 602–606.

Lacey, P. A. (1980). The role of the librarian in faculty development: A professor's point of view. In *Library Instruction and Faculty Development: Growth Opportunities in the Academic Community* (N. Z. Williams and J. T. Tsukamoto, eds.), pp. 17–28. Pierian, Ann Arbor, MI.

Lin, P. (1994). Library instruction for culturally diverse populations: A comparative approach. *Research Strategies* **12**, 168–173.

Lipow, A. G. (1979). Teaching the faculty to use the library. In *New Horizons for Academic Libraries* (R. D. Stueart and R. D. Johnson, eds.), pp. 262–267. Association of College and Research Libraries, Chicago.

Lipow, A. G. (1992). Outreach to faculty: Why and how. In *Working with Faculty in the New Electronic Library: Papers and Session Materials Presented at the 19th National LOEX Library Instruction Conference* (L. Shirato, ed.), pp. 7–24. Pierian, Ann Arbor, MI.

Lubans, J., Jr. (1983). Chaos or order. *RQ* **23**, 135–138.

Marino, S. R., and Jacob, E. K. (1992). Questions and answers: The dialogue between composition teachers and reference librarians. In *The Reference Librarian, No. 37. The Reference Librarian and Implications of Mediation* (M. K. Ewing and R. Hauptman, eds.), pp. 129–142. Haworth, New York.

Mark, B.L., and Lee, S. K. (1992). Liaison program + information technology: Getting your foot in the door. In *Working with Faculty in the New Electronic Library: Papers and Session Materials Presented at the 19th National LOEX Library Instruction Conference* (L. Shirato, ed.), pp. 107–119. Pierian, Ann Arbor, MI.

Matthews, J. R., and Lawrence, G. S. (1984). Further analysis of the CLR online catalog project. *Information Technology and Libraries* 3, 354–376.

McCarthy, C. (1985). The faculty problem. *Journal of Academic Librarianship* 11, 142–145.

McInnis, R. G. (1978). *New Perspectives for Reference Service in Academic Libraries.* Greenwood, Westport, CT.

Moran, B. B. (1990). Library/classroom partnerships for the 1990s. *College & Research Libraries News* 51, 511–514.

Nitecki, D. A. (1993). Conceptual models of libraries held by faculty, administrators, and librarians: An exploration of communications in the "Chronicle of Higher Education." *Journal of Documentation* 49, 255–277.

Nowakowski, F. C. (1993). Faculty support information literacy. *College & Research Libraries News* 54, 124.

Oberg, L. R., Schleiter, M. K., and Van Houten, M. (1989). Faculty perceptions of librarians at Albion College: Status, role, contribution, and contacts. *College & Research Libraries* 50, 215–230.

O'Brien, T. V., and Warmkessel, M. M. (1994). A mingling of minds: An in-class "conference" on educational theories. *Research Strategies* 12, 174–181.

Piele, L. J., Pryor, J., and Tuckett, H. W. (1986). Teaching microcomputer literacy: New roles for academic librarians. *College and Research Libraries* 47, 374–378.

Ruess, D. E. (1994). Library and information literacy: A core curriculum component. *Research Strategies* 12, 18–23.

Schloman, B. F., and Feldmann, R. M. (1993). Developing information gathering skills in geology students through faculty-librarian collaboration. *Science & Technology Libraries* 14, 35–47.

Schumacher, M. (1989). Instructing the academic search service user: The faculty connection. *Research Strategies* 7, 33–36.

Scully, M. G. (1986). Study finds colleges torn by divisions, confused over roles. *Chronicle of Higher Education*, November 5, p. 1.

Sheridan, J., ed. (1995). *Writing-Across-the-Curriculum and the Academic Library.* Greenwood Press, Westport, CT.

Simmons, H. L. (1992). Information literacy and accreditation. In *New Directions for Higher Education, No. 78: Information Literacy: Developing Students as Independent Learners* (D. W. Farmer and T. F. Mech, eds.), pp. 15–25. Jossey-Bass, San Francisco.

Southern Association of Colleges and Schools, Commission on Colleges. (1995). *Criteria for Accreditation*, 9th Ed. The Association, Decatur, GA.

Stanford, L. M. (1992). An academician's journey into information literacy. In *New Directions for Higher Education, No. 78: Information Literacy: Developing Students as Independent Learners* (D. W. Farmer and T. F. Mech, eds.), pp. 37–43. Jossey-Bass, San Francisco.

Stark, M., and Waltz, M. A. (1988). Thumbing the cards: the online catalog, the faculty and instruction. In *Teaching the Online Catalog User* (C.A. Kirkendall, ed.), pp. 35–69. Pierian, Ann Arbor, MI.

Steffen, S. S. (1988). Faculty as end-users: Strategies, challenges, and rewards. In *Bibliographic Instruction and Computer Database Searching* (T. B. Mensching and K. J. Stanger, eds.), pp. 17–21. Pierian, Ann Arbor, MI.

Stephenson, W. K. (1980). Library instruction—The best road to development for faculty, librarians and students. In *Library Instruction and Faculty Development: Growth Opportunities in the Academic Community* (N. Z. Williams and J. T. Tsukamoto, eds.), pp. 81–84. Pierian, Ann Arbor, MI.

Stephenson, W. K. (1993). A departmental approach to bibliographic instruction. In *Bibliographic Instruction in Practice: a tribute to the legacy of Evan Ira Farber* (L. Hardesty, J. Hastreiter, and D. Henderson, eds.), pp. 27–40. Pierian, Ann Arbor, MI.

Swierenga, R. P. (1984). Bibliographic instruction in historical methods courses: Kent State University. *History Teacher* 17, 391–396.

Talbot, C. (1989). A natural environment for knowledge. *Research Strategies* 7, 53.

Thomas, J. (1994). Faculty attitudes and habits concerning library instruction: How much has changed since 1982? *Research Strategies* 12, 209–223.

Thompson, G. W. (1993). Faculty recalcitrance about bibliographic instruction. In *Bibliographic Instruction in Practice: A Tribute to the Legacy of Evan Ira Farber* (L. Hardesty, J. Hastreiter, and D. Henderson, eds.), pp. 103–105. Pierian, Ann Arbor, MI.

Tierney, J. (1992). Information literacy and a college library: A continuing experiment. In *New Directions for Higher Education, No. 78: Information Literacy: Developing Students as Independent Learners* (D. W. Farmer and T. F. Mech, eds.), pp. 63–71. Jossey-Bass, San Francisco.

Werrell, E. L., and Wesley, T. L. (1990). Promoting information literacy through a faculty workshop. *Research Strategies* 8, 172–180.

Preservation and Digitization: Trends and Implications

Eric C. Shoaf
Brown University Library
Providence, Rhode Island 02912

I. Introduction

Preservation as a library focus became institutionalized in the late 1970s when libraries began to react in an organized manner to the deterioration of books caused by poor-quality paper. Prior to this time the book repair unit was the main area for preservation efforts in libraries but the nature of the "brittle book" problem, as it was called, changed all that. Preservation soon became a midlevel department in most major research libraries. As the magnitude of the brittle paper problem was realized several reformatting programs, both institutional and cooperative, were lauched to ensure that brittle books were preserved for future scholars. At the time the preferred format for reformatting was microfilm, the somewhat old but well-developed and familiar technology, which has the additional advantage of relatively low cost. As the medium of choice microfilm was further developed, notably through the works of Gwinn (1987) and Elkington (1992) with standards put in place that were acceptable to both the preservation community and to funding bodies. Microfilm has been used to reformat hundreds of thousands of brittle volumes from some of the largest collections of research libraries through the early 1990s. The development of the technology and concomitant standards for its use, as well as low cost, made microfilm an important wrench in the preservationist's toolbox.

Certainly microfilm has become entrenched as medium of choice for preserving deteriorated library materials. However, any researcher knows of the disadvantages in microfilm use and attendant eyestrain, lack of random access, and rudimentary copying systems. Some microfilm produced prior to the development of standards has shown signs of deterioration. These drawbacks and the rise of new forms of reformatting technology, notably digitization, have not only provided the preservation professional new wrenches but

ADVANCES IN LIBRARIANSHIP, VOL. 20
223

also a new toolbox. Although microfilm has not and is not expected to be replaced as the archival medium of choice, it is clear that digital technologies provide a powerful complement to present-day microfilm technology.

As early as 1982, the Library of Congress (LC) began research in the use of optical disk technology for image preservation and retrieval. LC's Optical Disk Pilot Project sought to experiment with developing optical disk scanning, digital conversion, storage, and retrieval and the results were positive. Such experimentation began before microfilming as a preservation reformatting tool had become entrenched. Nugent (1986), writing about the new optical disk technologies at the time, noted "they appear to have been designed specifically for libraries" and outlines specific uses for the technology including preservation. LC has since become a major contributor to the use of digitization in the preservation field. Experimentation and research with digital technologies has led to a new conceptualization of the way research libraries will deliver information to scholars in the future as well as how that information will be preserved, and it has raised serious questions for those charged with preserving information already in library collections in traditional print format and information that will be acquired in new formats created from a rapidly evolving technology. The trends and implications of this new technology are explored in this chapter.

II. Preservation *and* Access

Central to the role of preserving in the digital environment is the understanding that retrieval and transmission of digital information has few physical limitations. Except for hardware and software compatibility, digital information can be transmitted and received anywhere in the world where an infrastructure to send and receive is in place. This new access technology is expected to seriously alter the way libraries acquire and disseminate information, but it also changes the role of preservation. Whereas before preservation was most concerned with physical permanence of information sources, whether original or surrogate copies, in the new digital paradigm the act of preservation also provides access in ways not previously possible.

Some preservationists have been moved to state that preservation *is* access, even in the more traditional setting, when the act of preserving information means that scholarly access is enhanced. Lynn (1994) notes that scholarship follows access and not collection, and that the greatest collections in the world have diminished scholarly value if access is inhibited. Indeed, libraries are moving from what Waters (1994) has called just-in-case availability of information to just-in-time delivery. To elaborate, the structure of the research library has traditionally been to acquire, catalog, and preserve scholarly information in case such information was needed. Many library collection development selectors believed that if a volume was consulted at least once in 50 years then they had done their job properly. But with the advent of multiple access points through digital storage, retrieval, and dissemination, the library is freed to acquire only core materials in certain areas of scholarship while the rest are available at other institutions through electronic means. Waters (1994) shows that when completely costed out a library can actually reduce expenditures and provide funds to be reallocated into other electronic programs or into preservation.

Access, while central to the workable concept of digital preservation, is an area where research and planning is ongoing but where considerable progress has yet to be made. A chief component of the growth and acceptance of microfilm was the adoption of standards for all areas of film production. No such standards are yet in place for digitization processes, although test-bed projects to identify and recommend standards for digitization processes are in place and are discussed in this chapter. Lynn (1994) draws the distinction between open access and free access. Although research libraries have traditionally maintained open access for scholars, free access has been limited by proximity to those collections. The promise of digital collections is that free access will be available to all, regardless of location. But this type of access is still dependent on the availability of a technological infrastructure that is not yet in place for all potential users. In short, the promise of access to brittle collections brought by digital storage and retrieval systems is still in the development stage and while expectations are high, at the present time many challenges to the development of the technology remain.

As a developing technology, digitization is an area in which preservationists have many concerns, some of which are:

1. What levels of resolution must be employed on the bit-map images that are scanned into digital format?
2. Should a conversion to optical character recognition (OCR) be carried out as part of the initial process or employed at a later time?
3. Should structured text formats such as Standardized Generalized Markup Language (SGML) be used for materials preserved in digital form?
4. How can quality control in image capture and storage be achieved?
5. How can the costs of digital technologies for preservation be reduced?

Some of these concerns, cannot be answered only by the development of digitization standards, but also rely on an institutional commitment and integration of digitization throughout the research library. As more institutions make this commitment such concerns may be minimized, but there are still unanswered questions that are preventing the financial commitment and infrastructure upgrades necessary for advancement in the areas of concern.

The growth and acceptance of microfilm as an archival medium has its roots in the maturity of the technology and the development of standards in which the technology is applied. Preservation microfilming as a reformatting option for research libraries grew to favor rapidly in the 1980s as specific standards were developed for identifying appropriate materials, preparation and bibliographic control, microfilm production and processing, quality control, and archival storage. Each step of the filming image-capture process has specialized standards such as density levels, reduction ratio, quality index measurement, resolution, and target location and arrangement. Some analogous steps in the digitized image-capture process for which standards are not yet in place are scanning resolution (in dots per inch), continuous tone, contrast, gray scale, and pixel level. Standards for microfilming were set for film processing, quality control, and archival storage and these techniques also have digitization analogues. A key implication of the new digital technology is that standards will have to be developed and approved by American National Standards Institute (ANSI) or other national or international standards-making organizations before use of digitizing for preservation can begin in earnest and be supported by grant funding agencies.

While the lack of standards is a challenge to be overcome, it is important to note that digital technology and new information access paradigms such technology provides are more useful to the preservationist than any that has come before. As these technologies are further developed, preservation of materials and their wider dissemination can be a significant part of planning for the future library that may be defined by holdings of specific core collections with virtual electronic access to collections at other holdings at remote locations. Library administrators are currently struggling with different visions of the future library, and other technological developments are closer to fruition that will change the way scholarship is pursued. Although the electronic book has yet to become a reality, several theorists have long predicted its arrival, including Lande (1991) who notes that "it is technologically feasible and has already been designed and costed out" (p. 28). But in reality there is no clear demand for an electronic book. Print publishing continues to rise and libraries continue to pour approximately 90% of their acquisitions budgets into the purchase of books.

However, uses of digitization are rising. For example, some universities have already put their reserve readings online and are prepared for potential court tests of copyright law and the fair-use standard generally applied to libraries and researchers (Enssle, 1994). Document delivery expectations, space and storage concerns, ruthlessly rising serials costs, and equipment needs all portend to changes in the library's methods of storing and disseminating information. Writing for the Commission on Preservation and Access, Marcum (1995) notes that

> . . . as the research library evolves as a place for discovering knowledge to an entry point to the world of information that is physically stored in many different locations in a variety of formats, librarians are forced to consider these questions of use costs and organizational implications. At the same time, we recognize that digital technology also erases national boundaries. Scholarship, even for the faculty member of small, isolated, or poorly funded institutions, promises to become a truly international endeavor. The ease with which technology allows us to distribute information to all parts of the world stands in stark contrast to the boundaries of language and cultural differences that are not accommodated by technical fixes.

So far the promise of such access and the erasing national boundaries in the quest for knowledge has yet to be realized. Central to such a vision of open access is an infrastructure, previously mentioned, which provides the electronic pathways on which digitized information travels. Such an infrastructure has been called the "information superhighway" by the popular press, and in effect does exist as an outgrowth of the Internet that originally linked government and university researchers. In one sense the system of fiber optic cable that has replaced the telephone wire in many parts of the world does represent an infrastructure for digital transmission. But to access and retrieve information, one not only needs to have a fiber optic hookup but also requires hardware capable of handling large blocks of digitized information, software that can locate, access, and download the information, and both hardware and software must be able to interface with the equipment that is used to store the information. The key problems are that there is presently more than one system that can perform the activities needed to acquire the digital information, and there is no truly international infrastructure that will allow access to anyone in any location. When viewed on a worldwide scope, large difficulties loom for those preservationists who want not only to digitally archive information but also to distribute it freely.

However, it is clear that the research library is poised at the cusp of major change in the storage and dissemination of information and the area of preservation will be no less affected than any other library unit. Although this change has been taking shape for the past decade, several major groups have been testing and researching the emerging technologies for use in preserving knowledge in the library of tomorrow.

III. Investigating Digitization for Preservation

A. The Commission on Preservation and Access

The Commission on Preservation and Access was established in 1986 to foster and support collaboration among libraries and allied organizations in order to ensure the preservation of the published and documentary record in all formats and to provide enhanced access to scholarly information. In this capacity the commission was an early supporter of digital technologies for preservation and has continued to encourage development of this technology by publishing reports of libraries engaged in digital preservation projects. The commission has reported on several different projects such as the Vision 2010 study sponsored by a grant from the Carnegie Corporation of New York for study of the implications of technological developments for higher education and scholarly communication in the next 20 years (Commission on Preservation and Access, June 1994). The study, conducted in partnership with the University of Michigan School of Information and Library Studies, involves individuals from a broad range of activities and professional experience including librarianship and preservation and foresees changes in scholarly communication which will revolutionize scholarly publishing. In another project showing the far-reaching effects of preservation and digitization, the Bibliotheque Nationale de France is in the midst of an ambitious project to digitize 300,000 books and microforms by the year 2000 (Commission on Preservation and Access, March 1995) with access provided by the French RENATER network and on the Internet.

The commission also publishes reports on grant funded research, task force studies, and other progress in preservation and digitization. Among the recent projects mentioned: "From Microfilm to Digital Imagery", which explores the feasibility of a project to study the means, costs, and benefits of converting large quantities of preserved library materials from microfilm to digital images. "Electronic Technologies and Preservation", which suggests ways that preservationists can take advantage of digital technologies being developed for the library of the future. "The Organizational Phase of Project Open Book", which reports on a very important project at Yale University to convert 10,000 books from microfilm to digital imagery and outlines design principles, key issues for user access, and specific microfilm concerns. "A Hybrid Systems Approach to Preservation of Printed Materials" describes a preservation system that uses microfilm as archival tool and digital imaging as access tool and promotes long-term use of microfilm as permanent surrogate. "The Setup Phase of Project Open Book: On the Status of an Effort to Convert Microfilm to Digital Imagery", the most recent status report on this project, concentrates on digital image quality, indexing structures, and production workflow and has found that criteria-driven selection for imaging is vital. "Joint Study in Digital Preservation Phase 1" is a report of the joint Cornell Unviersity/Xerox Corporation study using digital technology to preserve library materials and which focuses on digital access to books previously printed on brittle paper. This project has been extremely successful and has resulted with approximately 2500 brittle books completely digitized, demonstrating the potential of digitization for preservation reformatting.

Another important study, "Intellectual Preservation: Electronic Preservation of the Third Kind", discusses the need to assure the integrity and authenticity of information as originally recorded since undetectable changes to digital texts are possible. This is a particularly important investigation since one of the drawbacks of digital technology for archival uses is that changes are possible that can compromise the originality of scanned digital images. Enhancement process use electronic algorithms to "clean up" or intensify a digital image in order to improve its contrast or legibility. Thus a heavily foxed paper-based text document could be enhanced so that the foxing disappears, or a low-contrast engraved frontispiece might be enhanced to improve the final image. For the user this means an improvement to the image but to the preservationist this constitutes a fundamental change in an archived image that is no longer true to the original. Another implication of digitization is data compression, where algorithmic techniques in which redundant digital data streams are reduced to much smaller sizes, resulting in lower storage and data transmission requirements. Again, this is good for the end user, but at some point the "redundant digital data streams" that are reduced can compromise the originality of the scanned image. This area has strong implications on the storage and transmission of archived data and its trueness to the original scanned images.

The commission has also reported on "Digital Resolution Requirements for Replacing Text-Based Material: Methods for Benchmarking Quality" tutorial, which provides a means to estimate resolution requirements for the use of digital imaging technology in conversion. These are calculated by evaluating the physical attributes of source documents and by applying Quality Index formulas used in preservation microfilming and are a key component in developing standards in this area. "Oversize Color Images Project 1994–1995: A Report to the Commission on the Preservation Access" provides results of the first phase of a project to identify acceptable preservation and digital access techniques for dealing with oversize color images associated with text. The report has particular implications for access to this type of material, as it was found that the ability to capture information outstrips the capacity for easy access and display with equipment available to most users and immediate online use of high resolution files is somewhat limited.

In addition to supporting and reporting on research activities, the Commission on Preservation and Access also creates task forces to investigate and report on trends and preservation and digitization and organizes workshops and symposiums to educate those in the field about advances. An example of the former is the Task Force on Archiving Digital Information, created jointly in 1994 with the Research Libraries Group, which is investigating the means of ensuring continued access indefinitely into the future of records stored in digital electronic form (Report of the Task Force on Archiving of Digital Information Research Libraries Group Press Release, 1995). However, in a disturbing move, cutbacks at the National Endowment for the Humanities (NEH) in 1995 meant that the Division of Preservation and Access saw funding reduced by 23% to $17 million. While this was less of a reduction than for NEH overall, the future for this area of funding looks less promising particularly if further cuts are made by Congress. The work of the Commission on Preservation and Access has been important in support of digital technologies for library preservation. Shortage of funding at this crucial juncture will endanger further development projects in digitization and slow progress in this area.

B. The Research Libraries Group

The Research Libraries Group (RLG) was founded in 1974 and has grown to include nearly 150 libraries and scholarly institutions. RLG has been at the forefront of developing technologies for preservation. RLG was an early supporter of reformatting efforts and helped to create and administer the Great Collections Microfilm Project in several phases which succeeded in preserving more than 100,000 brittle and at-risk volumes in the 1980s and early 1990s by reformatting to microfilm. Membership in RLG may be enhanced for institutions by choosing to be part of the PRESERV program, which offers intensive preservation support on an individual basis and also provides specialized programming. A Task Force on Photograph Preservation has developed ground-breaking projects to explore the use of digital technology to improve access to photographs. Other ongoing projects include exploring intellectual control of shared imaged collections, developing guidelines and models to assist institutions in beginning local digitization projects, and testing and displaying a range of digital models for photograph collections.

RLG uses the strength of its member body and the expertise of its staff to research and organize experimentation into new digital preservation technologies. An example is the Digital Imaging Technology for Preservation Symposium held at Cornell University for practitioners in 1994. Theorists in scholarly communication, collection management, and preservation were among the presenters as were those overseeing test-bed digitization projects at Yale and Cornell Universities, which have already been outlined. In addition, this symposium was the first time that vendors were invited to join a large-scale discussion of this sort and to demonstrate their products for the preservation community. Although the symposium represented the state of the art at the time, Kenney (1994) noted in her address that "while interest is high in the use of digital technology, the knowledge base—including the development of commonly accepted protocols and standards for the use of digital technology in a preservation context—is low" (p. 12). There were other calls for the development of national standards for digitization such as those which were created for preservation microfilming and which would enhance the climate for grant proposal acceptance and for long-term archival security. However, rapidly changing digital technologies do not readily lend themselves to such standards and more research and testing will be necessary that will stall progress and may cause support for digitization to drop.

C. National Digital Library

The Library of Congress (LC) has been a leading proponent of digitization since the early 1980s. Their initial digitization project was titled American Memory because of the 210,000 items from two dozen collections on American culture and history (all in the public domain), which were digitized. At first access was available at 44 test sites across the country, but more recently the collections have been made available via World Wide Web over the Internet according to the Library of Congress Information Bulletin (1994). The important leadership role of LC was acknowledged in a historic document signed on May 1, 1995, which establishes a National Digital Library Federation. Fifteen of the nation's largest research libraries, including LC, and the Commission on Preservation and Access agreed to "cooperate on defining what must be done to bring together from across the nation and beyond digitized materials that will be made accessible" according to the Commission on Preservation and Access Newsletter (Number 80, June 1995). The federation hopes to develop a distributed, open digital library accessible across the global Internet. Since the key institutions represent by their holdings most of the important scholarly and historical collections in the country, this digital library when complete would represent the largest and most complete group of scholarly collections available anywhere. In announcing the federation several goals were identified, many of which have direct implications on the further development of digitization for preservation. These are the establishment of a collaborative management structure, development of a coordinated funding strategy formation of selection guidelines that will assure conformance to a general theme, adoption of common standards and best practices to ensure full informational capture, to guarantee universal accessibility and interchangability, to simplify retrieval and navigation, to facilitate archivability and enduring access, and the establishment of an ongoing and comprehensive evaluation program. The group also expects to define and promote archival strategies for digital information, which is ephemeral and dynamic and to establish preservation standards for new digital materials. The document notes that "The time is now ripe to establish a national digital library of sufficient size, scope, and complexity support a meaningful text of the effect of distributed digital libraries on equitable access, on learning and scholarship, and on the economics and organization of libraries" (Number 80, June 1995). The National Digital Library Federation will be a powerful influence on the growth of smaller-scale local digitization projects as guidelines are developed which will encourage funding opportunities. Such opportunities are already being acted upon as reported in the Library Journal (1995) where Bell Atlantic announced it would give $1.5 million to the National Digital Library Federation (p. 11). While the federation has yet to actually do anything, its creation has important implications on the establishment of standards for digitization, standards that can only be developed through cooperation and agreement on a national and international scale and without which access will be limited.

D. JSTOR: Journal Storage in a Digital Age

The JSTOR or journal storage project began as a demonstration project funded by the Mellon Foundation. The basic outline of the system was described by Bowen at the Council on Library Resources Conference in Washington, DC (Bowen, 1995). It was initially conceived as an electronic database containing the back runs of 10 core journals in the fields of economics and history with the idea to scan and store all the pre-1990 issues of these journals to improve access and preservation and to reduce shelf space and associated capital costs. The project has been centered at the University of Michigan and early results are promising, although further investigation is warranted.

In one of the easier hurdles, copyright permissions were received from all 10 journals selected. This had been considered a serious threat to the viability of the project, but it was found that publishers are most concerned with revenue competition and since there is little demand for journal issues more than a decade old there was little threat to their revenue stream from this project. This outcome also ensures that future issues can be added to the JSTOR collection in perpetuity with the additional bonus of cooperation from publishers. Several other features of this system are a searchable table-of-contents index, complete optical character recognition (OCR) software that enables users to link with text for search terms, and access online through the Internet. However, some questions remain. For example, how can the system be made to be economically self-supporting and how can pricing and access structures be developed without severely impacting use of the system? Clearly, a significant number of institutions would need to buy in to the service to keep costs low but few are willing to step forward until others already have done so. While libraries are quick to recognize the implications on storage space once back runs of journals can be removed from shelves, it has not been proven that digitization is less expensive than storage of print volumes.

Presently, Bowen continues, it is anticipated that JSTOR would ask libraries to make two types of payment for access: a one-time charge for acquisition of permanent rights to the database and an annual fee to cover recurring costs of maintaining and updating the database and associated hardware. It is noted that for the project to be economically feasible on a national scale at least half the current subscribers to the journals would have to become paying subscribers. It will be no small undertaking for this to happen. Libraries are being asked to purchase access to materials they already own in print form with the only incentive to do so being use of OCR technology. Although the concept that JSTOR provides offers a tremendous increase in access and indexing for the 10 selected journals, its viability as a digital access tool appears limited.

E. Other Digital Preservation Projects

Several ongoing digitization projects, some already mentioned, are discussed. The Making of America project, a collaboration between Cornell University and Xerox Corporation is now several years old and is reporting success in digitizing brittle books for preservation and improved access. This project has focused on obtaining a quality digital image comparable to that obtained through conventional reformatting techniques and at an affordable price. One interesting finding of the project is that faculty called in to evaluate the digital images often preferred the scanned images over the originals because of the slightly heightened contrast that makes them more readable in many instances (Kenney, 1994). Cornell has been successful in establishing a test-bed for exploration of preservation reformatting using digital technology and has preserved well more than 2000 books by this process. Of further interest for researchers is investigation into OCR applications for the digitized brittle books, which promises new and unique research capabilities. But OCR technology concerns preservationists who believe that it may further damage image originality as the compression algorithms and image enhancements previously mentioned.

At Yale University, Project Open Book has taken a different tack. This project is exploring the potential for conversion of microfilm to digital images. Since much of the preservation reformatting done through the years has been on microfilm, this project is a necessary step in learning how to migrate data across different types of media and to develop the technology to allow such migration. Conway and Weaver report (1994) that they expect in the project to convert 10,000 volumes from microfilm to a digital library. The project is scheduled for completion in 1996. In addition to overcoming the unique problems associated with converting microfilmed images to quality digital images, Yale expects to also provide access to the growing digital library over the campus network and will consider the costs and benefits of using service bureaus for digital conversion and document structure editing. The important implication of the Yale project is that it builds on the accepted archival medium of microfilm and uses this base for creating digital images that can then be manipulated through enhancement algorithms and OCR technology. The solid base of an accepted archival medium for the reformatted image coupled with the access and search technology of digitization is the hybrid system that may be the trend of preservation reformatting in years to come.

As reported by Yvonne French in the Library of Congress Information Bulletin (1995), a project at LC expects to digitize some 35 manuscripts from the Federal Theatre Project Collection as part of the new National Digital Library Program. The focus on manuscripts is to help develop digitization standards for this type of material, which is complicated by the existence of both dark typewriter ink and light pencil markings. Much of the experimental work is being performed by an outside contractor experienced at document imaging. When completed, the collection will be accessible on the Internet.

Henneberger (1994) outlines a project at the University of Georgia to scan rare maps and make them available on the World Wide Web. Microfilm has an integral role since the image scanning is taken directly from preservation microfilm for several reasons: (1) the known preservation qualities of microfilm, (2) the large variance in map sizes from a small 8×10-inch page to large maps several feet wide and tall, and (3) microfilm was found to provide the best contrast, image quality, and sharpness. Initially the scanned image is stored on a CD-ROM in "tiff" format but is later transferred to "jpeg", which compresses the large images to make transmission easier. On average each "jpeg" image is only one-sixth the size of the original scanned "tiff" image. The CD-ROMs with the map images are available for local use in the library, and at present approximately 25% of the collection has been made available on the Internet through the World Wide Web. The author concludes that the project has been a success but cautions that because there are presently no national standards for digital imaging, they proceed cautiously and made as many provisions as possible for quality scanned images and the ability to easily convert existing images to a future standardized form.

In a digitization project at Oregon State University, Krishnamurthy and Mead (1995) report on making a major manuscript collection available via the Internet using a digital technology. As a means of providing easy electronic access to the Linus Pauling papers held at the library, the project was developed over a period of years and while the authors report that the actual scanning was straightforward, other more difficult issues needed to be dealt with. A printed finding aid needed to be converted to digital format and linked to the image database. Public access was accomplished using a Local Area Network Novell server linked to the campus and also to the Internet; however, database access is currently restricted to local users. Software allows full-text/free-text search capability and search results can be viewed on the screen as OCRed text or image, or both on a single screen. Another issue of concern was copyright. Since the donor gave permission to access and view the original papers without restriction, it is the intention of the library to extend the same access rights to the digital database. However the authors point out that this permission to examine digital data will not be an authorization for users to publish them. No exclusive rights to examine or publish material will be granted. Original papers of the Pauling Collection are currently housed in a highly secured, climate-controlled environment and will continue to exist in their original state so that they are preserved even as greater access for their use has been created.

F. Digitizing as a Preservation Option

Digital conversion of text and images is an exciting reformatting option for library preservationists. But even as test-bed projects of the early 1990s demonstrated the promise of the new technology, concerns about its long-term viability were growing. Among the advantages of digitization for preservation is the unparalleled access it provides. The ability to transmit digitized documents over great distances in seconds coupled with the technology available to provide OCR software for research and scholarship are impressive advances in their own right. Applied to unstable or unusable paper-based print materials, the advantages of digitization for both preservation and enhanced access constitute a breakthrough in information delivery. Digitizing rare noncirculating materials and making them available electronically eliminates the need for scholars requiring primary sources to conduct on-site research visits. OCR technology provides search techniques and capabilities previously unavailable. Formerly difficult to access information can be made freely available to all.

Preservation librarians, while inspired by these technological breakthroughs, are approaching digitization cautiously. Development of the technology is proceeding at a rapid rate, which means that both software and hardware platforms presently in place will be supplanted in short order. Preservationists are concerned about the long-term stability of electronically preserved texts and images with such rapid changes in data systems. As these systems change the data they store must be migrated to the new system and there is speculation that minute changes to the digital data accompanies such migration. Further, even as the technology becomes fixed on more permanent platforms, test-bed projects such as that at Cornell (1994) have demonstrated the need for periodic "refreshment" of data. The concept of refreshment is defined as periodically copying stored data onto a new storage medium, presently a computer-driven hard disk, to ensure access and reduce disk failure. The refreshment process raises questions about minute data loss as does migration discussed above. Preservationists are concerned that over the long term, hundreds of years, these minute changes in data can add up to something more substantial so that some of the original data elements, text or image, may be lost.

Another area of concern is the preservation of electronic data. This has been somewhat overlooked since digitization is seen as a preservation strategy in and of itself. Yet with the unstable nature of an evolving technology, changing software and hardware platforms, and little research in the area, the preservation of electronic data formats remains an issue of importance for preservationists. Two possible solutions to the issue are the migration and refreshment of data previously discussed. These solutions bring with them concerns about possible data loss already mentioned and they also add to the costs of technology. Perhaps the best solution to the problem is merging the older stable technology of microfilm with the new digitizing technology to produce a hybrid system wherein microfilm becomes the archival medium for long-term storage and digitization serves as more of an information delivery and access system for text-and-image data. The Yale Project Open Book has already shown that this is a viable alternative. Further, it builds on the strength and acceptance of microfilm as the medium of choice for long-term preservation while harnessing the attributes of the new electronic technology to provide access not heretofore possible. This issue is discussed again in the following section.

IV. Keys to Development of the Technology

Many of the projects outlined in this chapter, and others at a variety of institutions, may only be temporary as technological changes in the computer breed quick obsolescence of both hardware and software. Presently, the most important need for digital preservation technology is accepted standards such as those developed for microfilming in the 1980s. Standards for image capture, bibliographic control, image ownership, resolution, data transfer protocols, indexing, access, file types, quality control, and regular data refreshment must be in place before large-scale projects can be undertaken and before funding can be sought from agencies who require such standardization of any grant-funded projects. The experiences at the two test-bed projects currently ongoing at Yale and Cornell Universities have contributed a great deal to the body of knowledge needed to formalize a standardization. One of the goals of the newly formed National Digital Library Federation is the establishment of such standards, although it will probably take at least 2 years to do so and, recalling the experience with microfilming standards, possibly longer.

As preservation digitizing standards are put in place, and as libraries continue to add digital-based formats to their collections, the focus will change somewhat. Just as preservationists have had to confront the problem of brittle paper in books, so too will they have to deal with electronic data that must be preserved. The problem for those responsible for preserving data in digital form is the nature of the medium and the high rate of technological change in both software and hardware. It is generally accepted that as the technology matures the need to migrate existing stored data from an older system to a newer one is a given and that data refreshment, i.e., recopying data periodically to maintain it, must be standardized. However, such practices are costly and as Graham (1995) has noted "no research library has taken on the provision, organization, and preservation of information with the same long-term commitment we have made for print materials" (p. 4). He further postulates that an institutional commitment is required for the success of any electronic system that attempts to preserve the record of human scholarship and that "whatever the governance structure, an institution wishing to benefit from electronic information will have to make a conscious commitment to providing continuous resources" (p. 4).

Electronic media are less stable and degrade quickly if not carefully protected. A system of such protection must be built-in to any digitization project. In 1992, the Commission on Preservation and Access released a report that stated that "new media are a problem [and] new media formats are a problem" (Lesk, 1992). It recommended a standardization of media formats, software standards, increased funding for preservation of computer-based archives, and budgeting for copying and refreshment. Funding appears as a major theme in each report about planning for the preservation of digital information and it is appropriate to say that the institutional commitment to which Graham alluded may be one of the most important missing pieces of the puzzle. Until acceptable levels of institutional commitment are in place the use of digitization technology for preservation will not be able to move forward at a pace sufficient for its general acceptance and use in library preservation.

V. Conclusion

The digital age is no longer the future, it is here and now. Libraries are moving from experimental testing to planning large-scale preservation programs using digital technologies. A major national focus was created in the formation of the National Digital Library Federation and there are great expectations that this group of institutions will be able to create acceptable standards for the use of digital technology in preservation and information delivery. Funding continues as a major concern, exacerbated by the fact that these new technologies require continual upgrading for use of new software and hardware developments, and because the data themselves are only preserved if they are regularly refreshed or migrated into new systems. Institutions choosing to use the new technologies will need to make a commitment to its maintenance or will need to enter into consortial relationships as a way of structuring the financing of digital preservation. Access issues will drive the development of the technology as much as preservation needs, and we will see that the two become further linked in the library of the twenty-first century.

References

Bowen, A. (1995). *JSTOR and the Economcis of Scholarly Communication*. Paper presented at Council on Library Resources Conference, September 18, Washington, DC.

Commission on Preservation and Access. (1995, October). *Commission on Preservation and Access Newsletter* No. 83.

Commission on Preservation and Access. (1994, June). *Commission on Preservation and Access Newsletter* No. 68.

Commission on Preservation and Access. (1995, March). *Commission on Preservation and Access Newsletter* No. 76.

Conway, P., and Weaver, S. (1994). The setup phase of Project Open Book. *Microform Review* **23**, 3.

Elkington, N., ed. (1992). *RLG Preservation and Microfilming Handbook*. Research Libraries Group, Mountain View, CA.

French, Y. (1995). Experimental theater: Project looks at digitizing federal theatre project collection. *Library of Congress Information Bulletin* **54**, 12.

Graham, P. (1995). Requirements for the digital research library. *College and Research Libraries* **56**, 4.

Gwinn, N. E., ed. (1987). *Preservation Microfilming*. American Library Association, Chicago.

Henneberger, B. (1994). Preservation and access of rare maps at the University of Georgia Library. *Microform Review*, **23**, 4.

Kenney, A. (1994). In *Digital Imaging Technology for Preservation: Proceedings of an RLG Symposium*, March 17–18, Research Libraries Group, Mountain View, CA.

Krishnamurthy, R., and Mead, C. (1995). An overview of the project on the imaging and full-text retrieval of the Ava Helen and Linus Pauling papers at the Oregon State University Libraries. *Microform Review* **24**, 1.

Lande, N. (1991). Toward the electronic book. Publishers *Weekly*, September 20, 28–30.

Lesk, M. (1992). *Preservation of the New Technology: A Report of the Technology Assessment Advisory Committee*. Commission on Preservation and Access, Washington, DC.

Library Journal (1995), **120**, 11.

Library of Congress Information Bulletin (1995), **54**, 20.

Lynn, S. (1994). In *Digital Imaging Technology for Preservation: Proceedings of an RLG Symposium*, March 17–18, Research Libraries Group, Mountain View, CA.

Marcum, D. (1995). *The Commission's Challenge.* Annual report, Commission on Preservation and Access.

Nugent, W. (1986). *IFLA Journal* **12,** 3.

Report of the Task Force on Archiving of Digital Information.

Research Libraries Group Membership Brochure. (1993). Research Libraries Group, Mountain View, CA.

Waters, D. (1994). In *Digital Imaging Technology for Preservation: Proceedings of an RLG Symposium,* March 17–18, Research Libraries Group, Mountain View, CA.

Index

ISBN 0-12-024620-1

90040